P9-CQA-468
This book
belongs
to

Doing Words

Doing Words

Katie Johnson

for Pat,
with best wishes –
Sorry I didn't get to
see you at work! Next time...
Katie Johnson
1-31-90

Boston 1987

Houghton Mifflin Company

Library of Congress Cataloging-in-Publication Data

Johnson, Katie.
Doing words.

Bibliography: p.
1. Reading (Elementary) — United States — Language experience approach. 2. Language arts (Elementary) — United States. I. Title.
LB1573.33.J64 1987 372.6 87-347
ISBN 0-395-42723-1

Printed in the United States of America

S 10 9 8 7 6 5 4 3 2 1

To Sharon Lowe Eldridge,
who dared with me

Contents

Author's Note

There will be times in this book when I will want to say things about children without naming them, when it isn't exactly Jessica or Shawn or Lisa who has done something worth mentioning, but any child. The question is, how do I refer back to "any child"?

If I write about Lisa or Jessica, I can always call that child "she," and refer to "her" work or learning or mother or whatever. I can call Shawn's work "his," and Shawn "him" if I need to use anything else but his name to speak about him again.

I could say, always, "children," and use "they" and "them." But one of the most important elements of Doing Words is that each child is doing what each child does, when each child does it, not in groups. And you can see by that very sentence why I need pronomial help.

They are just little words, you might say, *he* and *she* and *her* and *him* and *his,* and you would be very right. But they are not small in their importance to the way all of us, *he*s and *she*s, think about ourselves.

And if there is anyone in this country right this minute who will tell you how much power even the littlest words have, it's me.

So I will use both formulations in this book when I want to make a general statement about what an individual child will do. The first mythical child might be a girl, the next a boy, and so on until the end. Wherever it feels right, I will use a name, because you will hear and remember the story better if the child has a name.

Plus ça change, plus c'est la même chose.

In this book there are all kinds of stories. Some of them are stories children in my classes wrote and I made copies of, some are stories they told me; some are stories I made up to illustrate how children in general learn to read and write. Some are sad; some are happy; some would be uncomfortable for the children who told them to see; some would be dangerous for the children who told them if their parents knew that they had talked about "home problems" with me. That's the danger of Doing Words: bringing things from the inside out can be scary. Because of this, I have changed all the names and altered all the personalities of most of the children. Only those in Chapters 7–14 whose completed drafts are quoted will have their real names attached: Gerald, Stephen, Eddie, Amber, Stephanie, Kyle, Jason C., Lance, Jamie, Caleb, Kris, Cory, Rachel, Jonathan, Tommy, Heather, Holly, Jacob, Becky, Michael, Weylon, Jason N., and Kevin.

Doing Words

Chapter 1

Doing Words, Or, Reading and Writing from the Inside Out

> Ged, speaking of power, in *The Wizard of Earthsea*: "It is no secret. All power is one in source and end, I think. Years and distances, stars and candles, water and wind and wizardry, the craft in a man's hand and the wisdom in a tree's root: they all arise together. My name, and yours, and the true name of the sun, or a spring of water, or an unborn child, all are syllables of the great word that is very slowly spoken by the shining of the stars. There is no other power. No other name."
>
> — Ursula LeGuin

RICKY CAME TO SCHOOL a few days after it had started, and he didn't want to be there. He stood by the door and sobbed all of his first day, except for recesses when his sister took him out to play. The second day he stood inside the door and wept a little from time to time, watching the other children getting Words and doing other fun-looking things during Word time.

"Would you like to come to the table with me, Ricky?" I asked a few times; but the big black eyes would fill at the sound of my voice, and he didn't come. He watched, though, and listened as the Words were read in the circle.

The third day he stood by the table, not speaking, as the other children went about their work during Word time, and finally he was the only one left. It was quiet, and I ruffled his hair once and smiled at him. "Would you like a Word today, Ricky, like the other children?"

He looked at me, not yes and not no. That was a big advance from the Monday, however, so I asked my regular question.

"What do you want for a Word today, Ricky?"

He hung away from me then, a little, and I could see that he didn't know what I meant. "You know those cards the others are reading?" I said. "Those are the words they want to read and learn." He was still there, so I chanced another downpour and asked, "Who do you love best?"

His face dissolved into tears again, but he choked out "Mom." So I briskly wrote *Mom* in big blue letters on a card while he eyed me and did a few of the jerky sniffs that come at the end of crying. "This word is *Mom,*" I said.

The sun, moon, and stars all shone at once in his face. "Mom," he breathed, taking the card. Then he looked back at me. "This says *Mom*?" he checked.

I nodded. "You can trace it and read it to some of the other children now," I said to him, but he didn't hear me. He had waltzed over to Eric, who happened to be nearest, and pulled on him. "Hey, lookit! This word is *Mom*!" And after that day he was fine: happy and reading and eager to come to school.

I am a teacher of first grade, and while I love it all, the best part is teaching writing. Ricky was one of my students a few years ago, beginning the writing program with his first Word. I have been teaching writing to first graders for the past twelve years — my first first grade should graduate from high school this June.

I have been working on this program of writing for all of these years, most of them with kindergarten colleagues. We base this program of writing, K–3, on the work of Sylvia Ashton-Warner, as she describes it in her book *Teacher.*

I call this writing program Doing Words.

Every morning, the first day of school and the last day, the wild day that is Halloween and the bursting day that is Christmas-at-school, we Do Words. From one word to whole stories, what the children want to write about is the most powerful stuff of all. We use it. In addition to good writers, we have proud ones; in addition to competent readers, we have confident ones. They know they have worth. They learn it through their writing, every day.

That is the one rule in the morning, at every level, on every day: you must write a story, you must get a Word.

"What is your Word today, Heather?" I ask a shy five-year-old on a beautiful fall day.

"*Daddy,*" says Heather softly, looking at her shoes.

Heather already has *Daddy* in her envelope of Key Words. I wonder if there is something special about Daddy today that is more Key than simply his name. Heather is scuffling her shoe on the floor.

"What's Daddy been doing?" I ask.

She looks up and her foot stops. "He went hunting last night," she says very fast, "and he shot a deer and it's hanging in the garage and it's all bloody." She is looking at my face, but she is staring at the carcass in the garage.

"Did you see it this morning?"

Heather nods. "Mama showed it to me when we were walking to the bus. She said it was a good big one." It is clear that Heather doesn't see anything good about it at all.

"She was glad to have the deer meat, probably," I say, in a vain attempt to make her feel better.

Another nod. "She said we would eat it in the winter." She shifts herself in the chair. "I could see its eyes."

"You didn't like to look at it," I say.

Heather shakes her head, looking at her shoes again. "But it will be good to have it in the freezer. Mama says." She looks up.

"What's your word today, Heather?" I ask again.

"*Deer,*" says Heather.

I print the word on the card, and Heather traces the letters, correctly, from left to right.

"What is this word?"

"*Deer.*"

"Good. Please read your word to a friend and then put it in the basket."

Heather moves away, and another child comes up to the table to get a word.

Doing Words is my adaptation of Sylvia Ashton-Warner's Key Vocabulary, adapted for the rural Maine children we teach. She defines the Key Vocabulary this way:

> I use pictures, too, to introduce the reading vocabulary, but they are pictures of the inner vision and the captions are chosen by the children themselves. True, outer, adult-chosen pictures can be meaningful and delightful to children; but it is the captions of the mind's pictures that have the power and the light. . . . the illustrations seen by the inner eye are organic, and it is the captioning of these that I call the "Key Vocabulary."

Organic writing is writing from the inside out. When we Do Words we take the images that are important to a child — "Key," in the American vernacular — and give them to him to read and write. Organic words are the captions to the pictures in the mind of the child. Key Words, the child's first words to read and write, caption his most important images, images that are part of his mind and soul. When we give such a caption to a child as a Key Word, to read and write and keep and remember, a bridge is laid between the world of his own person and the outer world in which his personality must function.

Most of the children we teach come from farm families, from rural households. Mama and Daddy are too busy to do much reading and were themselves not scholars. They almost never write. It is not enough, then, to teach reading as a skill, to teach writing as an activity, and hope to create readers and writers who will want to read and write more and more.

Skills must be taught, of course. The structure and elegance of the language in which these children are reading and writing must be transmitted. Not first, however. First comes the desire and the eagerness. The child must be hooked by his own excitement and confidence to take cards and then pages of black squiggles and turn them, inside his own head, into *The Billy Goats Gruff* or *Charlotte's Web* or *All About Dinosaurs.* If he first takes the black squiggles that represent his own most important images, and finds out that he can connect the two, he will effortlessly transfer this connection to other words that he might not have chosen first.

In other words, if the child has the opportunity to get onto that bridge from the inner man out, if he has the opportunity to spend the earliest part of his school life releasing his own images, he will be able to take in what the school and the world expect him to understand and remember.

When he reads his own words, Key Words for him, first, his curiosity is aroused about all words. His interest is hooked; his eagerness is channeled entirely without his knowing it. He is his own primer.

After he has moved out across his own unique bridge, then you can tell him, occasionally, what he is to write and read; tell him, occasionally, what you would like him to think: but only then. The worst thing a teacher — or any adult — can do to a child is to reject that which is important to him, which may define him for himself. Unfortunately it is also one of the easiest things to do, especially in crowded classrooms and in the hurrying life of America today.

You may not say, of his painting, his block tower, or his clay model, that it is bad. You may not even say, "Oh, why don't you . . ." fix it some way to make it more acceptable, implying that it isn't. It can be a rejection to simply say "What is it?" "Tell me about this . . ." painting or whatever is a much less judgmental way to find out. Exactly the same kind of care must be taken of his writing, of the captions he asks for during Words, the captions of his inner illustrations. No judgment can be made. If it's Key, it's Key. Let it be: it is the child.

Not using these organic images and their power is a waste of you both. Teachers sometimes say they can "get" the child to read and write with a "story-starter," like "If I had a pirate ship . . ." or "Last summer on my vacation I . . ." To do this, though, is to waste the infinite amount of material in the child's own head, his own life, and what is more, to implicitly inform him that what *he* can think of to write about isn't nearly as good as what *you* can think of. This is to be a molder, not an educator; a pusher-in, not a drawer-out. It is immensely counterproductive for you, as well. The children have a lot of energy for their own ideas and images, and if you want them to use yours, you have to spend your energy instead. You have to think up the ideas, and impose them, and keep the odd corners rounded off and the lids on the boxes you intend the children to stay in. Bear in mind the old Grimm tale: when Cinderella's stepsisters cut off their toes and heels to fit into the glass slipper, not only was it no fun, but it did not work.

Helping, or at least allowing, children to bring their own most important images into their school activities is one of the reasons why writing should be done in school, and done even at the youngest ages. Writing is one very good way for humans to get some distance on problems, to get in touch with what is going on inside ourselves at any age. When a five-year-old's first Words include whom he loves and what he is afraid of, and when a fifth-grader writes in her journal about her anger at her mother, it helps them to deal with their inner selves, just as it helps grown-ups. Writing at any age is cheaper than psychotherapy.

Another reason that it is important to continue to teach writing in school, and to greatly increase the amount of writing done in elementary schools in America, is television. All the children in our schools today have been brought up to, with, and sometimes by television. All they have to do is listen and watch. Television can blot out their own images, and gives them an unfair assessment of their own images as wrong, to speak only of the visual side of television. And as far as language is concerned, they merely listen: no conversation is expected by the screen, and any talking is probably discouraged by others watching. Many children spend many hours in such a passive state. When they come to school, then, they have no experience in respond-

ing in conversation, they are not at ease with active language at all. They do not know how to organize their thoughts into speech. Writing is a way to help them do this. Indeed, it is what writing does.

Doing Words is a beginning. Learning to write and learning to read what you and your friends write is only part of the learning associated with Doing Words. Awareness of the language is a corollary learning, the fascination of finding that *knee* really starts with *k,* the light bulb discovery that *glove* has *love* inside it. This awareness is probably not surprising, since young children are readily fascinated by language. Other intangibles, which not even the most cumbersome of skills lists might include, develop as children Do Words in kindergarten and first grade: sharing; respect for the work of others; eagerness; self-confidence.

Each child makes his own way to learning to write and read. I don't think these subjects are taught at all: the teacher has to provide the atmosphere and the opportunity for them to happen to/with/by/for a child, but that is all she can do. The mind of each child is as intricate as the activities of reading and writing are; the collective mind of thirty-children-plus-teacher in a classroom defies any definition but its own existence. There can be no single path, no sequence that all children follow. Each makes his own, and I follow them. The paths may all be rather similar when traced out, but the tracing of them is a unique movement and achievement of each one.

This tracing begins long before the child gets to school, of course. Children come to school, even to their very first Key Word, with language already part of them. By the time they are five, normal English-speaking children have already accumulated an active vocabulary of about two thousand words. There are more words in English than in any other language, so that may not seem like much, proportionally speaking, against the 200,000 or so possible; but an adult's working vocabulary is only about six thousand, so the child has really accomplished a prodigious deed in those first four or five years.

Not only vocabulary, of course, has been acquired. The structure of the language, later in his life to be known as grammar, is part of him too. He has listened to others, he has blatantly copied the usages of others, and he has also made connections of his own. When a word works for him, he uses it over and over; when it doesn't work, when no one understands him, he will change to another formulation and try again. Each child who is born, in a very real sense, reinvents the language from the sound up.

What is of the most interest here is that he does it entirely in terms of context. Children learn new patterns of speech and new uses for words and new formulations for their needs and thoughts in the context of what they are doing or wanting or needing. Memory isn't their strong suit: absorption is the way they learn.

I can say to you, another grown-up, "Remember when we were talking the other day about planning the reception for your mother's birthday? Well, I've had another idea about it." And you will be able to pull back that conversation we were having and we can go on from there, discussing it further.

I can't do this with a young child. Sometimes, very seldom, a young child of less than five will do this to me, or to you: "Remember, Mommy, we saw these elephants before in that big book at Granddaddy's." Or, even more rarely, "What does temperature mean?" referring to a conversation of days or weeks past. This becomes more common as the child approaches six; it happens fairly often in school.

Far from being in the front line, then, of teaching children how to read and write, I am, as a teacher of the early grades, merely the one who helps them codify all that they have already learned, all that they are already using. I don't teach them their language: they already have it. Even the teachers of English as a Second Language (ESL), whom I admire hugely, are working with postinfants. ESL students have already connected themselves to the world with language. They are already school age or often older, and they have acquired a language that worked for them in the context in which they were living before they came to English. The real work of teaching language is done by the most amateurish of all humans, the babies and the parents.

Who, after all, is the teacher of the infant? Who lets the baby know which early signals he is using to connect himself to the world are the ones that will work for him? The baby is the prime mover, actually, in his own learning: it is he who first makes the vocalized labial movements that are interpreted by an eager parent as *Mama*. When she repeats it and makes soothing and nurturing noises back, he begins to learn from her as well as from his own experimentation. The very young child works through a fairly predictable sequence of behaviors in his unending quest to understand and be part of the world around him.

He works from the inside out when learning his oral communications skills, just as he will later learn to write and read when Doing Words. He learns in wholes, acquiring the language that he needs to express a context, a situation of his life. Just so will he learn to read by acquiring Words, captions that name and encompass entire stories and complicated images in his head. A child is — a human is — first and foremost an egocentric being. Altruism, sharing, self-denial are human traits that come much much later in our social and psychological development. The child has to be egocentric: no one else can assimilate him to the world but himself.

It doesn't do any good to tell a child about a thing — he has to find out. He has to structure the known world for himself, each child does. The classic principle, let him touch the stove so he'll know what hot means, is sound, but has been a source of disagreement among parents and parental advisors since the Neanderthals discovered fire. There must be a Chinese proverb about this that I can't remember right now.

And they learn absolutely incredible amounts of stuff in the first four or five years. Leaving aside language, they learn to walk, skip, run, hop, catch, throw, bend, balance, dance, sing, and draw. You have to learn these things by and for yourself — nobody else can do them for you. Mom can tie your shoes, yes; Mom can tell you when you're tired, yes; but she can't walk for you and she can't use your eyes and ears and fingers and toes and nose and tongue and voice for you. The child is the only one who can walk with his feet, sneeze with his nose, taste with his tongue, run sand through his fingers, laugh with his voice. And these achievements can be doubled, because children can also do them backwards or upside-down. The child does what he does for and by himself.

Children learn — acquire data as they interact with their world, and put together bits of it to make new formulations — from the first breath they draw. It doesn't seem unreasonable to me to assume that they are doing this before they are born, too, although it's as hard to talk about such a thing happening as it is to talk intelligently about heaven. (There are no eyewitness reports in either case, or at least none that I have heard of that I can believe.) They don't wait to learn until they suddenly become five and can go to school. They are learning all the time. Any and all people, and animals, and events, and pains, and joys, and puzzlements are all teachers for a new child in the world. With these bits they invent their own systems for integrating themselves into the world. What I am giving the child of age five and six, with Words, reading, and writing, is a new mode of description and communication for all this data he has discovered and collected: a new bridge.

The beautiful thing about Doing Words, from the teacher's point of view, is that you don't have to work. All I do from 8:45 until 10:00 every morning is listen, spell, and chat.

"What do you want to write today, Jenny?" I ask one day in October.

Shrug. This little one has big circles under her eyes: it's harvest time and everybody cuts the corn at Jenny's farm.

"Did you help Daddy with the corn last night?"

"Yes." Sigh. "But I don't want to write that."

"What do you want for a story today?" I ask again.

Silence. "I don't know. I can't think." She slumps, chin in hand. Her bangs fall into her eyes.

I smoothe back the wispy strands of hair. "How about that one? *I can't think.*"

Grin from Jenny. "Okay. Yeah. *I can't think of anything to write today.*"

So we go over the words, I write for her the ones she needs, and she trots off to her seat to write it. Later, in the reading circle, she will eagerly share this story and concur, good-naturedly, with the triumphant cries of "You did too write!" and "You tried to trick us!" which will greet its delivery.

This is the central language arts experience of the day. In among the words and stories also appear beginning sounds drill, rules for using apostrophe *S,* when to capitalize, what a period is for, when to say *were* instead of *was,* why *brang* is *brought.*

By ten o'clock every child, every day, has achieved something to be proud of. Every single day every child will have done something that he can display to the whole class, and there is no one else who has done the same thing.

And he can read it. It is meaningful to him, it makes sense, because he wrote it. It's not something to read out of a textbook written by a committee in Chicago in 1978, it came out of his head that very morning, his own head. None of this, of course, can he verbalize, but it's reflected in his enthusiasm for all the other reading he must do. The unrelated and often moribund vocabulary of the school's basal textbooks doesn't seem to bore the writing readers. Enthusiasm for reading other people's writing has been generated by writing and reading their own.

The inner child has been heard.

If I had my way altogether I would have nothing in the room except tables, chairs, paint, chalk, clay, blocks, puzzles, scissors, paper, pencils, plants, animals, magazines, magnifying glasses, and books. There is so much slick printed stuff around today that a teacher can (and sometimes feels pushed to) fill her room with: highly colored and expensive cards, pictures, and posters — cute cures for every painfully separated skill. They call these things "visual aids." Visual aids — what can that mean except eyeglasses? These things are not aids to anything, they are substitutes for organic vision. The use of them will overlay, if it doesn't smother, a child's own Words. Using them only means that the child will have to wade through the overlay, if he can, before he can find himself, find his own bridge to reading, writing, and the world.

As the Words program has evolved over the past twelve years, I have identified six stages. All the children seem to pass comfortably through these stages between the beginning of kindergarten and the end of first grade. I like to think of these stages as Movements: there is something satisfyingly symphonic about the way organic writing works with children. In this chapter, Heather was in Movement I; Jenny in Movement IV.

There is a major shift of emphasis during Movement V, corresponding to the major shift of emphasis in writing instruction everywhere during the past few years. This is the shift to process writing, that is, working through drafts and revisions just as "real" writers do. (I will explain this more in Chapters 7 and 8.) Organic writing and process writing dovetail into each other neatly at Movement V. For the first four Movements we give young children the confidence that they can write anything, and we give them the language to write it in that anyone can read. Standard English, legible penmanship, and correct spelling are part of Doing Words from the beginning.

Movement I is Sylvia Ashton-Warner's Key Vocabulary. After a little conversation with each child, a Key Word emerges. The teacher writes the Word on an unlined, oaktag card for that child, the child traces it with a finger, then reads it to the class. Words are kept in large manila envelopes and the collection is read every day. By Christmas, the average kindergartener has between thirty and fifty of these Key, personal Words.

Movement II is done the same way, except the Words are sentences, longer captions for the Key images of the child. The teacher writes on the card, the child traces and reads. Every day, all the cards are read to a friend. The envelopes are getting very fat.

Movement III uses sentences chosen by the child in a conference with the teacher as before, but now the teacher writes the sentence on a lined card and the child, after tracing it, prints the sentence on lined paper. The papers are read every day, before and after the new sentence.

Movement IV has the child printing two or more sentences after the conference with the teacher, and the words needed for that printing are written by the teacher on a large card in a list. The child retrieves the words and prints them in a booklet made of lined paper. The booklets are read. This is usually the last Movement in kindergarten.

Movement V extends the retrieval of words to a personal dictionary. Stories are written independently and are often continuing from day to day. Each day's work is read, and stories are posted for others to read.

Movement VI incorporates the whole writing process, adding revision and editing and group peer conferences to the teacher conference, continuing drafts, and publishing of Movement V. Children may write in either a booklet or on many papers in a folder. As the children come to use the writing process exclusively, the differentiation of genres and audience is expected in their writings.

Movements I and II will be described and discussed together because the line between them is very wavy. In Chapter 3, I will try to describe Doing Words in a classroom where the first three Movements are in simultaneous use. In Chapters 6 and 14 I will describe how Movement V works for me in first grade. In Chapters 8, 9, and 11 the writing process of Movement VI will be described by showing children at work in this Movement.

None of the lines between the Movements is rigid. It sometimes happens that I guess wrong about where a child can best work, but the longer I teach writing the less often I guess wrong. When you goof, it's not a very big goof; just back up one Movement and things will be fine. Don't be afraid to: the power of their writing, writing what they want to and sometimes have to say, will not be defeated by being in the wrong Movement. They'll let you know, by the way they write, where they should be. Where you start depends on what grade you teach and how much language awareness has preceded your tenure of any group. Movement I may be begun anywhere in kindergarten, or at the beginning of first grade. If the kindergarten has done a lot with penmanship, Movement I can be combined with Movement III, so that Key Words are being printed right away. In any case, don't skip Key Words. If you begin in second grade, begin with Movement IV if nothing was done before; begin with Movement V if possible. In third grade begin with Movement V. More directions for these late starts are given in Chapter 13.

Kim has written her story today with no help from me, at the very beginning of Movement V. She has brought it to me to be checked. It goes like this, and is beautifully printed. *I am playing with cheryl. We will play jumprope.*

"Very pretty printing, Kim," I say to her, drawling the repeated *pr* as I always do. "But just look at poor Cheryl in your story — doesn't she have a name today?" I point to the lowercase *c*.

"Oops!" says Kim, one hand going to her mouth, pencil and all. "Capital *C*!" And she scoots off to fix it.

This may be teaching — I know it's fun.

Doing Words works for all children. Curriculum and content they choose themselves, admiration and success every day — how can it not work?

Chapter 2

Movement I, Or, How It All Starts

> A human being should be able to change a diaper, plan an invasion, write a sonnet, balance accounts, build a wall, set a bone, comfort the dying, take orders, cooperate, act alone, solve equations, analyze a new problem, pitch manure, program a computer, cook a tasty meal, die gallantly . . . specialization is for insects.
>
> — Robert Heinlein

MOVEMENT I is the Key Word Movement. Sylvia Ashton-Warner used Key Words as a bridge between the two cultures her New Zealand Maoris had to live in, a bridge from the Maori to the European.

These two cultures were radically different. In rural Maine, the differences between the native, local culture and the expectations of nationally patterned school systems are much more subtle. The gulf of comprehension between, for example, New York City children who have never seen a cow, and the children of rural Maine, who have never seen a fire hydrant or, in fact, a water system that serves more than one house, may not seem to be as deep as between a European child raised on Jesus and a Maori child who believes in the ghosts of his ancestors. The subtlety of the differences within American culture makes them dangerously easy to overlook or dismiss.

A bridge is definitely needed to bring the children of rural Maine across into literacy, to enable them to be comfortable with and excited by the printed and written word on which their school lives are built.

On another level, too, every child ever born lives in her own culture, inside her own head, and needs a bridge from that inner person into the outer world, no matter what is in that outer world. In this sense, then, Key Words are necessary as a bridge for all children, for all people at the accession of literacy.

The first Word is a hook. It is a deliberate emotional hook to cause the child to invest herself in her card, in reading her Word because it says *Daddy,* or *Frankenstein,* or whatever is the caption for an important image for that day. She is hooked by her own ownership of and commitment to the Word, hooked by the Word to reading and writing.

To do Movement I you will need half to three-quarters of an hour, a manila envelope for each child, a marker, and lots of cards. The ideal cards are manila oaktag sheets that you have cut into strips three by twelve inches. Manila is the best color, because it is the cheapest of the tag papers for one thing, and because it is neutral.

Some years, though, we have used anything because we ran out of tag. One year we discovered that the local printer's shop had boxes and boxes of strips just that size, left over from cutting off the ends of the town reports before binding, so we used those. They had the outstanding advantage of being free, but the paper wasn't as heavy and the cards were not as durable. Tag is best. It bends and twists many times before it tears. These cards see quite a lot of action, a lot of holding and showing and reading and sharing and putting-in-and-out-of-envelopes, before the first two Movements are over.

The arrangement of the room, and the decision about who moves during word time, you or the children, is a new decision every year. For me, it depends on the children. If they have not had much training in working independently, it is best to have them stay put and you circulate. Go to each one and scooch or bend down to be at their level. You could also pull along a chair of your own, to be comfortable and seem more relaxed. If the children have learned already to be a little self-directed, then you park yourself at a table (or at your desk if it's uncluttered —

mine never is) and the children will come to you, one at a time, for their Words. On the very first day of Movement I, you will need to explain what it is all about.

"Today each of you is going to have a Word to read and keep," you might say. "I'm going to ask you what Word you would like to have and I'll write it down for you." You really don't need to say more than that to fives and young sixes. They are fascinated by anything new, anyway, and will probably clamor to be first.

Sit at your table and call a child or two, if you don't have a passel of them draped around you already. Sit the child down next to you. Print the child's name in the upper left-hand corner of the card and ask, "What's your Word today?" On the very first day you may have to ask some other questions, like "What did you do when you got home last night?" or "Who do you love best?" but not often.

Most days most children will have a Word all ready for you. "*Mama,*" the child will say, giving the most classic Word of all.

So you print it on the card in your best printing, perhaps saying the letters as you do so. Then you ask, "What is this Word?" This is an invitation to read it.

"*Mama,*" says the child.

"Right," you say. "Now will you please trace these letters for me with your finger?" The index finger of the hand the child uses to write is the one I have them use, pretending it is a pencil. One of the other teachers I know who is Doing Words has them trace with the thumb and two fingers pressed together as if there were a pencil being held there. That works very well too. At the beginning there may be letters the child doesn't know how to form, so you do it with your finger and the child copies you.

The point of the tracing is to learn letter formation, so you need to watch it very carefully. If a child traces one incorrectly, like making *l* from the bottom, say that it has to be done "this way," and show her how.

When the tracing is all done, the child has to read the word again. "Good," you say. "Now go read it to a friend and put it in the basket on my desk," or wherever you collect the day's Words. And the child does these things while you talk to the next one.

"What's your Word today?" you say again. This time a whole story pours out. You learn that Grammy came over the night before and helped Mama make all the pies for the dinner for the wedding of Aunt Lisa and her boyfriend which is coming up. You ooh and aah appropriately and then you say again, "What's your Word today?"

The child may say over the first sentence of her recital, or the last one. Perhaps she will say "Grammy came over last night and made pies with Mama."

"Do you want *Grammy*?" you may ask. And she may say yes, or she may say *pumpkin,* which she hadn't mentioned yet, because it's her favorite kind of pie.

It is a good idea to have the letters of the Word named a couple of times a week, and if there is a capital letter, mention why. After a few weeks, and certainly in Movement II, you can begin to ask what the child thinks a word like *pie* might start with, and begin the phonic connections as well as the printing ones.

After everyone has a Word, and all the Words are in the basket, it's time to read. The next part of Doing Words is sharing all the Words for the day aloud in an all-class group.

Have all the children sit in a circle on the floor or a rug (this works infinitely better than moving chairs in a million directions). Some years I've even had a special reading rug which we unrolled and rerolled for this time. Sit with them — it's no good listening from across the room while you get ready for the next activity. Nearly everything in all the Movements of Doing Words and in all the steps of the writing process needs to be modeled, and listening to other people read is no exception. Children do not come knowing how to trace letters, how to read aloud interestingly, how to be helpful about their peers' writing, how to develop twists of plot, any more than they come knowing how to tie their shoes or multiply. You have to model all these things, some more than others, some more for some children than for others. This is also known as teaching.

When everyone is sitting together, pass the cards around in the circle until all the children have recognized and taken their own. They don't seem to use their names, written by the teacher in the left-hand corner of the card, at all for this process of claiming their own words. The name in the corner is meant to draw the eye of the child unconsciously to the left as she begins to read and trace her Word. This unconscious movement of the eyes appears on skills charts as Demonstrates Understanding of Left-to-right Progression.

Choose a child to read, and that one chooses one, and they all read today's word aloud in turn. Then they put the new Word into their envelopes with all their other Words and Word time is over for that day.

It is the child's responsibility to get a Word each morning. If she doesn't, she won't have anything to read in the circle when all the day's Words are passed and read. The next day she will get her Word for sure.

Every day the children read all the Words in their envelopes to each other, usually first thing. Once a week they read them all to the teacher or another adult. If there is a Word the child doesn't remember, it is removed: that one isn't very important after all. It is the Key Vocabulary, the important captions, that will be the hooking words. "That one isn't very important," I say as I quietly take it away. There is no censure in this; if it's not key, if it isn't remembered, why let it clutter up the envelope? The envelopes hold only the most current and vital Words.

One way to start a child in Movement I is with fear or love words. Fear words are easy to get but require careful handling. Several kindergarten teachers I know always begin Doing Words around Halloween, the second week or so of October. All the Halloween words are fear words, every single one. The whole illusion is scary for young children, because they are not at all sure that it is, in fact, an illusion.

Love is easier, although I don't mean to imply that it requires less careful handling! Mostly it takes the form of I-loves. "Who do you love?" is a sure-fire question in kindergarten and even sometimes at the beginning of first grade, before it becomes too giggle-bound. It's a very powerful question when it works. It worked with Ricky in Chapter 1, and with many other children.

"What do you want for your Word today?" I asked Daniel, with his straw-straight hair and his deceptively trusting blue eyes. I asked it gently, because Daniel was fearful of his own and all other shadows, and it was a wonder that he stayed close to me long enough to hear the question.

Daniel ducked his head and looked away, with a little murmuring noise. I smiled, moving my head a little so he would see me. He cleared his throat. "Do you know what you want for a Word today, Daniel?" I asked.

Surprisingly, he made a definite nod. He cleared his throat again, and I waited. After a third clearing and another jerk of his head, lowering his chin, he said, "Yes. Yes, I think so."

I smiled again, willing myself down to his speed. "It can be any Word you want, you know," I said encouragingly. He watched me. "Is it someone you love?"

Another frightened jerk of his head, but a little smile mirrored mine. "Yes." He cleared his throat. "But it's not any body," he added anxiously.

"Who do you love, Daniel?"

Then the smile came all the way out, and he looked at me for a full instant. "It's my dog. Her name is Emily." He looked away, and down, and back at me, with an almost smooth movement. Then he looked at me again, straight on, and said without clearing his throat, "I love Emily."

When he got the card with Emily's name on it, he loved the card, too. *Emily* helped Daniel trust his Words, and me, and himself.

Love is there, a major force and resource in the lives of fives and sixes. It's an odd child who doesn't have at least half the other children's names as Words after a couple of months of getting

Words every day. Often the deepest feelings about friends are heavily disguised, as by *very* in *Tony is my very very very very very best friend*; but it's there. It's been there since birth, the most basic need humans have that isn't connected to their bodies.

The very first thing a baby needs to understand is where and how to get nourishment. Mammalian instinct operates as an infant suckles, and at first the baby will simply drink milk from a real or rubber nipple and sleep, waking to feed again, feeding to sleep some more. A very new first-time mother said to me of these first days, with some puzzlement, "Will doesn't seem to want to play much." Her baby is still inside himself. As yet he has no awareness of the world, at all, except in terms of light and warmth. It is unlikely that he is aware that the nipple is part of a being separate from himself: it hasn't been so very long ago that he was, in fact, a part of that nipple-bearing being himself.

It doesn't take long at all, though, for Will to begin to command that nourishment, and to get his first glimmer that it is not part of himself. Weeks before he can consciously smile at Mommy and know that she is outside of himself, he has learned that a certain kind of action he can make — perceived as crying or wailing by the interested parent — will bring warmth or feeding to him.

Rest and/or sleep is the other very early activity the baby learns that allows him to make rudimentary distinctions between his states of being. He begins to know that being asleep is different from being awake. That's all: just knowing that there is a difference is a basis for later learnings and judgments about what the difference is, how to get from one to the other, and how to manipulate himself and his world to get what he wants.

As important as these two, but harder to classify as physiological, is love. Growth is more congruent with the child's own personality when love is present from day one. (We won't go into whether that day is the day of conception or the day of delivery.) Studies have been done which demonstrate that even plants grow to be more healthy and productive when they are loved. One of my daughters, for a tenth-grade biology project, recreated one of these experiments on all the windowsills of our house. She planted the same bean seeds in the same soil in the same kind of pot with the same fertilizer and watered them correctly for two months. She put them in windows on the same sunny side of the house and gave us strict instructions on how to behave with them.

The plants in the hall downstairs were not spoken to at all. She wouldn't let us say even hello. The ones on the hall windowsill upstairs were actively reviled: my, aren't you an ugly plant, we had to tell them. The plants in the living room window were actively loved. How well you're looking today, we said. This went on day after day, and I wondered a little if the guilt I felt at being so mean would have any effect on them. The plants in the living room window were much bigger, much greener, and (we thought) much happier when the experiment was over. I was convinced. I don't remember whether the biology teacher was or not.

If the beans absorbed our love from the air, however they could possibly do that, and it helped them to connect with their life force, why does love not do the same for maturing humans as well? How much more so, I would think, is that the case for humans, as they expand their cell use and learn. Humans, too, can give back love, and it becomes even more powerful. Fear is equally important but runs a greater danger of being stifled as the child is growing up to five. Fears come early in the infant child's life, and by the time children come to school they each have a personal catalog, depending on what experiences they have had. Sometimes the power of the fear is too much for the child, blocking out other experiences and growth. Words are a way to deal with a fear; talking and writing about scary things diminishes their power.

Lisa was terrified of snakes, but one day she wanted *snake* for her Word. She could read it when she went over her cards, but a week or so later when her teacher was tidying up the shelves, she found Lisa's *snake* in behind the puzzles. She thought little

one

of it and simply put it back in Lisa's envelope. Over the next week or so that card kept turning up in odd places, and the teacher always put it back.

Finally she tumbled to the fact that Lisa didn't want to have *snake* in her envelope; so the next time it turned up under the rug, the teacher "lost" it too.

Jim, intensely preoccupied with a fire he had seen when he was three, used to ask everyone he met if they knew about it. If they didn't — and sometimes even if they did — he told them. Over a period of several kindergarten days he got these words: *fire, fire engine, fire truck, smoke, Joe's barn, flames.* In addition to the release these Words provided for Jim, knowing and reading them was a powerful lesson in visual discrimination for a young five. Jim has stopped talking about the fire so much now. Somehow the power of the fire's images to lock up his mind has been lessened by captioning them in Words.

Words can relieve an emotion-ridden image on many levels. Not least of these is that the child gets to talk about it, both with the teacher and with the other children when they read their Words together. It is also helpful to get the caption into another medium, written down. This takes away some of the ghostly fear enveloping the image it captions, like Heather's *deer* in Chapter 1.

When children are in school, these feelings of love and fear are no less central to their lives than when they were Will's size, so I use them, use their power to connect young minds to the work of school, and incidentally give them back my acceptance of their feelings.

Every day is a new collection of images to share, a new delineation of the class as the answers to "What is your Word today?" pile up in the basket. One year, the first day of Doing Words in kindergarten, these were read in the circle:

> Blackie. Mommy. Duchess. baby. Wayne. Mommy. Easter. horse. Smiley. Horace. Snoopy. fire. Gloria. Grampie. Mommy. Francis. Darren. Dad. fire. Tiny. zebra. Mom. birthday. WonderWoman. Chieftain. rocket. Mama.

This group of children was well grounded at home: six named their mothers first (Gloria is a mother), nine named their pets.

When Words time starts, about nine o'clock, children are chosen to pass out the envelopes. They flounder around for a little while, deciding whose name is on the envelope. The teacher doesn't say a word. *Dicky* and *Danielle, Jason* and *Jarrod,* are not the same and Dicky will be outraged to be handed Danielle's envelope. They soon learn to tell the difference, all of them, because all get a turn to pass out the envelopes. It is the best visual discrimination lesson they will have. There is nothing more important than the self, and the children use the energy of that importance to learn through Words.

After the envelopes are passed out, all the children read all their cards to a friend. There is a lot of interchange and conversation during this reading — it is not silent reading by any means. If Keith is reading with David and David has *dumptruck,* Keith may want to get *dumptruck* when he comes for his Word. But it will be his own *dumptruck* then. If he got it just because David had it, and not for reasons of his own, it will probably not be in his envelope long, because he won't remember it.

Even though some words are common to all the envelopes, each child's set outlines a unique pattern. Here is Mac, just before Christmas:

> Mommy. monster. Batman. spiders. rain. elephant. Big Foot. Superman. police car. Bionic dog. Bionic man. Bionic woman. Bionic Mac. explosion. Winnie the Pooh. gorillas. Princess. spacecraft. outer space. giant. snowmobile. sea monster. crowd. robot. space academy.

Every day the teacher hears four to six of the children read through their whole envelopes of Words, managing in this way to hear everyone's Words once a week. After the teacher hears an envelope, she gives that child the Word for that day. Usually there are a few children hanging around, fascinated by another's Words. Sometimes, there may be a collection standing around the table and one on her lap, too. This is especially true of Fridays when everyone is tireder and therefore seems to be younger.

"What's your Word today, Brad?" she asked on the second day of Words last year.

"Mama had a baby," said Brad, who is the youngest child in his family.

Carefully not saying that, she commented, "Oh, is this a new baby?"

"No," said Brad patiently. "She had a baby when she had me."

"Of course!" said the teacher. "What Word do you want today?"

"*Mama.*"

The most Key Word there is, I think, is the Mother name. Brad's was certainly not the only *Mama* in the envelopes, perhaps not the only one in the basket that day, but his formulation of it was absolutely unique and personal.

The typically Key child always has Mama, and almost always the rest of the family, the dog, the cat, the neighbors, relatives, and classmates and, of course, the teacher. It's easy to teach children that proper names need capital letters when so many of their first Words are names!

Sally, bright and stable at home, started with the dog and got the whole family right off the bat, ending with the horse. Then she got her teacher.

> Duchess. Mama. Dad. Ronnie. Emily. Mommy. Gwennie. Silver. Mrs. Eldridge. hunting. light bulb. ghost. witch. Santa Claus. Santa's helper. snow angel.

For Sally, *light bulb* was a Key Word because one blew up at her house during a thunderstorm. As they talked about it, the teacher thought *storm* would be the Word to caption that experience, but for Sally *light bulb* was the code for all the events surrounding the storm, including her fright.

Similarly Christy, after telling the teacher all about a very scary windstorm at her house deep in the pinewoods, wanted *night* as her Word. *Wind,* pulled out of the conversation by the teacher, wasn't Key for her.

Of course having one Word that captions a whole experience

or emotion can be a disappointment, too. Once Scott spent all morning immersed to his elbows and the backs of his eyes at the sand table. When he came for his Word he wanted *sand*. When it was printed on the card, his glow faded.

"Oh," he said blankly. "Is that all there is?" It should've been five miles long.

The same words are Key for different children in different ways. Even the closest children have unique sets, even identical twins and best friends. Paul and Bobby are first cousins and best friends and often operate as one personality in the classroom and as a whole team on the playground. They have many of the same Words, and often read their Words together, but they never get the same Word on the same day. They are independent, and the Words program fosters this independence by allowing each of them his own vocabulary. These two were unusual in that they asked for their own names. Bobby got all the members of his family, except Mom, right off. Paul never did ask for his mother.

> Bobby. Brutus. Peppy. Dad. Kevin. Linny. ladder. horse. Grammie. snowmobile race. Spiderman. Lone Ranger. Six Fifty. Eight Hundred. Dragster. Evel Knievel. Mom. liquid cool. Clarence's Six Fifty. Brandy. Motorcycle. Diamond Real. Santa Claus. Zorro. green machine. T.X. Duchess. Big Foot. Rudolph. Kawasaki.

Paul's cards began this way:

> Rambler. Paul. Robby. Daddy. snakes. dark. Superman. baseball. Astro. Evel Knievel. Eight Hundred. Lone Ranger. Tonto. rabbit hunting. deer hunting. Santa Claus. liquid cool. Cobra. Bear. T.X.L. fire. plane. new jeep. green machine. pickup truck.

These two boys are oriented to male things and machinery of all kinds. In that classroom, even without the names in the corners of the cards, the teacher would know that the snowmobile names belonged to them.

There are mornings when a child doesn't know what she wants. That's when talk happens. After she chats with the teacher for a minute — rarely longer — about a few dozen subjects, either she or the teacher will be able to pull out an important Word from the discussion.

To have this one-to-one conversation with every single child every single day is one of the best features of Doing Words. Besides talking about things that are important that day to the child, other problems can be spotted during the individual contact of Words time.

Children with speech difficulties or health problems are noticed at once, of course. When the child traces the Word, with the teacher watching closely every day, all bad habits of letter formation can be caught before they become permanent. It will also be evident in tracing which children haven't decided on their handedness. Those who trace one day with the left hand and another day with the right will need particular attention when they begin Movement III; indeed, in a few cases a child might not be given a pencil to print with until the handedness is settled.

Because a Key Word is a caption for an image or an experience, it is occasionally more than one simple word, one discrete collection of letters with a single meaning. *Lone Ranger,* in Bobby's envelope, is strictly speaking two words. So are *light bulb, Santa Claus,* and *fire engine.* In Movement II, sentences and longer phrases are the rule, and would not be questioned; but even in Movement I the Keyness of the caption may require two words, like *light bulb.* In a way, it's the fault of the language that *fire engine* and *light bulb* aren't one word in the first place.

Sometimes, however, in Movement I the caption has to be a whole sentence. Rarely, very rarely, the image cannot be captioned in one word.

Holly came for her Word one day and said, when asked what she wanted, "My lips are dry." She was, indeed, rubbing them nervously with her finger. Their dryness wasn't the important thing: the Key thing was that "Daddy hit Mommy." This was very scary. With gentle questioning this story emerged.

"My lips were dry, so Mommy climbed up the ladder (to Holly's bedroom in the loft) to get some stuff for them and she fell down and didn't get up and I went and called Daddy and Daddy hit her in the face." So Holly described the incident, making a sideways slapping motion when she said "Daddy hit her." She knew that Daddy was trying to help Mommy, to wake her up, yes, she knew that. But it was very scary that Mommy fell and that Daddy had to hit her and, somehow, it was Holly's fault. For her it had begun with "My lips are dry," and that was her Word. For Holly, those four words, really a sentence, had only one meaning and stood as the caption for the whole event. Because of this story, the teacher knew that Holly needed some special caring that day. She traced the whole thing in a matter-of-fact way, which also helped dispel some of the scariness.

Dan, too, had a special Word for which the label "sentence" was utterly irrelevant. At age two he had been run over, entirely by accident, by his mother. The teacher knew that about him long before he ever came to school. Dan was a pretty, gentle, seemingly happy-go-lucky child: but he had trouble remembering his Words. He had a small core of his brothers' names, the dog, and a couple of classmates, but his envelope never got very fat. He went along for quite a while this way, smiling and doing what he was asked to do and looking content. He was being very protective of his inner imagery, however, and not at all willing to share it with the class or the teacher.

Finally, in the beginning of May, he came to the table for his Word one morning with his same happy look and said, "I know what I want today. I want *I got ran over.*" The teacher stared at him, knowing it to be a special moment. "I did too," Danny assured her, misinterpreting the stare. "When I was little. But I'm not hurt or anything. I got ran over."

So the teacher printed that on the card. For both of them, it was all one Word. And after that, he remembered his Words, read them easily, and was at peace with himself.

There is a lot of talking that goes on during Words. That is because talking is the way children communicate at this time of their lives. They have known no other way to use language as a means of printing themselves on the people and world around them.

Oral language runs a great risk in school of being eliminated or being frowned upon so heavily that children won't feel comfortable. "Be quiet" is an admonition heard entirely too often in school. At home, before the child comes to school, during the early growing time, being quiet should be the child's own choice. There are often quiet, searching moments in the life of a two-year-old or a three-year-old, even though, as with everything else in life, we remember the tantrums, not the naps, when we review a day at home. Some of the excitement of discovery has to be shouted out, often the joy of being loved has to be crowed about; fear and pain have special noises too, and conversation accompanies all of these events. Talk, after all, is the hallmark of humanity. Without the power of language, we are not humans. The wonderful work of our great brains cannot be shared.

Young baby Will does learn to play, from the inside out. He discovers that he can move certain parts of himself, beginning with his mouth, and depending on the reaction he will build on the first, probably accidental, movement and expand his repertoire so that he is, in fact, communicating with another human outside himself. He learns to do this in tiny incremental steps, adapting to the animate and inanimate inhabitants of his environment. Somewhere along the way he learns that he is separate from all those inhabitants, too. There are prerequisites and consequences in this development; there is an order through which children grow.

Language develops in just such sequential ways: Will also experiments with sounds, and how they affect his environment, learning about sound and about speech by using it. At first he doesn't know he is making the sounds, but when he becomes aware of this he begins to use them and invent more, building his repertoire of communication. But language is not thought.

Thought, the abilities of awareness, comprehension, projection, imagination, problem solving, and abstraction, are all developing and redoubling in an exponential way, paralleling but not dependent on the physiological and social changes that are occurring in the first five years of the child's extrauterine life. It develops in spurts, with plateaus in between the spurts. Time is required to pass while repeated use of a new ability is made, in both realms, thought and language. Thought can occur without language; it cannot be expressed without language. Language is the tool to express thought.

There are indeed some incredible things that instinct can require of an animal species on our planet, and unfathomable things happen in the aging of mountains and the flares of the sun; and thought, the growth of neuron connections and the use of the cells in the frontal lobe of the human species, is an unmatched phenomenon in the known universe. But of all the things that are accessible to our understanding at all, the acquisition and development of language stretches us to our most distant edges.

When they come to school, children are still deeply involved in the amazing development of language, and they find it as fascinating as I do. (Maybe this is why I stay in first grade.) Doing Words we both use this fascination and foster it, all of us capitalizing on their excitement and paying close attention to the way each one's language is growing. In Movement I, we capture a discrete part of the child's thought, using oral language, and with it introduce her to reading and writing, the other languages she may, because she is a human, use to express herself.

James had about thirty-five Key Words in Movement I, his tracing was good, he remembered his Words, and his eagerness was constant. In his envelope were every member of his household, including the rabbits; *teacher*; *E.T.*; *mountain*; *van* (because they had to spend the night in it once); *tractor-trailer*; and ten or so members of the class, as well as his own Halloween persona, *Frankenstein*. Then one day he wanted *Jacob*.

"You have *Jacob*, don't you?" asked the teacher. "Is there something special about Jacob today?"

"Jacob is my friend," said James with a little shrug. That's special enough for me, said his shoulders. So the teacher printed

Jacob is my friend. James traced it and read it and put it into the basket as usual, and read it in the circle at the end of Word time. He had moved into Movement II.

Movement II is a continuation of Movement I, and is different only in one respect. The cards, marker, envelopes, and basket are the same. The reading of the cards in the envelopes daily to each other and weekly to the teacher are still part of Words work; and the other activities (see Chapter 3) are still in place.

But these Words are sentences.

The line dividing these two Movements is very fluid. It is hard to say where to begin Movement II; it is easier to say that Movement II Words are usually not quite as Key, although they are always important and nearly always autobiographical. The "friend" formula begins here.

As the days went by James had *I love Courtney, My father's got a new car, I love Shannon, Power Puncher, I love Mrs. Eldridge, My father is gonna go ice fishing, We're moving into our cousin's house,* and more.

During these days James was tracing all the letters correctly, naming them on request, at ease with the whole routine. He was also framing the words as he read them, and making the correct responses when asked why the first words had capitals and the sentences had periods. So after a month or so of this the teacher gave him a writing book and they were off, with *Our bus was late coming to school,* into Movement III (as we will see in Chapter 4).

Notice James's Word, *My Daddy is gonna go ice fishing.* The construction *gonna* and its variant *gonnu* are absolutely endemic to the speaking patterns of the rural children I deal with. That doesn't make it correct, I hasten to say. One teacher I work with has always felt, however, that this pattern should be left intact at least during the first two Movements, and she does so. Very occasionally she gets a parent complaint on this, more often for *brang* than for *gonnu.*

In first grade I don't accept these constructions, even in Movement II, and the children adapt themselves readily. They would in kindergarten, too, but I think that the kindergarten teacher's position has some validity even though I don't agree with it. These first ones are sentence captions of their own making, for their own images; and our first purpose is to get those images and captions flowing into the school world, to connect the inner child to the requirements of a radically new existence in school. Later, when the sentences are less Key, certainly in Movement III and beyond, it will not disrupt their flow to have the standard imposed. "You can say it that way," I tell the children, "but you have to write it like this" as I write *brought, going to,* etc.

Movements I and II can begin the year of first grade, too. Because the children are more able — or are probably more able — in the area of fine-motor coordination and control, the tracing stages can be much shorter. Never leave out these Key Word and Key sentence stages, however. The unlocking of the child's mind through Key Words is essential. If the Words belong to the child, the child will give his whole self to them, and thereby make his commitment to learning. These two Movements involve no writing as such. They involve enthusiasm and commitment to words and to reading, and during them the children are hooked to the idea that what they have to say is important. Pride, self-confidence, eagerness, as well as visual discrimination, letter formation, alphabet recognition, rules for capitalization, sentence sense are collected in the envelopes as surely as the oaktag strips. They form the underpinnings for the next Movements, when oral and reading work are joined by transcribing, composing, and the creative work of writing.

Chapter 3

The Creative Vent, Or, What Is Everyone Else Doing?

Play is the specific occupation of childhood.

— Jean Piaget

IT'S ALL VERY WELL to extol the virtues of speaking individually with every child every day, as you will do when you are Doing Words. It's all very well to say that you will have time to find out what is on each child's mind through this conversation, and that you will have time, also, to correct bad habits of printing by watching every child trace every letter of every word in Movements I and II. These two movements may last, in a kindergarten, from October to January.

But where does this time come from? If you spend two or three minutes with each child, uninterruptedly, during the hour of Word time, who is with him the other fifty-seven minutes? Or, as teachers invariably ask me, "What are the other children *doing* while you talk and trace and print with each one?!?"

The tone of this question is usually half-incredulous, half-suspicious. The implication of the tone is that my classroom must be a zoo. Visions of the worst features of open classrooms, of Summerhillian permissiveness, of scandalous misbehavior scamper across teachers' minds at the mere thought of children having Nothing To Do for that time. Behind the question is really another question, the eternal teacher-fear above all fears: "What if I lose control of my class?"

Teachers need to know how to corral and control children when it is necessary to do so. This chapter will not pretend to teach this to teachers who don't know how. Each teacher must find the ways she can be comfortable with children, while at the same time enacting and upholding discipline and order all day long. Each teacher must strike her own balance between chaos and compulsion. Structure and order must be imposed for safety as well as sanity, and the varying tolerances for noise and movement must be taken into account as a class is organized. Twenty-five or thirty bodies in a cube thirty feet on a side for hours on end must be handled in very different ways from a family of even six children in a whole house. Put enough desks and chairs and coathooks and bookshelves into such a cube, leave enough room between the pieces of furniture to walk or sometimes march around, and insist that there be a rug to sit on for reading aloud, and you will not have much room for freedom, let alone wild abandon.

During Words each child reads, gets a new Word to trace and read, and, in the later Movements, writes. While all the children are doing this, each child may choose to do other activities available in the room. Sylvia Ashton-Warner believed that children are both creative and destructive. "As you widen the creative vent," she wrote, "you atrophy the destructive one." She believed that reading, writing, dancing, singing, drawing, painting, building, thinking, dreaming, spelling, printing, pretending, acting, sculpting, and above all conversation are elements of the creative vent. They can all be occurring simultaneously in a primary classroom, she said, and they should be. The idea of "seatwork," so popular in America, doing pencil-and-paper exercises for their own sake, was anathema to her.

If you allow for activities of the creative vent, there will be movement and conversation during Word time. Most of the children, if asked, will tell you — or a visitor — that they are playing before and after they get the day's Word. They are right. I describe their play as children using and directing their energy through the creative vent. (It really can look chaotic, or, as the speech therapist said on one of her weekly visits, "Do you let your children play all morning?")

This play is, however, very hard work.

"Imagination is often erroneously associated with the mind at play rather than with the mind at work," said an expert at a conference I went to once, and he turned my thinking on its ear. I had erroneously assumed all my life — I think the Puritans had something to do with this — that imagination was only operating during play, and that if work was fun there was something wrong with it. Somehow I had always had the suspicion that play wasn't okay, play was somehow not as good as work. I have that feeling even now. Play isn't as good as work. But it takes great effort to use the imagination, as much as to do physics equations — and perhaps they are the same thing. Perhaps that's not a good example, because I've never known a physicist who wasn't wide-eyed and smiling as he worked. That expert freed me from most of those Puritan bonds, so that I could better see what I was looking at when children played, could see that they were working.

Imaginative play is the expression used to describe the hours and hours of games my girls would engage in, upstairs, with their Barbie dolls, telling the dolls what to do, telling each other what to tell the dolls to do, telling each other what the dolls were doing. They would do this for many whole Saturday afternoons, creating the plot and the action and the characterization and the histrionics of the piece as they went along. This was imagination, in the same way that a novel is imagination, with reflections of truth and logic imbedded in it: nobody ever said that writing a novel or a playscript was anything but work! The girls would wear themselves out, but never wear down.

For the first few years of children's lives, and indeed for the lucky ones longer, play itself has been their work. Daddy goes to the city, Mommy cleans the house, child plays. I think the child, of the three of them, has accomplished the most at the end of the day. Daddy may have traded six or seven million dollars,

Mommy may have washed every curtain and folded 900 socks, but the child has discovered, depending on how many months he has been alive, that his hand is attached to him; that he can throw his toys up and they will come down; that some sticks pushed across the wall or the book leave marks; that he can stack his blocks but not his stuffed animals; that the red paint will change color when it runs into the yellow paint; that he can put some letters onto his paper in a certain way and it will mean his own self, be his name; that he can block the water running down beside the driveway with stones or sticks, but it will still keep running; that as hard as he looks he will never find two stones or two leaves that are the same; or any number of very important groundings, and usually several. That's quite a day's work, and he's been playing all the time.

At school, the same kinds of things can be allowed for, and can be considered work, if only we don't think of schools as factories instead, where little minds and brains are lined up for filling, and only one person can do that filling. When you ask what the most important things are at typical schools, ask any kid when he gets home "what did you do in school today?" he will tell you about recess. That's still where the important stuff goes on for him, in his nonprogrammed or self-programmed time. That's how he's been learning, and that's still where he gives his fullest attention. He knows that his play is his work.

Play has been thought of as "mental waste matter," and in some eras has been considered harmful to children. "An idle mind is the devil's playground." "Quit fooling around and get to work." "What are the kids doing?" Dad asks, or Mom asks. "Oh, they're just playing." The implication of all these is that what they are doing is not important at all — frivolous, unnecessary, useless — not like the way adults occupy their time, with *work*. And yet the toddler in his sandbox, the preschooler with her fingerpaints, the first grader playing school, the nine-year-old roaming the fields collecting bees or damming streams or building clubhouses are all learning learning learning. And they are working hard. They are experimenting and processing and collecting data as hard as any high-powered forty-year-old researcher paid to do work in exactly those ways.

So, as the child is growing up before he comes to school, real school I mean, he has been doing work all the time. No nine-to-five for the under-fives! They are encouraged mightily at the beginning. "Look, John!" cries the new mother. "The baby can touch his nose!" The baby has discovered his nose by accident, and worked to repeat the movements that caused such an interesting feeling for himself. Later he will begin to manipulate his actions for the positive response of his parents, too, which is another kind of work grown-ups call behavior modification or, in its extreme forms, public relations.

When the three-year-old plays with all the things in the bathroom cupboard, taking them out and putting them in an order that interests her, then putting them back, her work is greeted with cries of less delight, but her operation has been concentrated work. It has differed from Mom's work on the same cupboard only in that Mom wipes off the shelves before she puts everything back, and in that Mom gets to call her task work.

A five-year-old likes to play with stones, or seeds, or nuts, or anything countable and collectible. When he drops them into a plastic container, they make different sounds from the sounds they make in a metal pail. The more there are in the container, the more the sound changes too. A child is likely to give a great deal of attention to this experiment and to get a great deal of satisfaction from it. He works hard, not only doing the moving of the objects, but also figuring out the parameters of the experiment as he goes along. Probably he also changes his givens and his goals several times in the course of it, which exhibits typical scientist work behavior, I think.

What kids are doing when they play through their days as preschoolers, then, is to work on their understanding of the world and their own place in it, and by extension on their understanding of themselves. If there is one thing a child needs before he or she comes into the regular, structured, real world of school, it is a positive view of his or her self and that self's place in the scheme of things. This is what parents must do, because there is very little room for it to occur in the huge groups present in the schools as they are now arranged. Lots of buzz words float around now related to this: self-concept, self-worth, self-image, usually prefaced with either "positive" or "negative." Stacks of books for grown-ups line the bookstore shelves, with titles like *I Ain't Much But I'm All I've Got,* and *How To Feel Better About Yourself,* so it may be a case of the blind leading the blind if parents are expected to help children know that the child has worth.

Here I get into one of the many circular reasonings I see in education in America. If the people who are now parents had no self-concept before they came to school, they certainly didn't get it from the schools, by and large. So now they are reading all those self-help books and are often unable to give their children the grounding the children need. (The complications that the growing equality and/or working of most mothers have brought into this mix are another whole subject.) So the children still, many of them, come to school without a settled sense of their worth. Let us leave aside the complicating questions of latchkeys, sexual abuse, multiparent families, weekend exchanges. Even among the 16 percent of the population who live in what we all still think of as the typical family, there are strains and stresses that inhibit the growth of children. That is the parent's main task: to give the child, to help the child to have, the idea that what he says and does and thinks and understands is appropriate and acceptable. Not fantastic, overwhelming, superior; just right. Baby bear's porridge sort of just right.

And because play is what the child needs to have been doing before his school years, as work, the activities of the creative vent echo that occupation when he begins his entry into the grown-up world with Words, at school.

It is the teacher who must determine what activities are included in the creative vent in the classroom. There are perhaps some cultural restraints on teachers that make certain activities unacceptable, such as dancing; just as importantly, there are personalities for whom some activities are impossible to countenance.

In many kindergartens, for instance, there is a water or sand table. I cannot imagine anything more unwieldy and discombobulating than a sand table and wouldn't have one as a gift. I, on the other hand, can't imagine life in a room of sixes without the constant availability of paint: one young teacher I worked with once used to actually shudder when I said the word *easel*.

The first rule of thumb, then, for "What are the other children doing?" is "Whatever you, the teacher, can stand and feel comfortable with."

The second rule of thumb is more political: "Whatever won't upset the principal or the powers that are in charge of you." This is something you have to work out for yourself, deciding how your principal will feel about dripping paint and daydreams during writing time. When the children in kindergarten are writing in standard English with elegant penmanship by Christmas, or first graders by Halloween, the issue will die a natural death. Principals like to see what they will see when you Do Words.

When a teacher has trouble Doing Words, and wants to give it up, it is seldom because the principal doesn't like it, nor because the children take advantage of the creative vent and indeed "play all morning": it is because that teacher is trying to Do Words alone, with no colleague to talk about the morning's work with, no teachers' room support. Such an individualized and personalized way of doing language with children in school can be scary for a teacher, and if no one else is there to talk it over with, it is hard to sustain. Everywhere I have worked, Doing Words with children in grades K or 1 or 2, there has been at least one other teacher in the building to talk to about it. I've also spent a lot of time on the phone with other lonely ones in other schools.

Whenever you try something new you need support: even when you try out a new recipe you want the eaters you cook for to notice and give you some direction about whether to have that dish again. When you are first learning to cross-country ski or scuba dive, it works a lot better if someone else is doing it too. It's the same with Doing Words: especially true of Doing Words, which looks and feels and is very dissimilar to the traditional, tightly structured and programmed ways of teaching language.

Here is a vignette to illustrate how Word time works with the creative vent included, of a kindergarten on a fairly typical winter day. I have made up this scene from stories told to me by kindergarten teachers, not only my colleague "Dorothy S.," in whose room I have placed this scene. Children are working here in Movements I, II, and III. (In Chapter 6, I will present the scene in a first grade, placed in my own room, where children are working in Movements IV and V.) In "Dorothy's" room we see a fairly traditional teacher with fairly ordinary mainstream children who are learning to write in untraditional and extra-ordinary ways.

Round tables, waist-high to a five-year-old, dot the kindergarten room. Twenty-seven chairs, red and yellow and orange, are pushed in neatly around them. Snowflakes of all shapes and patterns hang from the ice-cube-tray lights, testifying to progress in learning to cut. Laminated cards of winter pictures rest on the chalk tray, each showing a numeral and number word: one snowman, two mittens, three sleds, four boots, five pine trees. Boxes labeled HALLOWEEN, VALENTINE'S DAY, ANIMAL PICTURES, SOCIAL STUDIES — INDIANS, and so forth balance on top of the cubbies against the back wall. All around the room shelves are covered with games, crayons, picture books.

Routine kindergarten paraphernalia. And every day these twenty-seven ordinary children, in their typical classroom with their conventional teacher, spend the first hour of every day Doing Words. The room is empty now, waiting for school to start. Dorothy is waiting, too, in the teachers' room, sharing a

few last sustaining drops of caffeine and conversation with her colleagues.

Word time starts right after the housekeeping details of the day are taken care of. The children gather down front where the calendar is added to and special news is shared. They take a few minutes to feel the wholeness of the group, to re-enter the experience of school as a special place where each one is responsible for his behavior so that everyone can do his best.

As a group they remind themselves of the class rules for Word time: when you begin an activity you finish it; when you get something out you put it away; when you forget these rules you will have to stay in your own chair for a while. They very seldom state the major underlying rule: you must get a Word.

Sharing time is over, and the twenty-seven well-used manila envelopes are passed out. Each child goes with a friend into a separate spot, where they read the cards in their envelopes to each other. The teacher, seated now at one of the round tables, sets out some cards of manila tag, some lined paper, a fat black marker and a fine one. As the children finish reading their cards, a few at a time join her. The others go to the blocks, the games, the sand, the doll corner, the chalkboard; to their own places to think or talk or do something special for themselves.

"What's your Word today, Charles?" Mrs. S. asks the first one.

"Kathy broke her arm yesterday!" bounces Charles, eyes wide and freckles popping. "We went sliding, down the hill across the road, you know, Teacher, and we were sliding and Kathy flipped over and Crack! went her arm. Daddy came running across the road and Kathy was screaming." Charles gulps.

"I bet she screamed," the teacher agrees. "That must've hurt. How is she today?"

"Better, she's at home. Mama said she could stay home one day. We took her to the hospital, Teacher, and she was crying and they gave her a shot to put her to sleep and she stopped."

"That was pretty scary." Charles nods, long slow movements with rolling eyes for accompaniment. There is a little silence. "What do you want for your Word, Charles?"

"*Cast,*" says Charles. "I want *cast*. Kathy has to wear a cast for a whole year!" His wide eyes stretch even further open.

"*Cast,*" prints Mrs. S. with her big marker. "Trace these letters for me, Charles." He does so, correctly, with his left hand. "What's this Word?"

"*Cast,*" says Charles. "I'm going to put it on the chalkboard." On the way he meets Milla; after telling her all about Kathy's arm, he writes his Word on the board. Then he puts it into a basket on the teacher's desk. A couple of children join Dorothy at the table. Charles goes right to the blocks, behind the plant-draped piano that divides the block corner from the reading shelves.

The teacher's aide for the building, who helps in several classrooms, is assigned to this room for this hour. She sits at a table on the book side of the piano. She is systematically reviewing each child's envelope of words, hearing the child read them. If the child doesn't remember a Word, she will discard it so that these envelopes hold only current, alive Words.

Leah and Jamie, working in Movement III, are writing I-loves at another table, sentence after sentence of them, using each other's Word cards: *I love Mama. I love Aaron. I love Grammy.* Nicole is at the chalkboard practicing *Nicole* and embellishing it with lots of interesting circles. Her Word for today was *pancakes.* Some unrecognizably spiffy ladies parade in the dress-up corner. Pegs, puzzles, coloring, clay occupy others in ones and twos.

Ellen is tracing her Movement II Word, *Mama has a headache,* which she has just been discussing with the teacher, who keeps an eye on her to be sure Ellen forms the letters correctly. On Dorothy's other side sits Aaron, printing on a paper that has red and blue and green rules. Aaron's tongue, halfway out, is making little movements as his fingers and brain work. He has traced the letters and is now writing *Leah is pretty.* Aaron is just beginning to put his Words into print.

Ellen finishes and goes to the desk to put her card in the basket. Travis, safe under the desk with a lap full of picture books, smiles a dazzling blue-eyed smile at Ellen and considerately pulls his feet in, out of her way. Ellen goes back to the writing table. She stands at the teacher's elbow until Milla finishes.

"Teacher," Ellen says importantly, "Travis's under the desk. Want me to bring him to get his Word?" Ellen graciously allows Dorothy to think she's in charge some of the time.

Dorothy glances at the clock, at Travis's toes, and around the room.

"Thanks, Ellen," she answers. "I think he's got time for a few more books before he comes." Ellen goes off to play, and Travis is safe for a little longer. He will come to get his Word, and he will probably not say five more words all day — but that will be five more than he was willing to let out in September.

Garry sidles up to the table and announces, "I'm going to play with the blocks now." He puts half a question mark at the end of this statement, as he often does, to be reassured that it's okay to make his own choices. Garry loves to build. He builds every day unless he has brought his toy cars and then, usually, a garage or a road must be constructed for their potential to be realized.

"Okay, Garry," the teacher replies, marker poised over Amy's card, mind poised over her story. "Did you get your Word yet?"

"No," grins Garry. He has one of those irresistible six-year-old grins. "I'm gonna make a tower and then I'll write about it."

"Okay. Let me see your building when it's done." Her concentration returns to Amy, whose front door opened by itself in the storm last night.

"Teacher," from Garry, ten minutes later, pointing to the rug. "Lookit! My tower is almost as big as me!"

"Wow," says Mrs. S. "It sure is. Is there somebody it is exactly as tall as?" After much sorting out of bodies, during which the teacher is still working with other writers at the table, Garry discovers that his tower is exactly as high as Linda, and with another big grin he invites her to help him knock it down, but being very careful that none of the blocks land on the clattery linoleum. Then he comes to get his Word, which is *I built a tower almost as tall as me and it's as tall as Linda*. This Movement III sentence takes two cards.

Another day he might find out how tall the tower is by getting the meter stick down from its place by the flag. On another day, when asked to look at a tower, the teacher might just turn with a glance and a "good," especially if Tina has had a tantrum or a water jar has spilled or the music teacher has been giving lessons. Or there might be a Crash!

"Teacher! John knocked down my tower!"

"Okay, no more blocks today, boys, put them away, please." The clean-up will be rebelliously slow this time, but it will be done, and there will be no more crashes that day.

By ten o'clock the basket has been filled and then emptied again so that all the children can read their Words in a big circle. Then the busy hum gives way to the business of getting ready for recess. Boots, hats, mittens, snowsuits, scarves, a few reminders about snowballs, and they're out the door.

In the teachers' room the teachers review Word time. "They do play well, this class," Dorothy says. "It's a good thing: I can't pay too much attention to their play, I've got to keep printing and talking." She flexes her fingers as she reaches for her coffee. "And I've got to get my letters right every time!"

"Did you hear about Charles's sister?" asks another teacher who lives near him. "What was his Word?"

"*Cast,*" says Dorothy with a smile.

"Really!" says the other teacher. "And of course you had to hear the whole story first!"

Dorothy nods. "I was sure he was going to say *hospital.* You really do have to listen. How did your morning go?"

"Not bad," smiles the other teacher. "I am still amazed that nobody cares that Lucie — the new one I got last week — is still on Key Words, while most of the rest of them are using dictionaries." She shakes her head. "And Marie, who wrote four sentences yesterday, chose her to read with first thing!"

"What was Lucie's Word today?" asks Dorothy. This is a child she would never teach because Lucie is in first grade already.

The first grade teacher grins and strokes her own hair in an exaggerated preening gesture. "Me," she says modestly.

"Yay," says the kindergarten teacher. "She's going to get the whole class, you watch, one at a time."

"That's fine with me," says Lucie's teacher. "You get them to be so good at writing they really don't give me much Key stuff — it's fun to have a Movement I person once in a while."

A bell in the hall signals the end of recess. Lines of red-faced, cheerful bundles of snowy clothing troop into the rooms. The two teachers watch them come.

"Did I tell you what Andy said yesterday?" she adds as they start down the hall. "While he was printing his Word he said, 'Teacher, I like doing this you know why? 'Cause then you know what you've read.'"

The two teachers move toward the stuck zippers, knots in bootstrings, lost mittens, and twenty-seven Words and writings to be read, all new today.

"I'm with Andy," Dorothy grins. "I like doing this too."

Here are some of the things that I have had and seen included as activities of the creative vent at various times with various kindergarten and first grade classes. Do put right out of your mind the notion of doing all of them at once or even in the same year: blocks, varied sizes of wooden ones and/or big cardboard bricks; Tinkertoys and Rigajigs and Legos, three of the jillion kinds of interlocking building systems; pattern blocks; inch cubes; dolls, and/or a kitchen; crayons and paper to color on, colored chalk and small chalkboards to chalk on; paint; trucks and cars; books, books, and more books; goldfish and gerbils to watch; the sink; the sand table; clay; puzzles; Developmental Learning Games of various persuasions and levels; and the toys and games children bring to school.

We always have crayons, and I wish we didn't. Crayons are an invention of the devil for a first grade room. I can't at this moment think of a single good thing about them except that they make a permanent picture. But crayons: roll off desks; leave ghastly marks on the floor; won't wash off the wall; break, especially the exquisite flattened points of new ones; provide no fine-motor coordination practice for children who are printing daily with pencils; use up paper, lots of it; don't blend to make new colors; and look dead on the paper. Crayons are good, perhaps, for a three-year-old with a mother who will pick them up and a father who will repaint all the woodwork and most of the walls. In many classrooms, where the janitorial service is limited to just a nearly daily sweep, crayons are a nuisance.

Chalk, now, is lovely stuff. The colors in a chalk box aren't boring red orange yellow green blue purple brown black, oh no! There are scarlet and lemon and turquoise and rust and chartreuse and mint and violet. Chalk is dusty, I grant you that, but it comes out of and off of everything, even the small chalkboards it is used on. A child who makes a chalk picture of a dinosaur or a mushroom or the inevitable house-with-apple-tree at 9:20 cannot, it's true, take it home at 3:00; but more often than not a picture crayonned at 9:20 has fallen to the floor and been tracked on into a ripped state long before 3:00. The small chalkboard is propped up and admired all day, certainly longer than the tower, which went back into the block box at 10:00. The next day, a new day, always brings new images to write about, new images to draw. Chalk is always new, alive. Besides, on a practical note, the children take much better care of the chalk.

Painted pictures are best. I don't begrudge a single square inch of paint paper. Painting is the most calming thing first graders do, at any time of the day, and all painted pictures get a strip of masking tape and a spot on the wall for a few days. The colors of paint blend and blend, endlessly fascinating.

They also streak; sometimes the blending and streaking are not the artist's idea.

"Mrs. Johnson." Kelly, one indignant hand on hip, the other holding a cerulean brush, has stomped across the room with her grievance. "Will you please tell Paul that he can't paint now, it's my turn and he is a pest."

"Paul," I call him to me. "You can't paint now because it's Kelly's turn. Don't be a pest. Come here and show me what you're writing today, I want to see it. Kelly, please tell Paul when you're finished, it's his turn next." And that will probably be that, and we will have two paintings to hang.

If paint is soothing, then puzzles are enchanting. Suddenly one Tuesday, as I sat at the table helping writers, it was silent in the room. I hardly dared to turn around, because often silence means the principal has walked in, and I'm never sure that the silence is sudden and perfect enough. But the door was still shut this time.

It was a puzzle, a big wooden one, of the map of the United States. One of the children had brought it from home and a whole lot of children, easily a dozen, were engaged in putting it together. They worked with no wrangling, no pushing, no oh-you-dummy-that-doesn't-go-there, but with elegant and total immersion in it. It was very calm and quiet. It was a group achievement that is not typical, but the concentration was not unique. Puzzles are quite appropriate to the creative vent.

We don't dance or sing during Word time. I'm sorry we don't. I've never been sure whether our neglect of these outlets of the creative body are due to my own reticence or to the children's. Certainly in this one, deep-seated way the sixes and sevens of my rural American classes differ totally from Sylvia Ashton-Warner's Maoris. My little ones like to sing at music time and to march and leap at gym and recess, but the most we ever see in Word time is the odd worm or dinosaur. There is not space in our room to jump a rope, nor, I fear, space in our souls to dance a hula.

When a story is finished there are fish to be counted, a gerbil to watch eat his breakfast, dolls to be settled. There might also be a set of measuring jugs in the sink, with instruction cards for liter experiments. The children's own inventions, like the U.S.A. puzzle, occupy a few. One year, tracing from a book of dinosaur pictures was very popular among the brightest ones. It's hard to distinguish, among "very bright" children, whether they are synthesizers or merely very well organized.

Whatever rules for behavior you have set down for any other part of the day have to apply during Word time, too: it is important to remember this. If children don't get to shout out "Teacher! Can I go to the bathroom?" in the middle of a math lesson, they don't get to in Word time either. Just because an activity is individualized doesn't mean it's licentious.

As the children work through the Movements, there is less and less time for other activities during Words. They're too busy writing. I always keep paints out, though, and for the antsiest classes I get out a cut-and-paste ditto every day in case I have to settle someone down completely. What can be used for the creative vent depends on what you can stand and also on what you have. Within the limitations of space and materials, everyone's organic needs for creativity and for sanity must be met as often and as fully as possible. Mine, too. And in any contest, I win. The test of my greater maturity is that I can circumvent most of the useless and soul-stifling confrontations.

Sometimes I have to go out to fetch paper from the supply closet in the hall and they will not know I have gone, except for the next one for story, who is left holding the pen. It is always a wonder to see what configuration they are in as I stand in the doorway as a stranger would. Two might be at the sink, some sets of two here and there in corners reading old or new stories, as many as eight on the rug with blocks, a few milling around. There may be a grand total of six actually at their desks writing. And all of them talking, talking: pretending, imagining, reviewing, informing, reading, arguing, learning. Sometimes I get a sinking feeling: Oh dear, they're not Working! I should sit them all down and Do Something!

But listen. Listen to the life in the sound, look at the life in the faces. The pulse of confidence, the light of self-esteem echo all around the room with the tone of organic expression.

Tone. That's what I look and listen for, from the doorway or in after-school soul searches. It is the responsibility of each child to make a path of his own through Word time each day. It is my responsibility to make a stable schedule and clear expectations; to cushion their efforts with love; and to give them limits toward which they may strive and against which they may test themselves as they grow.

Tone is a function of order. The deep sense of order, unconscious, shines through the chatter, the energy, the movement of the room. It will look unstructured, but it will feel calm. And every child, every day, will have satisfied himself a little.

Once in a happy while I have one of those moments that keep me teaching, when all the personalities — mine, theirs, and ours — fuse into a humming light, when I look around and see everyone immersed in his own person and flowing in his own energy.

That is glorious. All my knots loosen and my *should*s become irrelevant. This is the harmony I am wishing always to glimpse, a woven vitality of independent spirits. It feels good. Such a moment, cherished for its own sake, makes bearable many other moments when cogs slip, tempers rub, and mist penetrates our lives.

Chapter 4

Movement III, Or, Who Keeps the Pencils?

> Harriet Vane to Peter Wimsey: "I've always felt absolutely certain [life] was good — if only one could get it straightened out. I've hated almost everything that ever happened to me, but I knew all the time it was just things that were wrong, not everything. . . . it seems like a miracle to be able to look forward — to see all the minutes in front of one come hopping along with something marvellous in them, instead of just saying, Well, that one didn't actually hurt and the next may be quite bearable."
>
> — Dorothy L. Sayers

THE ACT of transcribing is a level of writing that precedes composing, says James Moffett, writing in *Phi Delta Kappan* in 1978. Children who have worked through Movements I and II have actually been composing every day, orally, with the teacher as transcriber. The work they have done in Movements I and II has been their own, as it will continue to be. Now they will be printing — writing down — their writing as well.

The children have become proficient in letter formation by doing all the tracing required in the first two Movements; they are at ease with and can explain the need for capital letters and periods. Most importantly, they are hooked to the notion that they can read their own ideas and images and adventures from their own Word cards. They have moved much of their own imagery from the inside out. They know that they can read, and they want to read. The idea of writing down their stories, to read anytime, is a very exciting one.

Movement III is the first Movement with pencils and paper, the first Movement in which the children will print their words and sentences from the Word cards the teacher has printed for them. They all have fat manila envelopes of Key Words and sentences they have been collecting since the beginning of Movement I, each envelope different from everybody else's. They have read them daily to a friend and weekly to the teacher; these cards are current personal reading vocabularies. Most of them have also picked up "sight words" from among the cards of the other children in the class, because they have been reviewing someone else's cards every day as they "read with a friend."

"What is your Word today, Donny?" I ask as I sit at the table with a can of pencils and some lined paper in addition to my usual stack of tag cards.

"*Tigers,*" instantly rejoins Donny.

"Tigers!" I echo. "What about tigers?"

"*Tigers are dangerous,*" says Donny, making a tigerish face.

"Tigers are dangerous," I repeat slowly, printing on the lined card as I speak. "Trace these letters, please."

Donny traces effortlessly. "You know what?" I say as I watch him. "I think it's time for you to start printing. What do you think?"

"Okay," he says, eyeing the paper and pencil I am putting in front of him. "I can do that."

"You sure can," I agree. I'm right, too, because I wouldn't have suggested it if I hadn't known that he was ready.

So Donny takes the pencil and prints *Tigers are dangerous* on lined paper, while I keep one eye on him and the other on the next child, whose Movement II sentence is *I went to Grammy's last night.* I watch one print and one trace, which is not as hard as it sounds. When they are finished with their respective work, they each go to read it to someone else.

To see these very small hands producing this exquisite printing is always, every day, a very exciting moment. I never get tired of seeing beautiful penmanship flowing off the pencil points of five-year-olds who are almost blasé about this remarkable skill they have grown into since they began Doing Words three months before. These pieces of paper, stapled into a small book, invariably overwhelm teachers and principals from other schools. "Those kids *couldn't* have done that!" I often hear when I display work produced during Words. When they are reluctantly convinced that fives have done it, the next covetous question is "How did you make them do it?" My answer, that I don't make them do it, they want to, is greeted with even more incredulity.

Parents don't find it incredible, though (unless they've had other children in other kindergarten and first grade programs, and then they are quite deliciously grateful). Parents usually believe that their children are naturally going to do wonderful things, so becoming eager readers and fantastic printers right off the kindergarten bat is entirely in accord with their fondest expectations. I'm very pleased to gratify them!

In a kindergarten classroom where Doing Words was begun with Movement I in October, Movement III will probably begin after Christmas. The line between Movements I and II is quite wavy, and the children can slide back and forth between those two Movements almost daily if they want to. One of the signals of readiness for Movement III is that the child is solidly in Movement II, getting and tracing and reading whole sentences every day. Another aspect of readiness for Movement III is that the tracing is accurate.

It is unlikely that more than a few at a time will be ready for Movement III. Children come to assured fine-motor coordination and control in their own time, and it is important to be careful not to push them into Movement III too fast. It is also easier for the teacher if there are only two or three starting at a time. The amount of work for both teacher and child is greatly increased in Movement III.

The line between Movements II and III is distinct, although at first glance, the work of Movement III looks much the same. The manila tag cards are still long and skinny, but now they are lined. Various teachers I have known, various schools I have worked in, do the cards in various ways. They can be lined in a color-coded way, with the top line red, the middle line green, the bottom line blue; or they can be fat blue lines at top and bottom with a skinnier blue line in the middle; or they can have unbroken top and base lines, a broken line in the middle. I really don't think it matters: children learn to fill with their best printing whatever size spaces and lines they have to work with.

The teacher still sits at the table, with a marker and these cards. She also has paper that matches them, and a can of pencils and erasers. She still asks the same question — "What's your Word today?" — at the beginning of each conversation with each child every morning.

But now, after tracing it on the card, the child will print the whole thing on the paper.

Things move a little more slowly now. These first printings are done under the eye of the teacher: each child who comes new to Movement III is carefully watched for the first few days. The concentration is intense as the child moves her pencil across the paper to match the marker-printed letters she is transcribing. She must not only choose and trace and read what she has to say today: now she must reproduce it so that anyone else could read it too. Spaces become as important as letters; beginning and ending punctuation are no longer merely intriguing; they are now essential.

Usually a child begins this writing on a single sheet of the lined paper, writing on the single sheet or sheets for a few days or a week. During these days, the teacher watches to be sure she judged correctly this child's readiness for Movement III. She makes sure that the child can, in fact, trace easily, copy accurately, leave spaces, understand punctuation, and form the letters as she has traced them. If this is all happening, then several of these lined sheets are stapled together into a book, the First Writing Book. A lot of pride is stapled in as well.

Each day's sentence is printed into the book right after the one of the day before. Sometimes two sentences are entered on a day, sometimes related to each other and sometimes not. Sometimes two days' sentences are related to each other, but not often and almost never at the beginning of this Movement. These are still, mostly, captions for powerful images or adventures.

The reading that is done at the beginning of Word time is now done from the books, not the cards, although the lined cards are kept in the envelope and the children can read them to each other as another activity in the time. All the Movement I and Movement II cards have now gone home, to be a very impressive experience for Mom and Dad. Later, the lined cards will go home. As each writing book, of six or eight stapled pages, is filled up, the child will want to take it home, too, to read to parents and siblings and grandparents, and anyone who happens in off the street. There is no apology necessary for these books. They are always beautiful: the children are understandably proud of them, and so am I.

Because the writing books go home, the home and the school can have a more nearly similar view of the child. Anything that increases communication between home and school is a Good Thing, I am convinced, and yet sometimes this gives me pause. Probably most of these sentences are pretty Key still. Certainly they will be personal, autobiographical snippets of the lives of the children. I muse about these connections; I brace myself for reactions to the intensely Key material the child has shared.

I got new shoes, wrote Kathy first in Movement III. Kathy was a self-possessed little someone whose home life was forcing her to be much more responsible than her years warranted. She started Movement III just after Christmas, and the shoes were shiny patent-leather ones for the holidays.

I have a cold, emerged the next day. This was a bad year for colds anyway, and Kathy's log house in the woods, where she lived with her father and little sister, got very cold when the stoves ran low.

I had to walk all the way home, a couple of days later, was a very Key story for Kathy. The main road is about half a mile from her cabin, and usually Dad managed to carry her, either in his Jeep or on his shoulders; but that night it had been too snowy for him to carry both girls. It took a long time to walk in.

None of the work was giving her any trouble at all. She printed easily and well, she enjoyed her Word and her writing and her reading. The sheet of lined paper she had been using for these first three days was stapled to several blank sheets with a construction-paper cover, and Kathy decorated the front of it.

Into this book went these poignant and Key commentaries on her life, one a day:

I am going to my mother's tonight.

I saw my mother last night.

I stayed with my mother.

My grandmother is coming today.

And after another week of writing, smugly,

I am on my second book.

Everyone knew about Kathy's family, knew that her mother and father did not live together, and didn't even speak to each other. They had "had a divorce," a word very difficult to explain to children who haven't had one. It becomes less and less difficult, unfortunately, because Kathy's situation becomes less and less unusual with every passing year. The images and experiences for which these sentences were the captions were in some indefinable way made easier for her by the matter-of-fact acceptance of her classmates as she read them. They knew how important their own stories were; so they knew how important these revelations were to Kathy. Sharing helps all the children to understand themselves.

Allan had nearly all I-loves for his Movement II Words, and I expected that he would continue them through Movement III. He did get going with one, but other Key sentences followed.

I love my Dad.

I got a new lunchbox. This is a Big Deal.

My dog's name is Sparky.

And the next two days

She licks everybody.

My Mom dances with Sparky.

In Movement III most stories are one-liners. They seldom bear any relation to yesterday's or tomorrow's, especially at the beginning of Movement III work. During the first weeks, repetition of a subject, such as Kathy's mother or Allan's Sparky, is merely a measure of how Key the subject is.

From my angle, "Key" is at once wonderful and terrifying: wonderful because of how much the children can grow by using their Key words and stories; terrifying, because I know too much about them as a result.

What am I going to do about the things the kids tell me and the things I can see? It's fine to talk about getting their key words out, and helping the children to connect their interior world to the outer culture, but the interior world doesn't exist in a vacuum. All the people who have been part of the child's life up to the moment of her first Key Word are part of that interior world, and they are often part of her story.

My daddy got his third deer last night was one I had trouble sitting on several years ago, because the legal limit is one. Kathy's *I had to walk all the way home* made me wonder if I should tell her father that a five-year-old shouldn't have to walk in deep snow for a mile. And then there was Rachel, with *Daddy threw Mama through the wall last night.* Is there enough to go on to call what happened to Rachel's mother abuse? And the next question to that is, if Daddy threw Mama through the wall, as big as Mama is, what about Rachel, who is only six and has a body to match? Is there something I should be doing about that?

And what about Paul? There has been no day this whole year that he has come to school with a washed face and combed hair. It makes me yearn to take the scissors to his hair, to get the snarls out, and to find a bathtub fast. Perhaps if I taught in a high school I could gently say to a person, Go to the locker room before school, here's some soap; but that doesn't seem feasible in the elementary situation. Or is it that I am afraid to do that?

The distance between teachers and administrators is pretty counterproductive often, because in my admittedly biased view there are many more good teachers than there are good administrators; but the distance between parents and teachers can be much more discouraging.

It's easy to talk to Sarah's and Laura's mothers, because I get away with saying "wow" a few times. How often can I productively say that they are doing everything just right? By which I mean they are covering all the learning objectives that six-year-olds in my district are supposed to cover. Since their behavior is never outrageous, I don't usually talk about it with Sarah's or Laura's parents. (It is of course interesting that both of these high-achieving children have two parents, together, the same two they started with.) But Laura, for all her wondrous behavior and brainpower, is a shy child who is having a lot of trouble making close friendships, and probably needs more guidance along those lines than I can give. Sarah — for all her fascination with, and exciting grasp of, school stuff — is a bossy little girl. What should I do about that?

In fact, although I sometimes say I'd like to have a whole class of Sarahs or Lauras or Craigs or Jasons, the bright and undefiant ones, it would be infinitely boring. The challenges are indeed great when dealing with the bright ones; but the challenges are constant when dealing with the — literally — great unwashed.

How much can I make of the correlation between being clean and being ready to learn? I remember Lee, who must be nearly grown up by now, and gorgeous to boot, I'll bet. He had a mother who pored over him before he came to school, who ironed his shirts to a crispness and who even shined his shoes. His hair, an unusual chestnut color, was ritually parted and watered and combed and slicked down every single day. What's more, she didn't seem to mind that we returned him on the bus to her every day looking as though he'd been through a combination cyclone and wind tunnel and mud bath — otherwise known as recess — because she turned him out again pristine the next day and he never said, or even looked, "I'd better not do that, I'll get messed up." What she gave him, with the soap and the comb, was love. Maybe it was love dressed as single-minded attention to his body, but that's a lot of attention even so. Grooming, they say of baboons and chimps, is an activity essential to the animals' social growth and self-concept within the troop.

Lee also got a lot of positive reactions from me and from the other adults at school, and, because he was a two-fisted sort of kid, got respect from his peers as well. Certainly no one ever said of Lee, as they used to say of Nat, "Ooh, I don't want to sit next to him! He smells!"

It was much harder for me to say anything to Nat's mother about his condition, because I felt that I was also saying it about herself, about the way she ran her house and by extension her life. Although my children went to school clean, I knew there were things that could stand improvement about the way I raised them, and who was I anyway to be so condescending?

The only thing to come back to is that I believe that being unwashed can interfere with the way the child can enter into his day and his growth at school. Grown-ups feel better about sitting down to their typewriters or running their board meetings or flipping their hamburgers if they think they look nice; and more so if someone tells them they look nice. Is this a learned response? It could be. Though I know that Chrissy, even at six, always grins and preens herself when I tell her how pretty her hair ribbons look today.

Being washed or not, feeling good about oneself is a factor in how a child learns at school. I wish I had statistics for that statement, but I don't.

Sometimes I think that when I hear about a problem during writing time I need to get on the phone right away and discuss it with the mom or the dad whose problem it really is. This scares me. Part of the reason it is scary is that I am not a child psychologist, nor am I a grown-up psychologist, and that is often what is needed. When Shane is in high gear, on a real tear one day, I think I should call his father and tell him. But I know, from talking to the other teachers who have known the indigenous families of this town for longer than I have, that Shane's father is not approachable, and in fact takes advantage of any opportunity to farm Shane out with aunts and grammys and the like. In truth, I only think I know this. I have never talked with

this man, although I have written several notes to ask him to make an appointment to see me. I don't really know what he would do if I told him that his son is behaving like a crazy person, and is crying and throwing things.

Of course, somewhere at the core of Shane is the fact that his mother abandoned him, and his father doesn't want him. Kathy is better off, because although her mother "went away" too, her father does do his bumbling best to take care of her. And what business of mine is that, anyway? Or, is it my business, and not the business of his later teachers, because I am his teacher when he is very young? And if so, why? Perhaps, if I didn't ask for and get the Key stories, I wouldn't know these things, I wouldn't have to worry about how ineffectually I resolve these issues, for me or for them.

If I didn't ask for and get Key stories, though, I wouldn't have whole children finding themselves and liking what they find.

Movement III is not always so Key. Sometimes these Movement III books read like a series of headlines, or titles for chapters in "The Life of ———." Kevin's are typical of this style:

Today I'm going to David's on the bus.
Donny and me read our words.
On Sunday I'm going roller skating.
I wish I had a new digital watch.
I'm on my second book.
My cat was stuck up on top of the roof.
I'm going to get a Dark Crystal book.
When I am outside I'm going to make a snow cabin.
On Friday I slept over at David's.
Today it is snowing.
David and me play chess.
David and I played CHips.
This vacation David slept over at my house.

(Can you tell who his best friend is?)

These stories, still one a day, are all autobiographical. They are important and personal, but perhaps a little less Key than the stories he was reading from his Word cards in October. He is already unlocked to reading, and now to writing. The inner child is at ease in these external media of print.

Luke, too, although he spent less time in the first two Movements, was in a very similar place in Movement III:

We gave all my kitties away.
I love jumping on beds. (This conversation started with "Boy, was my Mom mad!")
My bunny is too big for his cage.
Today I found a dead bird. I left it with my Mother.
Today my mother smelled a skunk.
I went to soccer practice last night.

This formulation "last night" that just went by in Luke's sentence is generic: it means "in the recent past." It is used interchangeably and indiscriminately by sixes to mean anything from yesterday to two weeks ago.

During Movement III the same kinds of activities of the creative vent (see Chapter 3) can be still available in the room. There is less time to do other activities, of course, because the printing takes longer to do than the tracing of the earlier movements. Indeed, the activities of the creative vent begin to atrophy during Movement III; as the children get better and better at writing their Words down, they will often come back and back for more sentences instead of doing something else in the time.

Every now and then, though, a Movement III story happens because of the creative vent itself. This is gratifying to me, and makes me feel justified in keeping these other activities available. Billy, a big but very young six, wasn't having much success with his Words. He was in Movement III, but wasn't much more interested in it than he had been in anything inside the schoolhouse. All he really wanted to do was play and fight.

One day Larry and Buddy were building a complicated array of blocks structures on the rug, and Billy was making a clay plane that was to be part of that scene in some way. When I called him for his Word he left the plane on his desk and joined me at the table. We had our usual desultory time, unsatisfactory from my point of view because I felt that I really hadn't hooked him to reading and writing. He read his own Words, and that was that.

"What's your Word today, Billy?"

Shrug.

"What've you been doing at home?"

"Nuthin."

"Do you have to help with the cows?"

First grin. "Yeaaah, I'm helpin' Dad milk." He had one eye on Larry and the blocks.

"Do you want to write about milking today?"

"No."

"What do you want for a Word today?"

"Oh, okay, milking," he said disgustedly.

So I wrote *I'm helping Dad milk* and he traced it, and read it, and started back to his desk to print it in his book.

There was a strangled, primeval cry from the rug and in a millisecond Billy was tugging on my jacket. "Lookit, lookit, Teacher!" he bellowed, holding out a lump of shapeless clay. "Larry smashed my plane!"

I had leaped up at the screech; now I motioned Larry to his seat with a glare. Buddy began to put the blocks away, noiselessly, trying to be instantly invisible. Billy stood there, breathing hard and bright red, his face as much of a shambles as the plane.

"That's awful, Billy," I said, giving him a quick hug. I still had marker and cards in my hand. "Want to write that?" And I printed, saying the words as I did, *Larry smashed my plane.*

Billy's tears receded, his breathing evened out, his eyes spark-spark-sparkled.

"Yeaaahhhh!" Reaching out his big paw he took the card, reading *Larry smashed my plane* with great relish. Then he brushed me out of his path, bulled his way back to his desk, grabbed the pencil, and began to write it.

After that day I didn't feel I had to pull his stories out of him.

I began to hear about the calf they were raising in the kitchen, about his tractor, about other things that were happening at home and at school. Stories came more easily, printing got straighter, and he was organically connected, at last, to the reading and writing world. He never did learn to add that year, but that's another story.

Stories can continue purposefully from day to day in Movement III, and as the children get used to writing, the stories sometimes do follow each other. There is no rule against it, although if it becomes a habitual thing it's probably time to move to Movement IV. When Robin's father had cataract surgery, Robin wrote about it nearly every day: sharing his preoccupation with this crisis in his family life seemed to ease it. These sentences went into the writing book for three weeks or so and show clearly when the crisis was over.

Daddy is going into the hospital tomorrow.
I'm going to visit Daddy after school.
I'm going to visit Daddy Saturday.
I went to see Daddy yesterday.
We had gym today.
Daddy's eye bled again.
I went to see Daddy last night.
We have a flood in our driveway. (This is about Daddy, too, i.e., his absence from home.)
My father is coming home today or tomorrow.
My father came home yesterday.
My father's eyes are getting better.
The ice cream man came yesterday.
I can't wait until Easter.

Another result of this continuing story is that Robin knows, like the shape of his pillow, the words *I'm, going, home, my, father,* and *Daddy,* at least, to read and to spell, and several other useful words to read: *today, yesterday, Saturday, home, tomorrow, eyes, visit.*

Weylon deliberately wrote a continuing story, using the cards of Movement III. It was late in the kindergarten year when he did this, and many of his classmates were already in Movement IV, discovering the endless delights of Once-upon-a-times. He wanted to do one too, but his spatial understandings and his fine-motor control and his all-around concentration weren't quite ready. He got around it, though, and wasn't he delighted!

Once upon a time there was a haunted house, he wrote the first day of the series.

People went into it. They saw dead spirits.

They were scared. Then they saw the door shut. This was the third day's addition.

Then the walls started to close. That was a Friday.

On the next Monday he added, *They saw a chain. At the top of the chain there was a window. They climbed to the top of the chain.* You can always do more on Mondays.

They got out of the haunted house.

And on the last day of this set, he wrote:

The end. I wrote a once upon a time story. It was very well received.

Movement III is the place for pages and pages of I-likes, too. You can write I-like nearly everybody, once you have the formula. A lot of formula writing is characteristic of Movement III. "——— is my best friend" is another type. For all practical purposes, this is independent writing, the beginnings of being able to use the teacher only as a resource. It is delightful, too, to be able to do it "all by myself" and to have it be beautiful.

Tony wrote, one day, with great diligence and concentration and no help, *I don't need you, Teacher.* When we all got to the rug to read, we found that Tony had written *Chris is my very very very very very very very very very . . . best friend.* There were twenty-seven *verys*. There was also a prolonged and slightly awed silence when he finished reading.

"I wrote *very* twenty-seven times," he said proudly.

"Boy, I guess Chris is sure your friend," I said. It was the most positive thing I could think of.

A little more silence; then Amy said, in a thinking-aloud sort of voice, "You know, I think we need a rule about *very*s around here. That was too many."

Much more diplomatically put than I could ever have managed; I applauded silently. And after some more discussion it was agreed, even by Tony, that four *very*s were going to be the limit. "We can tell you like him a lot with four," summed up Sharon.

"I-loves" tend to be more common in Movement II, and "I-hates" I don't allow at all, if they emerge in a conversation before writing. I always ask "Why?" and get an answer, and it's that answer — "Jennifer doesn't like me" or "School is too hard" or "Kyle won't play checkers with me" — that serves as the story for that day. I admit to a strong bias on this point, against the negative feeling at all, but that is only part of why I don't allow them. Imagine, if you've written an I-hate in your book it's there forever, nearly in granite, and who knows? Maybe tomorrow that very Jennifer or Kyle might be your very very best friend. It would be too bad to want to read your book with her or him in the morning and have to read the I-hate first thing!

If Doing Words begins in first grade instead of in kindergarten, the progress will be a little different. It is important to remember that the purpose of Movements I and II is really two-fold: first, to release the child's imagery and hook him to reading and writing through his commitment to his own personal subjects; and second, using the energy behind that commitment, to teach him how to print, and what punctuation is for, and the difference between words and sentences.

If you begin Words in first grade instead of kindergarten, then, it is important to assess whether either of those two purposes has already been accomplished in another way in the kindergarten program that preceded you. If the children come to you already trained in penmanship, etc., you can begin right away with the printing-in-books of Movement III. If you do this, however, *be sure that what they are printing is their Key Vocabulary.*

My experience is that the older they are the harder it is to release that Key imagery, the harder it is to get them onto the bridge from the inner man out. Unless they do get in touch with their own, they will be dependent and unsure writers later, in this program or any other. It is already harder to get Key Words — that is, the kinds of words and stories they would be asking for in Movements I and II — from six-year-olds than it is from fives, but it isn't impossible.

If, at the beginning of first grade, it is up to you to teach all penmanship, then you must start with Movement I. After a week or so, though, I would include in the work of Word time other penmanship practice — a double dose, so to speak. I think it can be said that sixes are more coordinated than fives, and it will take them fewer days to become printers. They will become better printers faster through the tracing Movements with Key Words and stories, although I and II can be shorter than they would be in kindergarten. You will see the majority of them in Movement V by Christmas with any luck.

It takes a little more effort to get from the outer man in than it does to get the inner man out. When I had a first grade class of wonderful printers who had not done Words, the most noticeable thing about them was that they had almost no self-motivation: they expected me to tell them when and how to do and think everything. Their Key imagery was well covered over.

Tina, in this group, was a very capable child who wasn't about to give anything Key to anyone. She started with *I like rainbows*. This troubled me because it was television-based for one thing; besides, rainbows are second only to unicorns in my book for sheer, insipid boringness. Tina skipped unicorns, for the time being, and went sideways into the equally boring (not that I said so, of course), *Pink is my favorite color.* Then she wanted another unrelated and external one, one I have rarely seen in any Movement, *The alphabet has a lot of letters*. This one started a brief flurry of alphabet-copying among these rote children.

Then we got a little closer to the true Tina with *We got to go to the beach a lot this summer.* This one took a considerable conversation to get. She wouldn't tell me what was good or bad about the beach, or even who *we* were, just that she went. The next day, reaching, as it seemed to me, for anything, she wrote *I have some socks that have hearts on them. I wore them yesterday.*

And after another week or so of this kind of thing — *Jennifer has a pretty shirt.* and *Today we have Art. I like Art.* — we finally came to the story that was immensely Key for her. This story began her interest in writing, and was itself a continuing story for several days: *Cabbage Patch Kids are cute. I wish I had one.*

You never know.

Similarly, Jean took a long time that year to come back to herself. These children needed to take the time to believe that what they really wanted to say was "okay," a belief that comes easily at the beginning of Doing Words in the kindergarten because no one has yet imposed other things on them as more legitimate than their own. Jean finally did, but first we had to work through:

Rainbows are pretty.
We have a goose and two ducks.
Unicorns like foxes.
I have three kittens.

We got a little closer to Jean's real life with *My mom got a new white car.*

Finally, when she was really ready for Movement IV, Jean asked for *I can go high on my swing set.* and *I went on the merry-go-round all by myself.*

One of the ways I knew that these last two were Key and the one about the kittens wasn't was to watch her face and look at the sparkle of her eyes as well as listen to her. She showed me as well as told me that these were the most important things she'd yet shared about herself. The same was true of Tina: Cabbage Patch Kids are pretty boring too, after all. But she stiffened up and became very still when she told me she wanted one, so I knew we'd finally reached the inside Tina.

Readiness to leave Movement III was hard for me to determine for many years. It was because of Tina, she of the Cabbage Patch Kid, that I figured out an easy way to know when to shift them to Movement IV. It's easy to tell if the child can trace well enough to go to Movement III; getting to Movement IV is a little trickier.

One day Tina came to get her Word looking a little self-conscious, not to say smug.

"What's your story today, Tina?" I asked.

"I like school," she answered softly — she's a very soft speaker and reader-aloud — and smiled sidelong at me.

Now this was the first of these that year, and we were still two weeks away from the first *I love Mrs. Johnson,* so I oohed and aahed a little.

"I like school, too, Tina," I told her. "What do you like best about school?" I put one arm around her waist, which I instantly realized was a mistake. Some kids you can't hug for no reason, and if you can't, don't. I moved my arm.

"I like school because I learn things," Tina expanded obligingly.

"I'm glad to hear that," I answered. "Is that your story?"

Tina nodded, so I began writing that sentence on a long, lined tag Word card. *I* I wrote, "*like,*" I said, pen poised. "You know *like,* don't you?" She nodded, so I drew a line next to the *I. School,* I wrote, *because. . . .* I stopped writing and looked at her again. "You know *I* goes here, right?" She nodded again, so I drew another line next to *because,* and wrote *learn things*. The card looked like this: *I* ——— *school because I* ——— *things.*

"Now read it to me," I said to her. She read it softly, framing the words with her thumb and forefinger, and I nodded in turn. "Tina," I asked her suddenly. "What do you learn in school?"

"I learn how to read," she answered immediately. This was gratifying, and also a little surprising, since most of her reading was in this writing book (but then, I'm always saying we write our reading).

"Good!" I said. "I love to read, too. Do you want to put that in your story?"

"Okay," she said. So I looked at this card with the lines in it for *like* and *I*, and I thought to myself: In for a penny, in for a pound.

"Can you do *I* and *learn* from this card and your head?" I asked her.

Nod. So ——— ——— *how to read* went onto the card. And she was quite right: she could do it perfectly.

The next day she was off into Movement IV.

Tina's mother and father were very interested in what Tina did in school. They had never heard of anything like Words before, and were a little skeptical, for the first month or so, that she was really learning. "Don't you do worksheets?" her Mom asked me anxiously.

I do remind myself from time to time that the parents are really the people who hire me. It is difficult to remember, because the school board and the superintendent get in the way of such a clear view. In fact it is often hard to see parents at all behind the school board and the superintendent; often parents are seen as adversaries to those very groups that are, supposedly, representing them.

Sometimes I think that there are groups in the world who won't work together on principle. Sometimes I think that if a magic wand could be waved, and all parents would come to conferences with teachers when asked, and all teachers would tell the *parents* first when something is not quite right with their child, everyone would still grumble and suspect each other.

Fifty years ago, or maybe even forty years ago, there were many institutions in everyone's life. There was school, there was church, there were Brownies and Boy Scouts and Rainbow Girls and Kiwanis. There was the nuclear family, with a father and a mother living together. And there was the extended family, which often included grandparents, usually seeming to be much older than the parents and certainly not trying to be younger all the time.

Each of these institutions had a part to play in the development of the child. It made sense for the school to be concerned only with academic and intellectual development. It made sense for the church to be concerned mostly with moral development, and philosophical or religious orientation. It made sense for the parents and the grandparents to take responsibility for the child's behavior, for learning about how people of all ages get along with each other: interpersonal relations and behavior management, we call it now. In all these different groups, too, there were different sets of people. All the children in a class didn't go to the same church, and there were children in church who didn't go to school together. The girls in the Brownies were not all in either of those groups. The children who were the most important to the development of the child were the siblings in her own family. The child learned from all these members of all these groups.

Now, there is just the school. By and large, the school has come to be responsible for the academic, intellectual, philosophical, moral, and social growth and development of the child. The extension of this idea is that teachers are now pastors, parents, grandparents, scout leaders, and incidentally teachers. They even provide breakfast, give flouride tablets, and check for head lice routinely.

But teachers still think of themselves as only responsible for the subject matter. They are trained to be only responsible for and proficient in transmitting the subject matter. They are not encouraged to take the time needed to be first of all a support for the child's ego, only secondly a distributor of facts.

As it teaches, Doing Words takes lots of time for the nonacademic because I believe that without a sense of self, without some clear good sense of who-I-am, math and biology and *Silas Marner* will not mean anything at all.

Chapter 5

Movement IV, Or, Retrieval and "Real" Writing

> Merlin to Arthur: "As I came toward an end it was to be seen that the tale fitted in with all that I had taught him in the past, so that now I was handing him the last links in the golden lineage and saying, in effect, 'All that I have ever taught or told you is summed up in you, yourself.'"
>
> — Mary Stewart

MOVEMENT IV is the beginning of independent writing. In Movement IV there is no more tracing, no more tag cards, not much supervision, and, usually, not anything like as many Key stories. Most of the children are over the bridge, now, from their inner selves out, and in Movement IV we often see the first of those wonderfully externalizing stories, Once-upon-a-times.

I'm always glad to get to Movement IV, even though I miss the shivers of seeing Key Words pull the kids into learning. I find this Movement the most exciting one because now they are really beginning to take charge of their writing. Here is where the children begin to put together, physically put together, their sentences and stories. By the end of Movement IV their writing vocabulary will be doubled, too, which means I have much less to do.

Movement IV is the beginning of dictionary work. In this Movement the child does not get all the words he needs to write that day's story or sentences from the teacher on a card to copy, but retrieves some of them himself. Each child has a retrieval card for words. This is a nine-by-twelve sheet of oaktag, usually colored. When he is ready to write, the teacher will meet with him just as she has always done to discuss his story. Then she will write for him the words he needs, and leave little spaces for those he will retrieve from the card or from his head. She writes the new words in a vertical list. When the card is filled up it looks like a phone book, or, in fact, a dictionary, with columns of words and little lines for spaces.

Movement IV builds on all the skills the children have learned — and by "learned" I mean that new buzz word, "internalized" — since their very first Key Words. They know how to print, know why there are capitals and periods on sentences and on some words, know that they read from left to right and write that way too, know that the sounds the letters make are in a fairly logical pattern and that they can figure out some words just because they know that. They know, almost incidentally, how to read. And they are usually still five or barely six, still in kindergarten if they began Words there, or solidly six if they began in first grade.

Each one has a lot of words stored in his head by this time, particularly the service words, the helping words that glue sentences together: *and, is, are, saw, to, the, my, it, in*. He also has some names and the very very Key nouns he has been collecting. The retrieval of words in Movement IV is therefore twofold: he must find on his retrieval card the words he needs after the teacher has given them to him every day, and he must find words in his head as well.

Each child has a writing book, as in Movement III, of lined paper stapled together and covered with construction paper or wallpaper. He can decorate it and put his name all over it, as many do, or smother it with rainbows or cars or whatever is his — or her — totem of the moment. The books are about ten sheets long at this point, partly because it is still hard for children this young, no matter how released their imagery is, to keep things neat; and partly because it's so much fun to finish a book and get a new one!

The same decision has to be made about whether the teacher moves and the children stay put, or the other way around, just as in the other Movements. I tend to start this Movement with everyone sitting and me moving, because I almost always start the year with the majority of children in Movement IV — but, as with so much else, it depends on the class. Although this retrieval is easy to do and perfectly comprehensible to children, it seems very hard for teachers to understand. A few examples will help.

When Greg got to the retrieval card stage, it was already late in the year and many of the children were already doing once-upon-a-times in Movement V. He wanted to do one too. The first day he had a new book and a retrieval card he asked for *Once upon a time there were three tigers*. The teacher printed it like this for him, vertically, on his card.

Once
upon
———
time
there
were
three
tigers

As the teacher and Greg discussed this beginning sentence, she asked him if he knew how to do *a* and he said he did. So she put the little line there in the list after *upon* to remind him that he would need to put a word there as he wrote it into his book.

Greg took this back to his desk and began to transcribe it onto his paper horizontally. He put in the spaces between the words himself, since they weren't obvious as they had been on his Movement III cards. At the end he put a period, and when it was all finished he showed it to the teacher again. After recess he read it to the class in the sharing time.

This line-for-a-word business is an instant gauge of readiness for this Movement. If the child just skips over the line as he's putting the words into his book, you know that he doesn't understand what's going on. If he does it two or three days in a row, move him back to Movement III. The same is true of the child who transcribes into a vertical list in his book, duplicating the list on the retrieval card. This is even more of a clue, really, because it is spatial, and should be more obvious than simply a missing word in a correctly horizontal placement.

Greg didn't have either of those problems, I am happy to say. The next day he wanted to add to this story with *They took a walk. They met a coyote.* So under *tigers* on his retrieval card the teacher wrote

They
took
______
walk
______
met
______
coyote

The lines stand for *a* and *They* and *a* in that order, which he could retrieve when he came to where he needed them in his transcription, *a* from his head, or from yesterday's writing, and *They* from the first of the sentences he was writing on that day. He knew he had two sentences, and put in both periods.

The third day he wanted to write *The coyote was their cousin.* He had to have several of these words, and used a line only for *coyote.* He probably could have gotten *The* from his head, but since it was the first time it had been needed since Greg started this movement, the teacher gave it to him. The first column was used up by this time, so these words were added under "coyote" and then at the top again:

The	their
______	cousin
was	

The next day he wrote *The coyote went home with them for two weeks. The end.* The teacher put these words and lines on his card:

______
______
went
home
with
them
for
two
weeks
______
end

After this sustained effort Greg fell back on autobiographical one-liners for a while. Under *end* in the second column of his retrieval card it says

I
spent
______
night
over
to
my
______
house

for *I spent the night over to my cousin's house.* When he and the teacher came to *cousin's* as they were talking about this sentence, she told him about apostrophe *S* and put one onto the end of *cousin* in the first column, where it had first appeared in the coyote story.

Greg's next story was *I got a new bike with two wheels.* (Don't tell me that's not Key!) For this he needed *got, new, bike,* and *wheels.* This sentence took him into his third column.

——————	bike
got	——————
——————	——————
new	wheels

With and *two* were part of the coyote story, and he retrieved them easily. ("Show me *with* on your card, Greg," said the teacher, and he pointed to it.)

Greg went on a couple of stories later to another bit of fantasy, which began *Once upon a time there were seven elephants.* For this his card had

——————
——————
——————
——————
——————
——————
seven
elephants

Imagine what a piece of cake this was for him!

Usually a retrieval card is good for four or five columns on a side.

This is not easy to do, this changing from a vertical to a horizontal writing. There is a fancy educationese word for it that I can't remember. All kinds of things are involved here: remembering that sentences start with capitals, that they end with periods; getting the spaces between the words, and getting them to be the same size, or nearly, throughout; keeping track of where you are in your list of words; remembering what words the lines stand for *and* how to spell them. That's a lot to be doing at once, in the spring of kindergarten, as well as all the same old stuff about letter formation, capitalization, left-to-right progression, and visual discrimination that has been developed before this Movement ever began.

The spacing problem is solved most neatly, we have found, by a rule of thumb, so to speak. Put the thumb of the hand you're not writing with on the paper next to the word you just finished writing. Put your pencil on the right side of your thumb, and begin to make the first letter of the next word. Take your thumb away, and there will be a nice space of about one-and-a-half centimeters left between the words. The thumb should be ball down, pointing to the bottom of the paper.

All of these achievements are important, certainly. To me the most important thing, though, in Movement IV, is the retrieval itself. I have heard such pride oozing through a six-year-old's voice when he says patiently, "No, Teacher, you don't have to give me that, put a line there. I already know that word." The same pride comes also through an impatient tone: "Teacher, that's already on my card! See?"

It may be tempting to hurry through Movements I, II, and III and get right into Movement IV, especially if the class is well able to print and can tell you about sounds and such. It is important not to hurry through them, however, even if the children come to Movement III very soon. It is important because the wonderful printing and the understandings of standard English are only the outward and visible signs of their evolution as writers. As wonderful and capable as their books may look, it is what is happening inside that is most important, that they see their own ideas and adventures as exciting and legitimate. Words provides a way for them to be in touch with themselves.

These are learnings that take some time. Time to be proud, time to believe in themselves, time to make the connections between what they write and what they read, and time to do a million I-likes. Time to grow in indefinable and untestable ways, too, needs to simply pass.

Movement IV can go on and on. Sylvia Ashton-Warner's Maoris had all their words entered on the inside back covers of their writing books, using the covers as retrieval cards, and were successful and content for as long as she had them. We do go on,

to Movement V, to the writing process, but the work in Movement IV is pivotal. Since Movement IV lends itself so well to continuing stories it is nearly a complete program. For years the kindergartners who came to me for first grade had been in Movement IV for up to five months, and that was fine with them.

The idea that because a child has done something successfully once, he can always do it again successfully is nonsense, now being borne out by education research on learning styles and retention. It is also borne out by every parental observation since Eve watched Cain try to walk to the tent flap. Children need time, to do things over and over again, to hear things over and over again, to try and to understand over and over again. Some need more tries, some need fewer; they all need time.

If I begin to talk here about reading aloud to children, please don't turn the page on the grounds that you've already heard this. Reading aloud is, next to saying *yes,* the single most important thing you as a parent or you as a teacher can do for your children. You need to hear that again and again, because there is so much that mitigates against your doing enough reading aloud.

Reading aloud isn't like going to the circus. If a child sees elephants only once in the years from birth to six or seven, he will probably have gained as much of an image — and a smell — of elephantness to last him. Elephantness is not a commonly or often needed understanding for the young child.

Language is. What you do when you read aloud to a child is introduce him to language uses he would not otherwise encounter, as well as to information and people and fantasies that make up part of his cultural heritage.

Just because you read aloud to your older child, in the first flush of mother-and-fatherhood, doesn't mean that you will keep it up with the others as they come along. If you think about the differences in the ways you have raised your children, if you have more than one, you will probably be surprised to notice that the older one got read to more. Even if you read aloud to them both, the younger one will have a very different and, I think, much diluted experience of it if the older one is sitting on your other knee. Ideally, you need to read three stories in a row: one to both of them, then one to the younger one alone, then one to the older one. There is a lot to be said — and I will probably say it somewhere — for that individual time. And even more to be said for the separate concentration on the language that each child needs to get.

"But they learn from each other," you say. "But it's good for the older one to practice reading to the younger one," you say.

Yes, very true. Both of those are quite true. *But they do not mean the same thing at all as you, Mom or Dad, reading aloud to your child.* It's a completely different thing.

Of course children learn from each other. Children need playmates, to use the old-fashioned word for "peers," as much as they need caring parents, two if possible. There are connections and emotional meshes that are impossible for a child to make with an authority in his life, with his mother or his father or his grammy, which have to be made in order for his mental health to be as good as it can be. How can a human learn to share his thoughts and his feelings — not the same things — with another human unless he can try them out on someone who has no personal stake in him other than simply caring? Siblings fill this need, because they rarely do more than simply care, automatically, for each other. It takes them years of being grown-ups themselves before they decide that they will like each other too, or that they can't stand each other in spite of being each other's closest relatives. When they are all young together, older siblings don't usually worry about how the younger one appears to the world. The parents very likely do.

"What will people think of me if my child . . ." takes drugs, flunks out of college, pulls his pants down on the playground, throws his food across the kitchen, smears applesauce on his bib, isn't toilet trained by the same day and month that his cousin was, to give a few examples from teens backwards. This is what I mean by a parent's "having a stake" in a child.

A parent can't and mustn't be everything to a child. A parent can and must be the first and therefore most important conduit to the child of his culture. Read aloud to your child, and be sure you read aloud things that you like. This rule is important for two reasons, one of them a child's reason and one a grown-up's reason. For the child's sake, read things you like so that he will hear your enthusiasm, so that he will learn that books, pictures, reading, learning, understanding, critical thinking, and the whole of civilization are available for his own enthusiasm. The way the world is set up these days, anyone who doesn't care about, have enthusiasm about, print and the printed word is going to be lost. So what if the print of our children's lives is going to be printouts, instead of the traditional Gutenbergian form: we still will be based on print for some little time to come.

For your sake, read things that you like so that the whole experience will be fun, and the intensity of it will be heightened by your own interest. You will then come away from your nightly book-time with a good feeling about yourself. This is an invaluable feeling for a parent to have, for which there is no substitute. It is pretty important just for being a human, too.

Imagine having a fifteen-minute slice of your life every day, even weekends, where you have a chance to sit calmly, be admired, get some snuggling physical closeness, and enjoy a story. You will even have a chance to exercise your talents as an actor or actress with the safest audience there is; you will have a moment or two to expound your philosophies of life and literature without contradiction; and you will experience unqualified love.

What more can a rushed human in today's world ask?

This is the bare minimum, I say firmly, for the care and acculturation of the young child. Beginning when the child is very young, this nightly performance is essential for both parents and children to grow, to share each other's thoughts and feelings in nonjudgmental, enabling ways. "I think I can, I think I can," says the little blue engine, pulling the train of dolls and toys and good things to eat to the children on the other side of the mountain. This is a lesson in altruism, confidence, and kindness that can be taught otherwise but never more succinctly to the readers of and listeners to the story of the *Little Engine That Could*. And the message of the little blue engine is a powerful one, which goodness knows all parents want their children to learn: I think I can, I think I can. The delicious joy of the last page is no less powerful, although its glee is so outrageously smug that it is less easy to see. "I thought I could, I thought I could, I thought I could." It's okay to be proud of your accomplishments, parents and children. It's okay. Take the time to do this. You both need it, just as the child needs time to experiment through Movement IV, to practice rearranging the world as many times as he can in his writing.

The children begin with one sentence in Movement IV. They can go on to two, or three, or a whole paragraph in one day, coming back to the teacher for help with each sentence for as long as the time lasts. They can do these sentences and stories about daily-changing subjects, or they can keep on adding to the same subject to make a continuing story.

Greg did both, backing in and out of one-liners, moving at will from autobiobgraphy to fantasy and back again. This is, I think, a normal pattern. Nobody in the adult world can produce exactly the same amount of writing every day: why on earth should we think children can? And the variety of output among the children in a class, even a whole class working in Movement IV, is as boggling as the content is on any given day.

While Greg was doing his stories about the cousins and the bike, Laura was constructing a saga that went on, finally, for twenty-six pages. It stands, still, as the longest story I know of written in Movement IV. She wrote it in early May of her kindergarten year.

I recommend that second grade begin with this Movement if no other organic work has been done before, and that it continue for at least a month so that the children can believe in their ownership of the writing, in their own ability to choose their topics, and themselves as writers.

Matt's first Word, on the first day of first grade, was *motorcycle*. It was clearly a Key word, hot on the tip of his tongue. He was a member of one of the few classes of my life that had never done any organic writing.

"What do you want for your Word today?" this new teacher he'd never seen before asked, a strange question he'd never heard before.

He looked at me, the beginning of a smile. Is she for real? the smile seemed to ask. I could almost hear the click inside his head when he decided that I meant it. But he had to check a little.

"You mean any Word? Any Word I want?"

"Yes," I answered. "A Word you want. Something you like? Someone you love?"

"Well," he said emphatically. "I know the Word I want. *Motorcycle*."

So I printed *motorcycle* and we talked a little about the motorcycle he said was his. He traced it, and read it to a friend.

That was all Matt did in Movement I. The next day he wanted a sentence, *Joshua is my very best friend*. By this time I had seen what incredible printers these children were, so I had made them books. Matt printed his sentence on the second day of school with no problems. It was spaced and punctuated correctly, the letters were well made, and he read it well. He had jumped to Movement III.

The next day he was absent. Then he came back with a long story about Joshua's dog, which took a considerable conversation — about three minutes — to get through to what he really wanted. I thought the important thing was that the dog jumped up on him, but what we finally came to was *Joshua's dog was trying to make friends with me*. Somehow this didn't feel at all Key to me, and I began to wonder if there might be a great deal that was much more Key that I wasn't getting from Matt.

Next he got *I made the shadow of my motorcycle jump*. This was actually because of a homework assignment for science. We'd been studying shadows and lights in science so this was certainly a topical sentence, if not Key. The next day it was both, a caption for a scary shadow experience in his bedroom: *I saw my shadow in the middle of the dark*.

Then he was absent again, but returned with a proud *I know how to put my motorcycle on the kickstand*. Next day, glowering, he told me about Billy, a bigger person.

"Billy stole my motorcycle."

"Did he bring it back?" I asked.

"Yeaah," Matt admitted unwillingly.

"Was it all right when he brought it back?"

"Yeaah." A flicker of a glance shot at me as he reluctantly added, "He gave me two dollars for the gas."

That day there were two sentences: *Billy stole my motorcycle. He gave me $2 for the gas.*

Then I shifted him to a retrieval card. He could print, he could read his words, so I thought he was ready. He was, externally. It took me the rest of the year to realize that neither he nor the rest of the class was organically ready. They had been Doing Words for only a month.

Matt's first sentence on his retrieval card was

Mikey
gave
me
a
toy
wrecker

The next day he had

My
______
motorcycle
can
jump
over
pipes
and
saws
______
tools

The first line was for *toy,* which he had the day before, and the second was for *and,* a couple of words up on that day's list.

The next day he mentioned the central person in his life, his Dad, for the first time.

______
went
jogging
with
______
Dad
when

______
got
home
from
school

After this sentence, with *I* and *my* and *I* on the lines, he was already into his second row of words.

I was beginning to have my doubts about that motorcycle, and during the conversation for his next story we talked about whether or not he actually got to ride it. He hemmed and hawed about it, but insisted that he did.

______
rode
______
______
all
the
way
to
Joshua's
house

I asked him if he remembered *Joshua* from his word cards, but he didn't.

That day he finished printing in jig time and came back for more. "What do you want to write?" I asked him.

"I don't know," he answered, with his charming and tentative smile. "What can I write about?"

"I don't know, Matt. What's new?" I looked him up and down. Same basic kid, same dirty face, same big blue eyes. "Are those new sneakers?"

"No," he said. "I got them for school," implying that September was at least a millennium behind us.

"Oh, yes, I remember," I said. "Well, I still like them. They're a nice color."

"That's what I want!" crowed Matt. "*The teacher likes my sneakers.*"

So I added, under *house,*

———
teacher
likes
———
sneakers

These one-liners continued for another few weeks. Toward the end of this time I stopped writing the lines for the words he knew, but only wrote the words he needed. The last column on his retrieval card looked like this:

flower
Popeye
Shawna
yard
them
they
biggest
littlest

He filled up his writing book with a story about his dogs, Shawna and Popeye. He needed other words, obviously, but some were in his head by now and some were on his card. When he needed *run* for the dog story, I told him he knew all the sounds in it and asked him to spell it for me orally, which he did.

Then he got a new book, another set of printing papers stapled together with a cover. Into this one he wrote, asking only for *myself,* this story: *My Dad hates me. I am going to kill myself. I hate myself.*

When he showed it to me I hugged him and told him I loved him and tried to get him to tell me some becauses for these feelings. He had nothing more to say, so I gave him a couple of special chores to do for me and he was quite happy by the end of writing time. He was so much happier, in fact, that when he went back to his desk to get his book to read in the circle, he was apparently appalled by what he had written. He erased the entire thing.

The next day I gave him a dictionary, and Movement V began.

Matt was, I thought, near the bottom of the middle of this class. Even on the second day of school they seemed rather lackluster and very young. I was mesmerized by their printing and didn't completely grasp that they had very little, if any, Key Vocabulary; that they were not, in fact, anywhere near in touch with themselves. I had been trying to compress Movements I and II into Movement III, to combine them, as it were, so that the children would be printing into books (Movement III) their Key Words and sentences (Movements I and II).

I did this much too fast. The result, by the middle of the year, was a large number of children with no organic connection to their writing. Many of them could only see it as another imposed chore: the diametric opposite of what I hoped for them.

Matt's class started the whole Words program in first grade with me. Because I moved much too quickly through the first three movements, some of them still didn't trust their ownership of their writing until well past Christmas, well into Movement V. I think now that a minimum of three weeks of Key Words, even if they are printing them, is essential and must not be skipped over no matter how incredible the printing is. I would move much more slowly with a class that has had no Words before, so that the children even out and become, by Movement IV, writers with Key Words and belief in themselves firmly under their belts.

Chapter 6

Movement V: Dictionaries, Or, Has Anyone Seen My Pen?

> I do believe that, indeed, education by and large serves to defraud humans of their own interests, and sometimes thereby of their souls, and that crazy horses are one consequence of the "education" of horses.
>
> — Vicki Hearne

WHENEVER I GIVE an alphabet book to a child, the child immediately goes over to a friend's desk and tells the friend in a quiet, proud voice, "Lookit. Lookit what I got. It's for my Words." Even the friends who already have their own are duly impressed. They were proud themselves, after all, when they got theirs. This has never not happened, in all these first grades. The alphabet book, the child's own personal dictionary and the hallmark of Movement V, is a Good Thing.

In Movement V the children extend their retrieving skills from a random list to a twenty-six-page booklet in alphabetical order, into which I write the words they need on the appropriate page. In order to shift into Movement V, a child has to be able to write the letters of the alphabet in order on the pages of that booklet. Writing goes on in Movement V as it has in Movement IV. Depending on the nature of the class, the children sit at their seats and I wander, or I sit at a table and they come to me. They must write, and they must also read yesterday's writing to another person during the writing time. At the end of the time we read everyone's writing for the day aloud in a circle, just as we have been doing since the first Key Words.

Each child thinks of what to write about and begins to write it. Sometimes the child comes to me to tell me the whole story and to get all the words she needs at once, before ever starting to write. As the children get used to it, as each one's independence grows, they start right in, only asking me for words they know they don't know, with the alphabet book open to the page the word they want starts with.

Those words are not necessarily the only ones they don't know, however, so another element of writing the children are responsible for during Movement V is to show it to me when they have finished for that day's writing time. "Have I seen your writing?" is a question I ask almost as often in Movement V as I asked "What Word do you want?" in Movement I. When I see it, instant editing takes place, so that the story is correct when it is finished. This correctness is no different from Movements III and IV, but in those Movements the children are more likely to be writing with me watching.

Not that I ever write on a child's paper. Never, never, never write on a child's paper. When corrections are needed, the child must make them if there is to be any learning. This instant editing is oral.

I like Philip. philip is my friend. David showed me this work, in his copperplate penmanship, at the end of writing time. He stood next to me, smiling his little smile.

"Nice work," I said. "Who is this that's your friend?" I asked, pointing to the second *philip*.

"That says *Philip,*" David told me patiently.

"I thought so," I said. "But how will I know it's his name?"

David looked again. "Oh, yeah," he said. "Capital." The smile grew to a big one. "I'll fix it."

When they begin Movement V they are not writing a whole lot, maybe three sentences a day at the most, so there isn't much to check over. But I still have to "see it." I still have to be sure that when it is time to read it the writer and I will both be able to. In general, Movement V stories are one-day stories, and therefore won't be worked on again.

Movement V used to be the last movement in Doing Words. There were many days in many years when all thirty children were doing one- or two-sentence stories with their dictionaries, before they or I had heard of the writing process, with its stages and its emphasis on continuing stories. It is logical, still, to begin second and third graders in the program with this Movement if they have done no organic writing before.

This chapter will take a morning of first graders in Movement V, word for word, to show that a whole class of children really can all do writing and the teacher really does have time to help them all in the space of an hour in Movement V. (Many people have skeptically asked how this can be.) With this group I sat at a table and they came to me; with a younger or more active class I would wander among seated children. It doesn't seem to affect the writing, only the noise level and busy-ness of the room. There were twenty-eight of them; it took about an hour to Do Words, including reading the writings aloud.

It is a Blue day. In my room you are either a Red, Blue, Yellow, or Green, an arbitrary assignment I make at the beginning of every year purely for organizational purposes. On a Blue day, the Blues get first crack at show-and-tell (if a Blue doesn't want to "use his time" he can give it to a child who is one of the other colors). Blues also get to be the first in lines, first to read, and chosen to run errands and help me.

On this Blue day the children are in pairs around the room, mostly on the floor, reading their writing books to each other. Andy is already in his seat, writing; four or five boys are heading for the blocks on the rug. Three girls are hovering around Debbie C.'s desk, investigating by feel and play the two Guatemalan dolls she brought for show-and-tell. A few are coming to or are on the bench by my table. Eric is wandering, yawning and twisting the hair on his forehead. There are the sounds of reading, chatting, working, thinking.

"Jerry, have you read?" I ask one of the rug ones as I walk to the table.

"Uh-uh," he says with a sheepish smile.

"All of you on the rug, read first please." I give each one a look. Then I turn to the first child on the bench. "Good morning, Robert. What's your story today?"

"*I got new pants and a new shirt and new sneakers last night. Mama went to the store.*" A happy boy.

"All new! Lovely — let me see the sneakers." He sticks out his foot; I reach for his alphabet book. "Mmmm! Now let's see, what words do you need? What page shall I put *sneakers* on?"

"*S*," says Robert. "And *shirt* too."

"Great," I say, entering these two. "How about *new*?"

"*N* page."

I turn to it. "Find *new*, Robert."

Another dictionary open to *S* appears under my left elbow. "I need *snowmobile*," says Andy.

I print it; Robert has his finger on *new*. "Good, Robert. Do you need anything else? You know *got*, don't you?"

Firm nod. "*G-o-t*."

"Good. Let me see it when it's finished." Robert takes his books and leaves the bench.

"Mattie?" She's all sprawled out, looking at the ceiling. "What do you want to write today?"

She focuses on me. "*Me and Tina read together*," comes her soft voice. "And I know *Tina* and *to* but I don't know *gether*."

"*Together* is all one word — on the *T* page — oh, look, you have it already. See?" Mattie straightens herself up enough to point to the word. I underline it. "What else?"

She mouths her sentence again. "*Read*." My hand doesn't move to find a page as I hold her eyes with mine. "It starts with *R*?"

"Yep! There you are!" I write *read*. "Now don't forget the date. Oops, I forgot to put up the date. What, Deb?" to another one hovering on my right.

"That's what I was coming to tell you — you forgot the date," says Debbie Lyn smugly.

"Thank you. Say, could you print it nice and big on the chalkboard? It's Novem. . . ."

"November 4. I know." Debbie Lyn — she's a Blue, thank goodness — hunts importantly for the chalk.

Tina's books are in front of me now. "Hi, Tina, what's —"

"*Me and Mattie read together,*" she says clearly. "*And we had pizza last night.*" All set, Tina is.

"Yum, pizza. Can you spell *pizza*?" A shake of the head. "Starts with. . . ."

"*P*," she says, pointing to her alphabet book already open to *P*. As I print it she adds, "I know the rest."

"Good. And Tina, no curly tails on your letters today, please."

"Mrs. Johnson, can I use the typewriter?" Tanya, a Yellow, asks politely. "Debbie C. says I can use her time." Debbie C. is a Blue.

"Is your story finished?"

"No, I haven't started it yet." She waits.

"Well, okay." I look up at the clock. "Until the big hand gets to the four, then zip! Do your story."

"'kay," smiles Tanya.

I give a quick look around the room. So far so good. Mrs. T., the volunteer, is working down a list of children she is checking for consonant-blend recognition. No mayhem on the rug.

Lisa, who is beautiful, has been queening it on the bench with Mike and Randy. Giggling, they are trying to hold her hand. She smacks Randy gently with her writing book. Both boys are shaking with quiet laughter. A protest is heard from Joanie, second from my end of the bench; no sound from Ernest, next to me, looking scared as usual.

"Hush, you three, I can't hear Ernest." I cock my head at him. "What's your story today, little one? 'Mrs. Johnson loves me?'" I am rewarded for this sally by a tiny grin and a quarter-shake of his head: quite a response from this silent E. "But you already know what you want, don't you?" A little nod. "Tell me."

Another book thrust under my nose. "I want. . . ." from Jackie.

"Just a minute, it's Ernest's turn." Still looking at Ernest, I put a hand on her arm.

"*My brother is helping me make a train,*" he whispers.

"How very nice of him," I reply. "What are you making it out of?"

"Wood."

Withdrawn is perhaps the best word for this child.

"You know, Ernest, if I give you *train* I bet you can do the rest yourself. You have *brother,* and *help,* I know. What do you do to *help* to make *helping*?" I ask as I flip to his *T* page.

"Add *i-n-g.*"

"Yes indeed. And here's *train.*" He gets up and goes, still solemn.

"I need *church* and *choir,*" says Jackie impatiently, "because I'm telling about what we're gonna do at Easter. I know *church* starts with *CH.*" Her book is open to *C.*

"Not just starts, listen: chur-ch."

"It ends with *CH* too!" she shouts in triumph.

"Yes." I write it. "And *CH* is like *G,* it can have more than one sound, because look at this," I say as I continue printing on her C page. "*Choir* starts with it, too."

Jackie figures this out right away. "Yeah, but the *H* is silent." She takes the dictionary from my stunned fingers. "There's *Cheryl,* too. That *CH* should be *SH,*" she tosses off as she moves away.

"Right," I agree feebly. Then I pull myself together and look at Joanie, next on the bench.

"*Christmas* starts like *choir,* too," Joanie says. "But I don't want that. I need *married,* I know," ticking off one finger. "My brother Ronnie is getting married on March eighteenth and Mama said we will have a party for his girlfriend next month." I smile happily back at Joanie; Penny, at my elbow, holds out her *S* page and whispers *snowplow.* "And my sister Karen and I are going to be in the wedding and. . . . I write *snowplow* for Penny and whisper back "Gum!" with a meaningful jerk of my head toward the wastebasket. "And," repeats Joanie with emphasis, "I am getting a new dress for it!"

Joanie jounces on the bench, already excited for March. Penny trots toward the wastebasket, eyes dancing: she tried!

"Lucky you!" I respond to Joanie. "This sounds like it's going to be quite a story. Would you like to read it to the second grade when you've got it written down?" More affirmative jounces from Joanie. "Well, now," I go on. "You know *Ronnie*. I'll give you *wedding* and *married,*" I say, writing these on the appropriate pages, "and what about *getting*?"

"*G-e-t-i-n-g,*" spells Joanie.

"Close," I agree. "But the little short words like *get* usually get an extra last letter before the ending, so it's like this." And I write it on her *G* page. The complete explanation of this rule about doubling the final consonant if it's preceded by a vowel is coming a little later this year, I think. Not too many seem to need it yet. "Now let me see it when it's finished and we'll see about second grade."

"Mrs. Johnson." Deborah, growing very fast and therefore uncoordinated, bumps into me. "Whoops, sorry. We have a reader."

Behind her is Sara, a beautiful, small, self-possessed five-year-old from the kindergarten next door.

"Freeze!" I call. All motion and sound is supposed to stop. "Freeze for Sara." I repeat. I gesture Sara closer to me, waiting for the silence to be complete. "Okay, Sara."

"*Debra is my very best friend,*" she reads, loud and clear.

"Good work. Thank you for coming." I draw a smiley on her paper as other voices echo "good printing, Sara" and "nice story." She is escorted to the door.

"Deborah, how're you coming on yours? Need any help today?" I give Deborah a quick hug.

She careens away, narrowly missing two desks.

"Nope, almost done," she throws back.

Mike is still squinched next to Lisa on the bench. "What is this, Mike," I tease him, "I-love-Lisa day?"

"No," giggles Mike, "but that's my story. *I love Lisa.*" He says this with a big grin: he knows better.

"Come on, Mike, that's a kindergarten story. What else are you going to say?"

"Oh, yeah," he adds in mock surprise. "Okay, okay, I know.

Me and Randy were kissing Lisa on the bench. I need *bench*."

"You can do *bench* by yourself, I bet," I tell him. "Spell *ben* for me."

"*B-e-n*?" says Mike.

"Right: now put on the *ch* sound."

"*B-e-n-c-h*."

"Great. Let me see it when it's written, please. Now Lisa." Mike walks away, Lisa slides down, I look at the clock. I look back at Lisa: she's thinking. To my left there is a game of block-toss beginning on the rug.

"Jerry. Gene. Mark. Rick. Come here for stories, now!" Building is one thing; playing and throwing the blocks are not allowed. I watch to be sure those four are moving.

"Lisa?" She is sitting very straight now.

"Guess what, Teacher, Chris is going to have a baby!" Chris, I've learned, is a neighbor of hers.

"That's nice for Chris, isn't it? Are you going to write about that today?"

"No, I don't want that. Let's see," she ponders, with one forefinger dramatically pointed at her temple. She takes the finger down. "I don't know yet," she reports, thrusting a smiling face close to mine.

"Well, why don't you go to the end of the bench and think of it while I do these boys."

"Okay," says Lisa cheerfully. At the far end of the bench she is joined by Carla, who has come for once without being reminded.

"Now. Randy. What do you want to write? About kissing Lisa, too?"

"Oh, no." The startlingly deep voice is embarrassed. "*My grandmother and grandfather are coming next week for two weeks*. I want to write about that."

"That sounds like fun," I answer. "What do you need for that? You know *grandmother*?" Nod. "*Grandfather*?" Nod. "How about *coming*?"

"*C-o-m-i-n-g*," he spells. "You have to take the *E* off."

"Boy, Randy, sounds like you've got the whole thing right in your head!" Randy moves away to his desk, looking pleased. Jerry, lately of the block tossing, is beside me, dictionary in hand.

"Teacher, I can do my story but I need *friend*."

"Gee, Jerry, don't you have that? What page will it be on? What does *friend* start with?"

Jerry thinks. I say it slowly. "*F*!" he says.

"Let's see, *F* page — yep, there it is. See it?"

He points to the word, delighting me. I make a blue box around it with my pen.

"Okay, Jerry, you've got it all now. What kind of printing?"

Grin. "Perfect." We exchange nods.

There are three on the bench now, several writing at their seats, and a gaggle of girls behind my desk with the Guatemalan dolls. It is nearly 9:25. Thomas and Glen are on the rug, five others are playing and kibitzing a checkers game at Dolly's desk.

"Last call for stories, now. If you haven't got one yet bring yourself to the bench please." This is really the first last call.

"Hello, Mr. Mark," I greet the next child. I flip his hair out of his eyes a little. "How's my friend Mark today?" I try to remind Mark at least once a day that I love him, because not many of the children do.

"Good. Guess what, Teacher. Today is my Mama's birthday and *my* birthday is in three more weeks!"

"Wow, that's soon, Mark!" The bench is filling up. An alphabet book open to *G* is smacked down on top of Mark's: I look up at Debbie C.

"*Guatemala*," she says. I write it, speaking to Mark.

"Well, Mark, be sure to tell your mom Happy Birthday from me, will you? Is all of that your story for today?" Debbie C. is gone; Ernest reappears at my elbow, hands in pockets, silent.

"Yeah. I need *birthday*," says Mark. "Wait, I think maybe I have it." He looks for his *B* page. I look at Ernest.

"May I go bathroom?" he whispers.

"Yes, Ernest."

Sunday
Monday

"Here it is, Teacher," points Mark. "I can write it all."

"Good. What will you do to make *Mama's*?" I ask, all innocence.

Big grin. "You know, Teacher. Put on possafee *S*, of course."

"Good boy. And show me when the story is finished, please."

"Here's a reader!" calls someone. In fact there are two readers, one from second grade and one from third. We freeze and listen; I give a smiley to each.

"Joanie, are you ready yet?" I ask when they leave.

"Almost; I'm on *girlfriend*," she answers, busy.

Gene is next on the bench. Gene is in a rut of I-loves at the moment which I allow, for him, because he can't sustain much else and his printing is still shaky.

"What's your story today, Gene?"

"*I rove the kindergarten*," he bubbles.

"You what? You mean *r-r-rove*?"

"L-love, starts with *L*, I mean," he corrects himself, smacking his forehead with his palm for emphasis.

"Right. I thought you could say that!" I give his head a stroke. "And you have *kindergarten* in your dictionary?" Nod. "Now. Where will all the words sit?"

"On the lines!" He knows this catechism; I wish his fingers did.

"I think I'll make extra lines so it will be even easier today," I say, and as he watches I trace blue pen lines over the ones in the writing book for the four words he is going to write. "There."

Carla and Lisa, together: "We don't need you, we know what we want."

"Oh. Okay. Do you have all your words?"

"Yep," laconically from Lisa; "I have some and Lisa has some," elaborates Carla. They go to their desks.

"Absolutely last call!" I call, taking Rick's dictionary.

"Excuse me, Mrs. Johnson, may I please go to the bathroom?" says Judie and "Teacher! Can I have a turn on the typewriter?" from Thomas, both speaking at once.

"Yes, Judie. May I see your story after? No, Thomas, I haven't seen you for a word yet. Get your books and come to the bench. Hi, Rick." This is a good solid boy. "All ready?"

One big nod. "*Me and Glen was playing in the block corner.* I need *corner,* I know the rest."

"Good. Here's *corner.* Would you say *Me and Glen was playing,* or can you make that better English?"

Swiftly shaking his head in one direction only, Rick corrects himself. "I mean, *we were playing.*"

"Right. And I don't need to say do your best printing, do I, because your printing is always the best."

Smiles all around at that.

"I can do mine too, I don't need anything," says Glen, right behind Rick.

"Okay, Glen." I give him a mock-fierce scowl. "How are you going to start all your circle letters?"

"From the top," he sighs; but his dimples are showing.

"Matt. Thomas. Heidi. Stories now. Put the checkers away, Dolly." Tanya comes with her dictionary open to *G.*

"I did my story already," squeals Heidi.

"Let me see it." Some days Heidi thinks it's still yesterday.

"Mrs. Johnson, I need *Guatemala* for my story," says Tanya.

"Debbie's dolls, eh?" I write it. "Why do I have to use capital *G?*"

"It's the name of the place they come from?" Tentative, but true.

"That's exactly why."

"Teacher." It's Jerry again with his green preprimer. "Me and Andy's gonnu read in the hall, okay?"

"Did I see your story, Jerry?"

"No."

"Bring it to me first, please." Jerry, going to get his writing book, pokes Andy, whispering, "She wants to see our stories first."

"Okay, Matt," to the next on the bench. "What's your story today?"

Dolly, twinkling, puts her *H* page down in front of me. "*Hawaii,* please," she says. She's bubbling with something!

"Hawaii! Who's going to Hawaii?!" I ask, printing. "Are you?"

"I know," chimes in Matt, who is Dolly's cousin.

"Don't you tell, Matt!" Dolly threatens him, hands on hips. To me she says, "You'll see when I read it." She loftily sweeps away, twirling the dictionary with studied nonchalance.

Jerry and Andy are back, books open. "Good, Jerry. You may read with Andy if it's all right with him. Okay, Andy," looking over his two pages. "Great. Bye." Heidi and Debbie Lyn both show me theirs too. "Debbie Lyn, what goes at the end of this?"

"Oh. Period."

"Yes. Good, Heidi. Now Matt, what is your story?"

Matt folds his arms tightly. "You know!" His face is one big freckled grin. I know? What?? Oh, yes, he used Gene's Blue time this morning.

"It's on the *S* page, right?" His arms hug tighter as he nods. "You showed it this morning?"

"Snowmobile suit!" he bursts out.

"Yes sir!" I write it fast. "Have you got *got*?" I ask; but he's halfway to his seat.

Now Thomas. "What's your story today?"

He rolls his eyes in his very expressive face. "It's a funny one, Teacher," chuckling to prove it. "*Jerry is a carrot.*"

"Oh, Thomas," I exclaim in mock dismay. "I thought Jerry was your friend!" Another chuckle. "Of course he does have red hair — is that why he's a carrot?"

Thomas begins a nod, to agree; then he changes to a negative shake. "No, you are silly, Teacher. A carrot has green hair!"

Now we are both chuckling. "Okay, okay," I give in, secretly delighted by this "slow-learner's" speed of thought. "Okay: this is your last vegetable story, please. Now. You know *Jerry*?"

"He's in my head," Thomas points. "*Jerry* is, *i-s. A. Carrot.* I don't know *carrot.*" I write it on his *C* page and underline it. "Can I write at the table today?"

"Yes. You're the last one, Thomas. Do a good job on Jerry."

I cap my pen. "Everybody to the rug, please, time to read." I get up, to shepherd and check as I go. Eric sidles up to my hip-bone, looking very tired. There is a new screamy baby at his house.

"But I didn't get my story yet," he says, dragging the words. I sit down again, on the bench, drawing him close.

"Are you a tired Eric today?" I rub his back a little. "Can I help you with your writing?"

"I don't know what to write," says Eric, leaning heavily.

"Well, how about that one? *I don't know what to write.*"

"No . . . not that."

"Want to write about what we're going to do this afternoon?"

"The movie?" I nod. "Uh-uh." He rolls his storybook up, unrolls it to show me a big rip on the back cover. "Can you fix my book?"

"Certainly. Let's find my tape." As we walk the ten feet to my desk several books are held out for inspection. "Yes; yes; good; period; that's nice, Joanie, you may go now."

Everyone is gathering around the rug. Debbie Lyn has pulled up a chair for me and Dolly is guarding it. I'm the only one who gets a chair. A few children are still finishing up at their desks. "Hey!" I notice. "Look at the blocks still out! Rick, Gene, Randy, Glen: blocks!"

I get the masking tape out, briefly dislodging Mrs. T. and Debbie C., matching pictures and blends, and tape Scott's rip. "There. Now it's all fixed. But what's going to be in it? How's your baby sister?"

"Good," drawls Eric. "But I don't want to write about her." He looks around, sighs. We are at his place now. He sits down, I perch on the edge of his desk. "Can I write about my book?"

"Sure — you mean about fixing it?" Nod. "Sure." I reach for his alphabet book, but he keeps a hand on it.

"I can do it, Teacher." A huge yawn, but the stubby fingers are curling around the pencil.

"Okay, Eric, come to me if you get stuck."

I move, finally, to the rug.

"Can I read first? I been good," says Mark. He has, too, which is refreshing.

"I'm sorry, Mark, it's a Blue day. Ask me first tomorrow. Today . . ." — I look around — ". . . Glen may read first." I sit down. "Glen, let's go then."

"You made a rhyme," says Heidi unexpectedly. I wink at her.

"Hello, Susan!" I have suddenly found this one, thumb in mouth, leaning on my knees. "I didn't see you today. Did you do your story all by yourself?"

A proud smile around a thumb is like no other.

For the next fifteen minutes each child will read his writing for the day aloud. Each one reads, shows his book to me if I haven't seen it, and chooses a friend to read next before sitting down to be a listener himself. On this day Andy has written about a ride he took with his brothers and his father; Deborah has written about a visit from her aunt, Susan about our volunteer for today. Judie's story is "*Robin and I are going to get some new books with are Christmas money. I want a book about horses.*" I don't myself say *are* and *our* homophonically, but this has happened before to Judie. I point it out and she goes to fix it, choosing before she leaves the circle.

Dolly's story is the high point today. It is another of her many cousins' parents who are going to Hawaii, and she has done an elegant job. Just as she finishes, and added bits of information are being provided by Matt, Jason from the second grade comes in to read. The travelers-to-be are his parents, and we all listen attentively to his horse's-mouth version. I'm thankful Dolly got to read hers first. Jason gets his smiley and leaves, and we go on. There are a couple of periods missing, Ernest has put an unnecessary capital *B* on *brother,* Lisa has made *S* backwards. As the reading progresses those who were still writing finish and join us on the rug.

"Randy. Sit still. We listened to you, now you listen. How are you coming, Gene?" looking quickly over my shoulder. "Need any help?"

"Yeah, I'm a little bit stuck," says Gene, not exactly in despair but close. I detail Debbie C. to "help him make his letters," and the reading goes on. Then it is a few minutes before ten.

"Good work, first grade, we finished in time for recess! Tina, can you bring the book box back to the bench — ooh, listen to that, bring the book box back to the bench, all those *F* words —"

"No! *B*!!" comes the chorus.

"— and we'll get ready to go. . . ."

"I didn't read yet, I tricked ya!" from Jackie, who's been sitting on her book. "Ha ha!"

"Oh my goodness, Jackie." Some are already halfway into snowsuits. "Freeze: we forgot Jackie!" I order inaccurately. She reads her description of church music plans to a less-than-attentive class.

"There. Now we're really finished. Thank you, Jackie."

Recess. Ah, recess. After zipping and tying all the boots and suits and hats and scarves and fielding "I can't find my other mitten" seven times, it's recess. An eight-minute cup of coffee. Maybe.

Time to put the blue pen away.

Notice that I expected much more of Jackie than I did of Thomas. Notice that I spoke differently to Ernest than to Joanie. Notice, as I'm sure you have, that each child in that group was working on a different idea. They were all moving through that hour in their own twenty-eight diverse says.

When I first got into primary teaching, allowing for each child to do what was appropriate for that child was an okay thing to do in school. It was called Individualized Instruction, and it was the savior of all things, the solution to all problems in the late sixties and the seventies. It was then considered to be a good idea to "take each child where he is and move him as far as he can go" along a linear spectrum of learnings and facts and abilities. It still is a good idea.

It is not wonderfully easy to manage, however. Soon Individualized classrooms ran big risks of being discipline nightmares, and since there was no concurrent attempt to help teachers learn to manage these new ways, nor to reduce class sizes, most efforts died. Straight-out-of-the-book teaching returned, known as

Back to the Basics, where groups of children are taught all together. Slowly the insidious idea returned, too, that there is such a thing as a "third grade work" and that all children can be expected to achieve it during that year. "Individualization" is now not considered to be a very nice word, and the pendulum has swung all the way to Mastery Management. Perhaps I will say more about that later; perhaps I will keep my temper instead.

I went into more detail about her story with Joanie and into more depth in spelling with Jackie because they were ready to deal with those ideas. Either they had them firmly tucked into their brains already, or the moment was right for those girls to discover those things that day. By Doing Words, even though it is a little more complicated in Movement V, all the children are fulfilling their own patterns and, by and large, matching that mythical list of What All First Graders Can Do. It is in Movement V that the huge and hideous American rearrangement of what was a perfectly good language, known as phonics, can be most painlessly inhaled by children. Sooner or later, in the course of a year's writing, everyone wants a word that begins with almost every consonant and consonant blend, everyone wants to write with words that have as many vowel patterns as there are! When they need them, we "cover" them. (I will go into this in more detail in Chapter 10.)

Just as the baby isn't ready to "play much" at three weeks old, children aren't ready to do other things until they are ready to. Everyone who has ever read a woman's magazine or had a mother-in-law knows that there are "right" times for children to learn certain skills. These "right" times are a little like the "average" family, which has 2.3 children. The only arena in which this is possible is in the inhuman arena of statistics.

The other day I was visiting a friend who has a six-month-old daughter. Carol was holding Molly, holding her up to say good night to her father and to me, and saying, in a typically hopeful way, "Wave bye-bye, Molly." Carol waved with her free hand as she said this, and Molly grinned. No wave. Carol doesn't see me very often, and she did want the baby to perform — no amount of clowning on my part would do. She kept waving and repeating "Wave bye-bye, Molly," for several minutes. Molly was watching, and giving every appearance of being a contented child, and then suddenly began to kick her feet up and down. "Oh no," said Carol. "She'll never get it."

But she had gotten it. Kicking her feet was her way of doing the same thing her mother was doing with her hand. Molly's understanding of the world was still limited to what the parts of her body she sees can do. Piaget calls this accommodation. When I explained it to Carol, she understandably was very proud of Molly, and I could leave content.

Piaget. Piaget is a name to conjure with and has been for fifty years or so. A French child-watcher whose work spans most of this century, Jean Piaget has laid the foundations for universal understanding of how children learn, how their behaviors build in predictably integrated steps. He has concentrated on the physical world, watching children develop and taking notes and notes about the sequences in which they learn, the ages they are likely to be when certain activities and abilities become their own, and incidentally, what joy can be had from watching, rather than directing, a child's growth.

To me, the most important of Piaget's many contributions to our understanding of the new generation is the idea of readiness. Your child will learn to wave with her hands, Carol, he would say, but she has to do several other things first in preparation for that. Then she will be ready. First she has to notice that parts of her body move; then that she can move them; then that some movements are waving movements, and she can make them; then that she has legs she can move, then that she can move her arms too, and that these parts belong to her; and finally, after several other steps I've undoubtedly left out, she will wave goodby to me on command with her hand. Before she goes through all the readiness steps herself, she might wave with her hand once or twice, and she might even happen to do it when Carol had just said "Wave." But until she has done all these intermediate explorations, she won't be directing herself to wave.

Sometimes the parent's expectation gets in the way of the child's growth, but usually the parent's expectation just gets in the way of the parent's appreciation of that growth, as in the case of Molly and Carol.

If you believe that each child has a pattern to follow, and is doing it in her own time, it's a lot easier on you as a parent or as a teacher to ignore or smile benignly at the people who say "Can't she do that yet?" The thing to do, at home, is to watch and to provide the growing child with whatever she is ready for — big balls before little balls, for instance; things to move before things to take apart; and so forth. (I think it would be nice if teachers could do that, too.)

It's too bad that the title Teacher has been reserved for a schoolhouse person, when all moms and dads teach like crazy too. When children come to school, though, somehow many parents think that they can no longer teach their children anything. After having been teachers in everything but name for three or four or five years, they suddenly go all shy about helping the child continue to assimilate his environment. I don't know how many times I've heard someone say that: I'd better wait 'til Jimmy gets to school to teach him his letters. Or, your teacher will tell you, dear.

Somehow parents get a fear of doing the wrong thing the minute the child steps into kindergarten. It's odd, since they've been doing the right thing for years. It may be because the parents suspect that their child will be judged by a different set of expectations, ones not based on that child's growth pattern but on some curriculum list in the sky. There's no reason why parents can't continue listening, talking, reading aloud, admiring, limiting, putting as much environment and challenge in the path of the child as will fit into the family's way. Especially if she is in a school where no one is Doing Words, where no one is allowing and encouraging children to believe in their own images and strengths, the parents and the family will be the only source of self-esteem the child may have.

It is hard in a classroom to juggle the readiness levels of many children at once; but it is absolutely necessary if the children are each to learn what each needs to assimilate the world. It's better for Joanie to come at the sounds *CH* makes on her day than on Jackie's because then she will be the ready one. I expect differently and I get differently. If I wanted sameness, I'd program robots for a living instead.

Chapter 7

Autobiographical Interlude, Or, "If Children Have To Spell, They'll Never Want To Write"

Know thyself.

— Inscription at the Delphic Oracle

ON MARCH 6, 1982, I went to a lecture given by a roundish and gracefully balding man of fifty or so who looked and spoke like a cross between a James Thurber character and Jonathan Winters, as gentle and as twinkly. He was Donald Graves, then deeply involved in his research on writing with young children at Atkinson Academy in New Hampshire. His lecture was straightforward and wonderful, and it set off a landslide of doubts in me about my own teaching of writing.

"Children need to write in school, even very young children, every day," he said. Yes, yes, I nodded from the fifteenth row. "Children can write what they want to write. When we give them topics to write on, we're saying we know better than they do what's in their heads." Yes, of course, I thought, I never tell them what to write. "And they have as many ideas of their own as a teacher could ever want. When we give them topics we cause them to be self-doubting and dependent, which I call 'writer's welfare.'" What a nifty way to put it, I thought, joining in the ripple of wry amusement that swept the hall.

"The way children write is exactly the way grown-ups and professional writers write, with many drafts and revisions. Editing comes last in the writing process. As a piece of writing develops, it is the content that is the most important thing." Well, okay, I thought. I certainly am interested in *what* they write.

"Concern about spelling and grammar should wait until a piece has been drafted and revised, when it can be cleaned up for publication." Cleaned up by whom, I wondered. They can clean it up as they go along. "Children left to themselves will invent their own spelling in a predictable way, and it can be used to measure their growth." What? Invent spelling? How can anyone read it, then? "And the teacher can write the message of the child's writing correctly as she types a piece for publication. To ask the child to do it all correctly would discourage him from writing." But what about printing? What about *ain't* and *gonnu* and *brang*? What about communicating by writing?? And it doesn't discourage them, they keep right on writing, every day. And they don't know enough sounds to even invent much at the beginning of first grade, never mind kindergarten. . . .

Applause began, pattering an echo to the stutter in my head.

"Wasn't he great?" beamed the woman beside me, a vibrant young special-ed teacher. This lecture was a special event for a course she and I were taking.

"Yes, he was, but . . . Jeanie," I burst out. "What is all this about inventing spelling? I loved what he says about writing, I agree with him, I have writing in my class every day but . . . but what good is it if nobody can read it? How does anyone know what the child is saying?"

"It works, though," she assured me. "The research shows that children who write with Invented Spelling . . ." (Goodness, I thought, it has a Name?) ". . . develop into standard spellers in a predictable way."

That stopped me in my tracks, and Jeanie stopped too. "In English?" I said incredulously. "The world's most illogical and impossible language to spell? In first grade?" We stood in the carpeted hallway, with people streaming by on both sides of us. I stared at confident, well-read Jeanie, baffled and frightened.

Graves was right about so much, I thought. Was he right about this, too?

Was I so wrong?

The next week one of Graves's co-researchers gave a talk on Invented Spelling, with lots of overhead transparencies and a don't-interrupt-me style. She explained that a child's first writings in school, in kindergarten and first grade, were pictures; the teacher annotated them by writing at the bottom of the paper what the child said the picture showed. As the child began to use letters of his own to label the drawing, the teacher also wrote the message on it so that they would both know what it said another day.

In this labeling, she said, children use beginning consonant sounds first, then endings, then middles. A picture of a boat, for example, would first be labeled *B* and later *BT.* They began to use vowels in their inventing last, all according to a system called letter-name strategy. This systematic invention of spelling made it possible for the teacher to read what the child wrote and to gauge what help he needed to move to the next phonic step. It didn't make any difference, she added, how the children formed these letters. It was the content that counted.

Somebody asked if they took home these pictures with their writings that sat on the page so untraditionally. "It depends on your own public relations, really," she answered. "I think the best thing is to keep the child's drafts. Then you can have a parent conference to show how much the child has grown in his writing."

Finally I raised my hand. "What if you think it's important for children to spell and print correctly?" I asked. I was trembling inside, feeling that I was summing up my whole existence with those words.

She practically snorted. "Can you imagine," she said scornfully, "that a child would want to write if he had to know how to spell first?!"

Yes! I wanted to shout. They do! They have!

But my confidence to say so out loud had been withered by her overheads and her righteousness, stumped by Donald Graves's logic and gentleness, and overpowered by Jeanie's greater intimacy with research. I had none of these in even the smallest measure. All I had were ten years of Doing Words, of children in kindergarten and first grade eagerly doing writing in standard English with standard spelling. All I had were ten years of teaching organic writing that had been working fine.

Mostly.

Now, as I relive those meetings, I think I know why those March days blitzed me so. I was ripe for the self-questioning they threw me into because I had a few doubts creeping in already about the way my writing program was going in first grade.

By March of 1982 the children in the class were writing a complete story every day, either autobiographical or fictional, a page or so each day. They chose their own topics, wrote about what they wanted to. Their writing was well printed and in correct English, corrected by them before Word time was over for the day. They used personal dictionaries and shared their writing with the class and with other classes. They were working well in Movement V, and felt good about it. Spelling, punctuation, penmanship, usage were carried along by the energy of a child's commitment to his writing because it was his own. They wrote with eagerness, confidence, imagination, and accuracy.

And I was not happy. I was disturbed, somehow, by their perfection, I was almost disapproving when they wanted to write more; and I was greatly puzzled by my dissatisfaction. There were several times that winter when I turned away from trying to understand it.

William, for example. Bright, arrogant William worked busily on his story and had done a lot before I got to him one day in January. It was a Monday, and the day before had been especially great:

> We climbed up on the roof and slided down into the snow. Suzy wouldn't slide. Me and Wendy slided down and went back

Shadows

> up again. Wendy got stuck in the snow. Then Jami came over. Jami wanted to slide to but

It wasn't finished, which was the only thing I saw. That was one of the rules in those days: a story should be finished by the end of Word time.

"It's time to stop now," I told William, and exasperation came out in my voice. Alarm bells went off in my head, too, but I ignored them.

"Can I finish it tomorrow?" he asked.

I agreed reluctantly; but of course he didn't. He'd felt something wrong, too, with me. I hadn't said out loud that he shouldn't want to write more: but we'd both heard it. I never found out why Suzy wouldn't slide, and that Monday I didn't make myself find out what was wrong with me, either.

Last night, wrote Maria, whose angle on the world was always striking, *I went down to the edge of my field and slid all the way down. There was a path that led into the woods and that is where I was.*

After a glance at this clear and correct page of writing, and a smile, I moved on to another child. I was vaguely aware that Maria hadn't been challenged at all by that morning's work, although she'd done what was expected. Soon after this she began writing jokes, using even less of her considerable talent. I told myself that it was good that she concentrated on the punny jokes. (*Do you know that it's raining dogs and cats outside? I just stepped in a poodle.*) This was rote stuff for her. She began to write in the *ha-ha*s with casual condescension.

At about this same time Eric, a year older, burst into enormous once-upon-a-time stories in second grade. Words poured out of him; every day he wrote a huge story like this one in his writing book.

> Once upon a time there was a wicked witch and she lived in a castle and somewhere in the woods was a hill and no one knows that the one that lives in the hill and the one that lives in the woods is a dog and the dog carries a sled with a seat and somewhere else is a rabbit and the rabbit is the one that rides the sled

> with the seat because it was snow on the ground. One day the rabbit went for a walk and then he saw a hill and it was a castle but he was looking for butterflys and he saw a butterfly and then he went for a ride on his dog with the sled with the seat and then he said giddyup and then he was going and then he was gone and then he went down the hill and the wicked witch saw the rabbit and the dog in her crystal ball and she was trying to get them and tried to get them but she did not get them the end.

Sometimes there were rattlesnakes instead of the witch, and Davy Crockett instead of the dog. His teacher and I were at a loss to know what to do with this material except to ooh and aah. Soon Eric's sagas shortened until by the end of the year he was only doing staccato pieces of family news.

William and Maria and Eric, and others like them, were pushing against the boundaries of organic writing. Their imagination, penmanship, story line, spelling, fluency, and motor coordination were all that we had ever asked for. We were proud of them, proud to complacency. They were proud of themselves. They, however, had metaphorically raised their heads and their pencils and looked around and asked, "What's next?"

I hadn't asked that. I was a little uneasy sometimes, yes, but in general I liked what was happening with Doing Words. Perhaps my very defensiveness should have given me the clue that my system was too pat. Meeting up with the writing process and invented spelling, apparently a unit, had the effect of making me doubt all the organic work we did and had ever done. Was I stifling the children? Would they do better (and what did that mean? more? differently?) if spelling and printing didn't matter? Was it or was it not important, centrally basic, that writing communicate?

That last question was the one I kept coming back to as I struggled to make peace between all that I had heard in those March meetings and had been watching the children do during years of Words. For me, if the children themselves couldn't read what they wrote, and if others couldn't read it, it wasn't worth doing. So I couldn't believe that switching to Invented Spelling would help the writers I was teaching. Why would I want them to become users of incorrect English when they routinely used correct English? As I fussed about this for the next year, the same answer kept coming back: Yes, it was important that writing communicate.

By the end of that year I had calmed down enough to begin to understand that my uneasiness with William and Maria and Eric had nothing to do with spelling. Gradually it dawned on me that just because invented spelling was not appropriate for my teaching style, for Doing Words, I didn't have to reject the writing process. Slowly I recognized that although I could identify four levels or Movements in organic writing during the kindergarten year, I had expected that Movement V alone would cover all of first and second grades. Finally I saw that moving into the writing process was the logical next step for organic writers. They needed the steps of the writing process, they needed some instruction about the literary conventions that define good writing, and they needed to be able to put their pieces together over time.

William and Maria and Eric had been trying to tell me this.

The writing process, or "process writing" as it is sometimes called, is the pedagogical opposite of writing for a product. As a way to operate in American classrooms, the writing process is a major, radical, night-to-day shift in emphasis and ownership. In the average classroom in America for many years past, writing a paper or a report or a story was usually part of the year's work in grades three through six, part of each term's work in various subjects in grades seven through twelve. The teacher assigned a topic, and a due date, and the student wrote about that topic and passed the paper in and got it back with red-pencil corrections and/or comments on the writing in the margins, which the student might read but probably wouldn't. Most of these efforts ended up in the wastebasket, unless the student's mother was determined to keep everything. Very little time, if any, was given in class to teach the student how to do the paper, and that time was devoted solely to generic how-to — what's supposed to be in a research paper, for instance, or beginning, middle, and end for a fiction story. Very rarely, and as good as never in the grades below high school, was any teaching time given to what was supposed to be in Mary's research paper, or how Eddie could shape his story's beginning or ending. In "product" writing, enormous emphasis was on getting it right the first time, so much so that at least two very undesirable things became common: hardly anybody ever thought of revising or changing anything they wrote; and, to be sure it was right, many children routinely copied reports from the nearest encyclopedia. Nothing could be further from the idea of ownership and learning, both basic to writing.

When writing is accepted in classrooms as a process, the papers and reports and stories are worked on by the students and the teachers together, in class time. Children are actually taught how to determine their own topics and how to focus them (prewriting); given time to simply write and get down onto a page whatever they want to say about the topic (drafting); encouraged to talk it over with the teacher and other students, shown how a section or a sentence might be rearranged, added to, or otherwise changed (revising); helped with spelling and other grammar problems that may be inherent in that piece of writing (editing); and then, only then, told to make a final, beautiful copy (publishing). When this effort is passed in to the teacher, then, the teacher is well acquainted with it already and can judge it (if there has to be a grade) on the basis of what it says and how much the student has learned in the process of writing it. No red pencils are necessary.

William was making a list of the elements in the story of his snowy day. He was prewriting it, remembering the parts. He needed me to see that, to legitimize his getting-ready, and to talk to him about other details he might like to include, such as the feel of the snow, and to ask what did happen to Suzy. The story needed much more than one day to do.

Eric's repeated retellings about the witch and the dog were

drafts of the same story. No wonder he gave up! He needed me to help him identify what needed revising, and to show him how to do that, and to say that it was okay to twist it and turn it until he had what he wanted.

Maria's piece about sliding was a powerful beginning. *The edge of my field,* very precisely located, and the path that intriguingly *led into the woods* were used to create a mood, to make the reader want to know more. It was an elegant little lead, not a story yet. She knew that, although she had no label for it. She needed me to recognize it too, and to confer with her about what she could make happen in that setting.

These children were ready for the writing process, for continuing and revising and reworking and conferring and doing all those things as many times, over as many days, as they needed to in order to make the best story they could make. I was ready for it, too, to wash away my uneasiness and to help them grow even more as writers. We all needed Movement VI, and now we have it.

It is pleasant to admire Donald Graves again. I am grateful to him, and to all my doubts. I am glad to have the writing process to use with young writers, and I am glad that I don't have to have invented spelling as well. Invented spelling may work for others, but I like Doing Words first. We can certainly write without it — English is just fine.

Invented spelling still fascinates me, just as New Math does. The theory behind the letter-name strategy seems sound, and the idea that children learn sounds in a certain sequence has diagnostic value which I do not ignore. But it isn't, for us who Do Words, necessary to our communication by writing. As Meg, now in third grade, says, "Well, of course you have to write it right — so when other people read it, they can understand what you said!"

Chapter 8

In the Process, Or, Another Day, Another Writer

> . . . she tried to think deliberately of something appropriate for sharing. But when she did try, there was only silence. Experience had taught her long before what that meant: if she was to have music at all, it must be what she heard.
>
> — Margaret Dickson

When we got home last night the cows were out, wrote Jacob on the fourth day of school. *Me and Andy and Luke and Ben went to get them into the pasture.*

Jacob had come to me for the word *pasture,* but that was the first I'd seen of this piece.

"Well?" I asked. "Did you get them? How many cows got out? Not all your cows, I hope." Jacob and all these brothers and one sister live on a dairy farm with a herd of fifty or so.

While I asked all these questions, my eyes widening with each one, Jacob's eyes were slitting shut, making way for a huge stretching grin. Slowly he shook his head, looking as if he'd swallowed a whole cow's worth of cream.

"You'll have to find out what happens tomorrow!" he crowed.

On this same day, Sam brought his writing to me at about 9:40 with the announcement that he was finished for today. As I was looking it over he added, "I already know what I'm going to put in tomorrow."

It took a little while for Craig to get to writing once-upons, but the first day he started one — which was about the A–Team, as they all turned out to be — he brought it to me grinning from ear to ear. "They're gonna be surprised when they read this, 'cause it's not finished," he told me happily.

This acceptance, by six-year-olds, that their stories are not "done" just because writing time is over or because they have come to a period is one of the major understandings that separate the captioning of the first Movements from the process of writing a continuing piece of work. Once-upon-a-time stories are the commonest vehicle for this continuing form, because usually a lot has to happen before "the end" can be put on.

In Movement VI the writing process is in place in first grade. The first stage of the process, prewriting, seems to come very naturally to writers who began in Movement I. They seldom, if ever, seem to need formal prewriting activities to get started. In second and third grades, particularly for children who did not work up through the early Movements, it is important and necessary to model several prewriting strategies children can use when they don't — or think they don't — "know what to write today." I will describe these in detail in Chapter 13.

The two most common prewriting strategies used by children in Movement VI in my class are thinking and talking. These children have had a conference with the teacher every day since the first day of Movement I, a tiny conversation about what they are going to write that day. This has been, for all practical purposes, a prewriting conference. The children are used to this, from the first "What's your Word today?" in Movement I to my checklist-filling "What are you working on today?" in Movement VI. They know that they can talk to me or to a friend if they're stuck for a subject. This very rarely happens, however, in my class. If I multiply the number of children writing by the number of days they were working in Movements V and VI this past year, I get about 2,000 answers to "What are you writing today?" Of these, over those months I probably heard "I don't know" only about twenty times.

In Movements V and VI, of course, stories are often if not usually continuing, so a very common answer — probably a thousand of those answers — was "I'm writing more on the same one I was doing yesterday," and I merely note *ct* on my checklist.

It's important to know what the children are doing every day in writing, what they are writing about, and what bits of the language they are discovering that day. It's important to know for my own sake, so that I have a glimmering of what might happen in writing time tomorrow; it's important for their sakes, because if they see me keeping track they'll know that I care about what they're doing; and it's important in case someone in a position of authority wants to know.

I keep records in my head, of course, as any teacher or any parent automatically does. I know on any given day to watch for Troy's backwards *P,* to notice if Heather's finally figured out when *S* has an apostrophe, to encourage Cory to begin some of his sentences about the giant with something besides "*The giant* . . ." I know that I need to remind Luke to look for words he needs in his dictionary before he asks me, to remind Craig that he needs to be writing instead of reading all of writing time.

In the early Movements the record keeping can pretty much be done internally. In Movement I most of this internal record keeping has to do with letter formation on the one hand and how Key the first Words are on the other hand. In Movement IV I need to be sure that I know which children need me to sit very nearby while they are writing from retrieval cards. In Movement IV, too, I should be aware of subjects repeated often, and of who is ready to do continuing stories.

In Movement V, however, and certainly in Movement VI, it gets to be too much to keep track of. Someone always slides through the cracks of my mind. Nothing is more scathing to my spirit than a child who says, "No, Teacher, I finished that dinosaur story last week! Don't you remember?" So I keep a daily checklist of who's doing what.

At the beginning of writing time in Movement V, I go around the room with my checklist, an ordinary 8-by-11 sheet marked off in a grid with children down the left side and days across the top. In the square for the day I put two things: a notation about the process and the number of sentences. Allan, for example, wrote two sentences on October 22; three on October 23; three on October 24; four on October 25; two on October 26. The four on Thursday were divided two and two between the two stories he was doing that day, the first two being a continuation of the story he'd begun the day before. On my notation *N* stands for a new story just begun that day that is about something not autobiographical, such as "Dinosaurs are very big and they have very sharp teeth." An autobiographical new story is noted by *A*, such as "I went camping with my mom and dad and my brother and we had fun." And *ct* says that the story is continuing from the day before. So, in the squares for that week for Allan it says: N 2, N 3, N 3, ct 2 N 2, A 2.

When Movement VI is well under way I use bigger spaces for the grid on the checklist and go around at the beginning of writing time to find out what each one will be working on. Other notations are always needed in Movement VI: whether a child is revising or editing or publishing. I also note the subject of the piece for that day in the space. I also enter C if the child has a conference that day, and make a few tiny notes about what was suggested in the conference. David, for example, on May 2, began a story about Richard, worked on it more on May 5, also on May 6, when he had a conference. Then he began another story about candy bars on May 7, worked on it again May 8, edited the Richard story on May 8, worked on the candy story May 9. The checklist looked like this for the first five days: Richard N, ct, ct C looks like, candy bars N, ct. "Looks like" is a conference note I made for him, when the other children in the conference told him that he needed to tell what Richard looked like in the story.

I go around the room first thing, asking "What are you writing today?" and filling my checklist. I never write "Prewriting" on it. The children who are writing continuing stories come to school most days with the next part all ready to go — they have done their prewriting elsewhere. Sometimes this continuity is astonishing.

Eddie, the shining hope of a family of hardworking parents and one older sibling, is a beautiful and endearing boy whose academic gifts are totally congruent with his background in all areas but writing. He began a story about a wolf on the first day of first grade and wrote it slowly, one or two sentences a day. He was sitting at the table with me while he wrote, because I wanted to keep a close eye on his progress with letters and sounds. Then, when he'd gotten to the part where the girl's father comes out with the gun, he was absent for several days. When he came back he was so busy being welcomed that he didn't reread his story before he came to the table, his writing book and alphabet book closed under his arm. I was talking to someone at my elbow; then I turned to Eddie.

"He pulled the trigger," Eddie said, blue eyes beaming. Not "hello, Teacher"; not "I know what I want." I didn't even have time to smile a greeting at him before he plunked his next sentence onto the air between us.

When children know what they want, they know what they want!

> Once upon a time there was a wolf. There was a girl. She was walking in the woods. The wolf got in back of her. He growled. She heard him. She ran. She was scared. The wolf ran after her. Her father came out with the gun. He pulled the trigger. When the daddy wolf heard the gun he ran into the woods. Then he saw a fox when he was walking in the woods. They got into a fight! He killed the fox. Then he took it to his babies. Then he saw the babies' mother dead. He took the dead wolf into the woods. He heard a river. Then he walked to the river. It was a waterfall. He dropped her into the water and she floated downstream. A guy was fishing. After he caught a salmon he saw the dead wolf. Then he put the motor up full blast. When he got to the wolf he got the net. He pulled the wolf up into the boat. When he got to land he dug a hole. He put the dead wolf into the hole. Then he put the dirt into the hole. Then he packed it

down! He went back fishing. The baby wolf walked over the dead wolf. He didn't know it.

I love this story of Eddie's. What I knew of his background would never have led me to expect a gem like this, so I was really watching a brain stretching to its limit as he did the wolf story. As a writer, I am envious of the seeming ease with which he knew where his piece was going even though he hadn't seen it for days. The story itself is almost existential in nature, which is not untypical of first grade stories. Their world is only beginning to make sense, after all; their control of it is still fragmentary, and sometimes their logic is more logical than adults can accept. Each of the characters in the wolf story has an identifying attribute that is plausible, and the story combines these features into a believable fantasy. In my experience, children seldom write the vapid "Run-Spot-run" stories of the basal readers, even when they have to read them. Children, that is, who are brought up on organic writing: they believe in what they themselves have to say.

Eddie and I talked about this story many times while it was in progress, and when it was finished. I didn't in fact think that it was finished, but he was patient with me. These individual conferences, no more than a minute long, can happen with writers who are in a prewriting stage, as Eddie was every day, or in the middle of a revision, or when a piece is ready to be edited, or any time, at any stage of the process. Gerald came to me one day at 9:15 in the grip of a classic writer's block. He didn't know that he had a problem with a name, but that's what it was. He'd already been whirling inside his own head about it for some time, so I was his second line of assistance. He said, in despairing wonder, "I knew what this story was about when I started it, Teacher, but now I don't know what they're going to do next." I expect Hemingway and Shakespeare would fervently recognize that sentiment.

He and I talked about it for probably three minutes, a very long time by conference standards. I asked him to tell me what had happened so far, who his favorite character was, what was his "best" part, and similar questions. Various other children put their dictionaries down in front of me for words while this was going on; some of them were caught up briefly in the discussion of Gerald's story and offered suggestions. Gerald finally hooked himself to a new idea and went off to write furiously until recess.

Conferences about work in progress are what make the writing process different from the old "product" writing. They give the writer many chances to bounce ideas off other minds, to see if an idea "works" in a reader's opinion. The flip side of this is the understanding that writing very seldom comes out perfect the first time. Children who have not been Doing Words and building their self-confidence as writers are reluctant, at first, to change and revise and talk about their writing — it usually takes a couple of months to convince them that it's okay. And sometimes a piece does come perfect the first time, as with Becky's story in Chapter 11.

The individual conference, between one child and the teacher, is only one of several kinds of conferences. Children can and do have conferences with themselves, individually and in pairs, all the time. The individual kind is what, in a discipline that didn't need buzz words, would be called "thinking"; the pair kind has been known for centuries as "talking." The first is virtually impossible to catch as it goes by in class; the second I rarely have leisure to listen to.

Child-child conferences are often the continuation of the reading to a friend that occurs at the beginning of Word time. Kathy and Amber often read together, and sometimes got so interested in talking that they didn't get around to writing at all. One day I was feeling more than usually concerned that Everyone Should Be Working, and I realized that Amber and Kathy were not in their seats and not at the conference table and not under my desk: not, in fact, in any of their usual haunts. Nor could I hear them softly discussing Life, as I usually could.

"Have you seen Amber?" I asked Jamie, who happened to be at the table with me. "Do you know where Amber is?"

Jamie, unfortunately, was the wrong person to ask. She was

very far away, on a journey to a country where horses turned into unicorns and she was big enough to ride them all. In this story the heroine's name just happened to be Amber, so Jamie was understandably startled at my question.

"She's in the pasture with the yellow unicorn," she answered. She looked at me then, really seeing me. "What?" she asked.

"Never mind, Jamie. Go on with your story." I got up from the bench. "I'll be right back."

The room was really working very well. Nearly everyone was concentrating on his or her own problems and delights, so I wished myself invisible as I made a brief tour. Pencils were being chewed, pages were being read over, friends were being consulted, dictionaries were being checked. Finally I came to the big chair in the corner, which was turned away from the room and toward the window. Stockinged feet were barely peeking over the top of the back. I looked over.

Amber was lying upside down on the chair, with her head on one arm. Kathy was sitting on the floor, with her head on the other arm of the chair. Both of them had small chalkboards in their laps for tables, alphabet books between their knees, pencils going like mad. They looked up.

"Hi," I said, feeling like an unpardonable interloper. "How's it going?"

"Good," they both said as one. The look, that interior-aimed look, stuck on me.

"Great," I said quickly. I turned around, almost holding my breath for fear I had broken their concentration, and walked back to the bench.

Sometimes no one needs you at all.

As children ask for words as they are writing I try to keep from telling them what I think they already know. Some of these requests demand a spelling conference on the spot. In a big class I try to have one of these with each child at least once a week — although the Geralds may not even need one that often — and with Jamie and Eddie at least once a day. That's what I *try* to do.

Cheryl, an average child somewhere between Eddie and Gerald in ability but with a much lower opinion of her own competence, was writing about her plans for the weekend. She came to me and asked for *spending*.

"You can do that yourself," I told her with a smile. She didn't believe it: one finger went up to her mouth, the fingernail slipping anxiously between her teeth. I put an arm around her waist to counteract the anxiety.

"Yes, you can," I said. "You know *end*, don't you?"

One tiny nod agreed. "Tell me," I said, pen poised.

"*E-n-d*," she said clearly, taking the finger out and, I was glad to see, not putting it back.

"Yep," I said, printing as she spelled. "Now what's on the front for *sp-ending*?"

"*S-p*," said Cheryl, a smile breaking over her face.

"And on the end . . . ?"

"*I-n-g*!" came a chorus, Cheryl and the others around the table answering together. She picked up her book. I kept a hand on it, holding her eye.

"See, Cheryl? It was in your head the whole time."

Group conferences are the most useful revision strategy I know of. In addition to that, in addition to giving a writer a sense of what has worked in his piece and some ideas for how to go on, group conferences are fun. I have one every day with one fourth of the class (last year, that was 7¼ children); the best size for a group is nearer four than seven. I have one of my color groups for a conference each day, so I have small conference groups when I have small classes. Group conferences can be arranged as many ways as there are teachers.

Conference time has its own special rules, both for the children at the table and for the rest of the class. The children who are not in the conference are to stay put and not interrupt us: no one gets to ask me for a Word until the conference is over. I remind them nearly every day that if they can't find what they need to spell, to write the beginning letter and leave a space. Except for extremely dependent and anxious children, this

works out pretty well. "When *you're* in a conference *you* don't like to be interrupted, do you?" is another line, but it is only understood by the most mature. That line works well in second grade.

For those in the group conference, the rules are quite simple. A writer reads aloud; each person around the table tells what he or she liked about it, something specific. Then we go around the table again, and each one asks a question or suggests a change or addition. The writer may or may not respond to the suggestions — first graders usually do, second graders often do, third graders usually don't — and then asks his own questions, about how his story might grow, for guidance from the group. Everybody has to listen, so they can help each other out. I have a wall chart with the conference procedure spelled out:

1. The writer reads.
2. Each listener says "I like. . . ."
3. Each listener makes a suggestion.
4. The writer asks questions.

Every conference proceeds exactly the same way. At first, I take it upon myself to say "What did you like?" to each child, and then "What can this writer do to revise?" to each child, but soon the writer says these things. Not surprisingly, they pay more attention to the writer than to me. This predictability is important; it contributes fundamentally to the nonthreatening atmosphere of a group conference. Children — or grown-up writers — won't share their writings and their souls if they don't know what's going to happen to them.

On Thursday the Greens brought their books to the table. There were two absent, so there were only five of them. Jamie read first, about her family's horse.

> Once upon a time a horse let Daryl have a ride. Daryl said we could ride him. The horse let me ride him last night. We made him run. When he ran he tripped Jessie with the rope. Daryl's mother said get away before he kicks you in the eye. He tripped Daddy with the rope. The horse will not let us pat him.

"What do you like about this story of Jamie's?" I asked the group.

"I like stories about horses," said Stephanie. "I'm writing about a horse, too, you know."

"I like the way she read it out loud," said Jason. "That was good. I could hear it all."

"She read it so you really wanted to listen, didn't she?" I restated in agreement. Part of my function in a conference is to model the kinds of responses that are appropriate for them to make.

"I like it when the horse tripped the girl," said Jacob.

"Yeah, me too, that was neat," echoed Craig from the end of the table. This echo sounded legitimate to me, that is, as though Craig was planning all along to say that it was neat when the horse tripped the girl, only Jacob happened to say it first. I accepted his echo for that reason. Often the response "I like that too" seems to be simply laziness, and I press that child for another response. I admit that this is a judgment call.

"I liked what the mother said," I commented. "She really sounded worried."

"That's a big horse," said Jamie, nodding.

"Okay, now let's tell Jamie what we need her to do to make this story even better," I said. "What do you want to know that isn't there?"

"The name of the horse," said Jacob promptly.

"And what color it is," added Jason.

"Well," said Stephanie, "I can't tell if it's a horse or a pony. Maybe she can tell that."

"If he won't let you pat him, Jamie," I asked in my turn, "what can you do with him?"

"Sometimes he lets us pat him," conceded Jamie. "But he didn't want to after Josh hit him."

"What'd Josh hit him for?" Craig wanted to know.

"Can you tell that in the story?" I asked quickly. Often if the writer tells such an episode at the table he won't write it into the story when he goes back to his seat.

Jamie nodded, beaming. "And sometimes Daddy puts his hand up and he stands on his back legs."

"Put that in, too," directed Stephanie. "I can see that."

I smiled. That "seeing" is another response I have often modeled, and Stephanie has internalized it. Good.

"Now is there anything more you need help with?"

Still beaming, now hugging the book, Jamie shook her head. She looked at Stephanie. "Your turn."

Stephanie looked a little smug and a little shy. "This is my porcupine story, really, but there's a horse in it too."

"You've been working on this one for a while, haven't you?" I encouraged her. She nodded and began to read.

> Once upon a time there was a mother porcupine. She had a baby. A fox chased her. The porcupine hit the fox. The fox saw her babies. A wolf pounced out of the bushes. A girl came. A wolf chased her up a tree. The porcupine got poisoned by the wolf. A python choked the wolf. The python went away. The wolf went away. The girl picked up the baby foxes. The girl took the baby porcupine and the baby foxes home with her. On her horse. The girl rode into the woods. The girl met three girls. Their names were Courtney, Cheryl, and Amy. The girls got on the horse. The girls rode away. the end.

"I liked the python," said Scott immediately. "Did he kill the wolf?"

"No," said Stephanie. "He just choked him, you know, squeezed."

"I liked it when she took all three girls with her on the horse," said Jamie.

"I liked it all," said Craig. "That's a good story, Steph."

"Thank you," smiled Stephanie.

"I liked it all, too," said Jason.

I didn't let that one go by. "Which part did you like most?" I asked him.

"I liked it when the wolf pounced out of the bushes," Jason decided.

Hooray! I thought. More awareness of language! "Good," I

said. "That word *pounced* gives us a picture of how the wolf moved." Nods from Jason and Scott greeted this statement, and Stephanie leaped one bent hand onto the table in a pouncing gesture. "Now, Greens, what do we want Stephanie to add or change in this story?"

"Did the other girls have horses?" asked Jamie. "How did they get to the woods?"

"Weren't they scared of the wolf?" I asked.

"How did they all get on that horse," asked Craig in a puzzled voice, "if she had all those animals on there too?"

"Oh, no," said Stephanie patiently, shaking her head in a slow arc. "The animals, the babies, were at her house. She took them home. Then she met the other girls after that."

"Oh!" Craig and I said together. "She went into the woods twice, then?" I added.

Stephanie nodded emphatically.

"Then what do the girls have to do with the porcupine and fox babies?" I asked.

"I don't know," said Stephanie, palms and shoulders up.

I rephrased my question. "Do you think they belong in the same story?"

"Yes," said Stephanie. "They went home with the girl and played with the babies."

"Great," I said, relieved. "Be sure to put that in as you revise this, Steph. It will be a lot clearer to your readers." I turned to Craig. "Do you have something started to read to us?"

"Not yet," he answered. "But I know what I'm going to write about today."

"Okay, Craig. Jacob?"

Jacob sat up straighter and read very loudly:

> "Me and Andy picked eggs. We picked eggs from under the chickens."

"That's an interesting beginning, Jacob," I said, summing up the I-like part for everyone because the beginning was so short. "What can we do to help this writer, Greens?"

"Where were you picking eggs?" Jamie asked. "Maybe you could tell us where you were."

"How do you pick eggs, anyway?" asked Stephanie.

"You put your hand under the chicken and take the egg," said Craig. "Right, Jacob?"

"And I got pecked, too!" said Jacob, eyes flashing. "That hurted."

"Can you put that in, too?" I asked. Jacob nodded. "But how do you do it? Do you put your hand right under the chicken?"

"No." Jacob began sketching lines in the air. "There's a tray under them, and the eggs come on it, and you pick them up. Me and Andy's gettin' paid, too."

"Sounds like you have a lot more to go on with," I said. "Are you all set then, Jacob?" Answering nod. "Good. Jason?"

Holding a blank page up for us all to see, Jason said he'd been absent yesterday and didn't have anything to read. "I don't know exactly what I want today, either, Teacher," he concluded.

The others were a little edgy at this. They were all set to go on their own pieces, and had already done a lot of brainstorming for each other.

"Looks like we're finished, then, Greens," I dismissed them. "You've all got good starts." All the Greens but Jason began to move away from the table. A few other children, seeing this movement, began to walk toward me with alphabet books. "Would you like to write at the table today, Jason?" I asked. "Then if you're stuck I can help you."

"Yep. Get my pencil, Teacher," said Jason, climbing over the back of his chair.

Correctly interpreting this to mean "I'm going to get my pencil," I turned to the first of the alphabet books lying in front of me, open to *D*.

"*Delicious,* please," said Gerald.

There were of course many other things that could have been changed or commented on in those Green stories. Some of them will be discussed if and when the piece comes to conference again, some will be brought up in individual conferences with me at the start of writing time, some will be caught during the editing conference with me, some will be changed by the writer without any prompting from anyone.

Why is that python in the porcupine story, for example, is a question no one asked. A couple of days later Stephanie decided the python didn't belong there and took it out herself. Daryl is Jamie's brother and so the next time I talked to Jamie I told her how neat it was to call her mother "Daryl's mother" since it was a once-upon-a-time story, but did she think it would be good to call Daddy "Daryl's father" to match? She thought about this a while. When that story was finally published, it wasn't fiction any more at all.

Publishing is the last stage of the process, and there are as many ways to publish as you can think of. Joanie in Chapter 6 went to second grade to read; Jamie's horse story was typed on the primary typewriter and bound in wallpaper. In Chapter 11, Holly's story was hung up on the wall, and Gerald's was sent to a state writing contest, to name but a few. Mount them and contribute them to pediatricians' offices or public libraries; send one to Grammy for Christmas; put it in a bottle in the ocean. It's all ritualized sharing, moving out to a wider audience. That's what publishing is.

I give the children in conference some ways to tell a writer what works. "I like the part where . . ." is easy and specific. All the responses I make myself are intended as models for them to use, and they pick up on them eventually. I said, of Stephanie's *pounced,* that it made a picture. I hear them, now, saying something "makes a picture" when they are talking about each other's work.

A really ugly Martian appeared in a story last week, and the writer told just how ugly by saying, *He was so ugly a mirror could break*. I was gratified when Woody picked that out as the "best part" and delighted when he interpreted his reaction for the group.

"'So ugly a mirror could break,'" he repeated with a grin. Then he gave a wriggle. "That says it all."

The function of the group conference, as it has been working, is to generate ideas for the writer, to help the writer decide on sequence, and/or to reinforce the words or phrases or actions that strike the listeners as particularly strong. The responses of the group show the writer which ideas in the story "work," that is, connect the reader to the writing. Of course, not everyone agrees on what works, and the writer has the final say. Sometimes disagreements are useful, forcing the writer to think further; sometimes they are just fun for all of us and incidentally reinforce the idea of ownership.

One day in February the Blues were having a group conference. Jason N. had just begun a story and had read his beginning to us.

> "Once upon a time there was a unicorn. It was the most beautiful unicorn in the world."

"Oh!" said Michael, bouncing on the bench. "Oh! That pictures silver in my head!"

I was speechless, overcome by the excitement Michael, of all people, was finding in the words of Jason N.'s story. Michael was as nearly uncontrollable as anyone that year, he flitted from idea to idea, and I hadn't really expected him to be listening. Jason N., however, felt no such awe.

"It's not a silver unicorn, Michael," he said with righteous indignation. "The unicorn in this story is going to be black."

"But those words," protested Michael. "The way you say it's the most beautiful unicorn in the world, that's silver, I see silver."

"No, listen," said Jason N., putting his notebook down on the table and lowering his head pugnaciously. "This is my story, and this unicorn is going to be black." He looked at me, then, for some support, and I nodded.

"Thank you, Michael," I said. "What does anyone else have to tell Jason, Blues?" And we went on.

It is possible to have two groups having a group conference at the same time, with the children working alone after they've got the model. I don't do it that way though. It might be better, because it can be argued, I'm sure, that a conference on a piece only every four days isn't enough.

But I'd hate to miss anything.

One of the aspects of Doing Words that is not easily predictable and may seem unmanageable is that every child is doing something different every day. From the point of view of the teacher's work, this can seem daunting. From the point of view of the child's growth, the diversity is essential. James Britton, writing in *Language and Learning* about how children learn language, says that "Operations undertaken by . . . pupils [must] offer genuine challenge, and result in the extension and deepening of their experience . . ." as writers and as speakers. This cannot be done, he says, where all children are doing exactly the same thing. "We must begin from where the children are: . . . there can be no alternative in the initial stages to total acceptance of the language the children bring with them." If what we really want is that the children each learn to use their own language most effectively, then to deny them the ideas and images they have already with them is counterproductive.

I believe, myself, that each child's learning has to be achieved (and often identified) by each child. I believe that individual, personal writing is merely a corollary to this.

But even I will admit that looking over a set of papers done by thirty six-year-olds is a lot faster and easier if they have all had to simply fill in ten blanks with words that will, if they've done it "right," be identical from paper to paper. That is much easier than keeping up with and helping thirty six-year-olds to develop thirty different papers every morning. Unfortunately it is also an utterly sterile exercise for the teacher. It was just as sterile for the children to do, and in addition was destructive in some measure of their belief in themselves as owners of their language. That's why I don't do writing that way. That's why I need to worry about record keeping.

It is important, of course, to know what you want to teach. That's what curriculum is for. But it is more important to realize that you can't teach children what they are not ready for. (You can teach it all you want, but the odds are that the children won't learn it.) The older I get, the more I believe in the theory that children develop in stages. I have to know where a child is, as Britton said, so that I can teach the next thing that child needs to know.

As the children develop as writers, and begin to routinely include more sophisticated constructions and usages in their writing, I make a big chart and hang it on the wall. Along the left side are the children's names; along the top are the skills I'm seeing the children use and need as they write. The first two are "capitals at the beginning of a sentence" and "ending punctuation." The list across the top grows differently every year in my first grade, and of course would look different even to start with in second and third grades. The children like this chart, because they can see what they are already incorporating into their writing. When Heather needed quotation marks a couple of years ago to make sense of the conversation she had included in her piece that day, I told her about them. (She always referred to them as "those little things when you talk.") She used them correctly that day, and I put a date notation — 3/24 — into the appropriate block. Whenever she used them correctly again, I added another date.

As I look at the checklist I can easily see who has a working knowledge of a particular skill by seeing which blocks on the grid are crowded with dates. The children love to watch me make these notes next to their names. It is a kind of carrot for them. There are always a few, too, who read across the top and down to their own line and find out where their empty spaces are and practice putting those in their stories. These are usually the oldest female ones. Having the curriculum on the wall, so to speak, takes a lot of the mystery out of why they come to school, and provides me with an instant subject for a lesson if we have a minute or two between activities and appointments.

When writers are well begun in the writing process, then, my concern is for the content of their writings and how they are using the whole process. And again, the very fact that I'm keeping track makes the whole operation even more important to the children than it already was. I follow them through their learning, even as sophisticated as it has become, just as I followed them through their own images with my cards and marker in Movement I. They are more linear now, or perhaps I should say that their progress more nearly doubles some lines of learning I can imagine them tracing. As long as they are Doing Words, however, I don't tell them what to do, any more than anyone told Will how to walk.

In school, which by its nature is still in the business of filling up little minds, writing provides the way for each child's own person to be validated.

Chapter 9

Problems in the Process, Or, What Do I Do When It Doesn't Work?

> There is something in such laws (e.g. geometry) that takes the breath away. They are not discoveries or inventions of the human mind, but exist independently of us. In a moment of clarity, one can at most discover that they are there.
>
> — M. C. Escher

IT NEEDS TO BE SAID again that every year is different, every class is different. In some schools children's learning styles are matched to teachers' learning styles, in some schools children are more, or less, homogeneously grouped even in kindergarten, and the variations in the way principals assign children to teachers are endless. No matter how class lists are arranged, however, there are "good" and "difficult" classes, groups whose group chemistry works to enhance all the individuals, and groups whose individuals rub against each other to flame status all year long and never achieve a good group feeling. These possibilities are inevitably present whenever humans are. It makes a bigger difference in groups of children who are becoming writers than in groups of children who merely do rote work assigned by their teacher or the system, because the writing process encourages and expects everyone in the class to talk to and support each other.

The class in Chapter 8 was, in these terms, a "good" class.

The following description is a composite to show a class that was very different. Many in this group had not done a year's worth of Words in kindergarten, which was only partly the reason why they compare unfavorably with the class in Chapter 8. The portraits of these children come from three classes I have had over the years that had an unusual number of mixed-up and/or broken-up homes, an unusual number of young children, and an unusual number of children with special needs, either academic or emotional.

We did writing anyway, every day, with each child beginning in whatever Movement was appropriate and moving along through the Movements as far as worked for each child. The published efforts of these children were rarely spectacular, by my lifetime standard, but they didn't know that. Each of these children worked, as all of them have, through Words and through the writing process in their own way. I include this chapter lest another teacher, reading as far as Chapter 8, has said, "Well, my sixes can't possibly do this kind of work. She's nuts."

With every class, writing happens before morning recess, in about an hour.

The institutional balderdash still comes first, no matter who the children are: lunch count, putting up the date, pledging the flag, singing a patriotic song, passing out fluoride tablets. And then, last but never least, show-and-tell. On a Thursday it is a Yellow day, so the Yellows get to do show-and-tell. I'm very fond of these five minutes: everyone, including me, sits still and listens calmly. I learn a lot. When the Yellows or their substitutes finish, I do a short oral lesson in front of everyone, a lesson that they have to actively participate in. This is a trick of Madeline Hunter's, and it's fun; a group activity is essential to starting the day in a "difficult" class. This day it's capital letters.

"Show me how to make your hand look for capital letters," I say, holding up my closed fists. Gradually the hands of the children go up and their thumbs and first fingers spread apart to make open Cs facing each other. "Now lowercase?" I ask, and the thumbs and forefingers come together.

"Now I'll say a sentence and then say one word from that sentence. Show me with your hands whether my word should be a capital or lowercase. Ready?" I catch a few eyes, look sternly at Tommy, open and close my own fingers with my eyes holding Angela's until she realizes what's happening. "'Today is Thursday.' Thursday."

All the hands open, to show that Thursday needs a capital *T*. "Good. Why?" Several hands go up. "Charlie?"

"Because it's the name of a day."

"Right. Now show me this one. 'Next week is vacation.' Next."

They show me, I ask why, someone tells, and we go on for eight or ten sentences like that. It takes about three minutes for this lesson. Yesterday we did a similar one on periods and question marks, Victor Borge style; tomorrow will be about the plurals *S* and *ES*. All these are done with hand movements for answers, and then some verbal justification. I do not introduce exceptions during this activity.

"Get out your alphabet books, please, and be sure you have a pencil. Yellows, pass out the writing books." Most children, by Movement VI, can keep their books and take care of them, so I don't have to have writing books passed out. These are young and antsy and self-doubting children, though, who tend to rip, tear, or lose nearly everything. This class would do better with tables, not desks.

"Don't forget to read yesterday's writing to a friend." There will be a uniform babble for the next four or five minutes while they do this. I have to tell them to do it, every day, because so many of them forget. When you are not at all sure of yourself, it is hard to be self-directed, even in the most predictable environment. They do this reading for the usual reasons: one, so that they will hear what they wrote and be doing a little prewriting, either inside their heads or with their partner, for this day's work; and two, because writing is made to be read, and when they know someone else will hear it they write more interestingly. I say this, too, at least once a week. There is also reading aloud itself, which is a speaking skill there's not enough practice of in the ordinary way.

"Teacher, I can't read my story from yesterday, remember,"

comes accusingly from Jessica. "Remember, it's getting published?" Jessica does her best to keep me on task, but it's an uphill fight for her.

"Yes, I remember. Did we edit it yesterday?" I look at my checklist, clutched firmly to my chest. Next to Jessica's name it says, under Wednesday's date, *edit*. "Right. Well, you're all ready to begin your new story then. You don't have to read." She smiles a dimpled and limpid blue smile and turns away.

"No! I'm not going to read to you, Tony! I'm reading to Mark!" comes from Edwin, and when I look I see a common sight: Edwin's eyebrows up into his head with frustration, his eyes nearly overflowing, backing up from Tony, whose best Al Capone face is thrust toward Edwin.

I move between them. "Edwin, go with Mark over by the table. Tony, you need to read with me. Please find me a chair." This Tony, when he is not absolutely terrific, is the bane of our lives. He needs this muscle-flexing action every few days for his own self-image as The Fonz, but it's a little wearing on the rest of us. Edwin, unfortunately, is a natural target.

On his way to get a chair for me, Tony is waylaid by Rachel, who says she wants to read with him. He comes back to his own desk, where I'm standing, for his book. We look at each other, and he goes back to Rachel. Edwin and Mark are doing fine.

As they finish reading to a friend, the children return to their seats. For the next several minutes I will move among them with my checklist, settling them and finding out what each one is working on. I ask each one the same old question.

"What are you writing about today, Tommy?" I ask the first one in the front row. "More about the Superheroes?"

"Yeah," answers Tommy, looking at me only for a second. He doesn't look at me directly if he can help it.

"Do you know what you're going to add?" I ask, looking at my checklist to see what was noted there during the conference he was in yesterday. "Need any help?"

"Nope," he answers, sliding the writing book a quarter of an inch nearer to the hand with the stubby pencil in it. "I have to tell about all the rest of them, you know."

"Okay, sounds good to me. How about you, Jeff?" I ask the next one. "What's your story today?"

Jeff points to his book. The words *I went to* are already there, and in fact he has his other hand on his dictionary; as I watch he turns to the *N* page. "I need *New York,* please, Teacher, I'm writing about my trip with my Dad."

"Oh, great, Jeff," I exclaim, entering *New York* on his *N* page. "I was hoping you'd tell about that." I note *New York* by his name on my checklist and *ct* by Tommy's. "Don't forget to tell what it looked like, please," I say to Jeff as I move away.

Angela is next, and as usual she has started a whole lot of writing before I get there. Today it says

> Ihav a Cat the Cat is pretty he has a flecolr to I like my Cat

"You're writing about your cat today?" I ask Angela after looking at this. She nods and smiles. "Good. I like your cat stories." Another smile. I point to the word *hav* in the story. "Tell me what's on the end of *have,*" I say.

"Silent *E,*" whispers Angela, looking at the eraser end of her pencil. She always whispers. While I watch she puts the *E* on. She looks up at me.

"Listen for the periods," I say. "'*I have a cat.*'"

"Period," says Angela.

"Right," I agree. "'*The cat is pretty.*'"

"Period," says Angela.

"Right," I say. "Read the rest to yourself and find two more periods, please."

Next to Angela are the three girls who do know what's going on with themselves, to whom I absolutely never have to speak, who are the exceptions in this class. Heather is busily adding to her story from yesterday, and looks up at me before I have a chance to open my mouth. "I'm still writing about the princess," she drawls at me.

Debby, next to her, smiles and lets me ask my question: "What are you writing today, Debby?" She looks at me as if I've been naughty and shakes her head. I bet her grandmother does it exactly that way.

"You know, Teacher," she says patiently. "We're editing today." I look at my checklist. Sure enough, it says *edit* next to her name.

"Yes we are," I tell Debby, "but not until after the conference with the Yellows" — I look at the clock — "so it'll probably be when the big hand gets to the seven. What are you going to work on until then?"

Debby looks around. "I'll start a new story about Mark." A smirk. "He's my boyfriend, you know."

"Okay," I reply, writing *Mark N* (*N* stands for *new*) next to Debby's name. "How goes it, Tina?" I ask the busiest writer in the place.

"Fine," she says absently. I look at her book, see that she's still writing about the trip to Florida and all the girls she went swimming with there, so I write *ct* on my list and move on.

At my elbow suddenly is Lorie, her alphabet book open to *M*. "Mrs. Johnson, I need *mine*," she says quickly. She's one of the few who call me by my name. "You know, like 'the purple bunny is mine,'" she adds as I write the word for her.

"You're writing about your rabbits?" I ask.

"Yep," she says. "About the ones I brought to school."

"Good," I answer, noting this on my list. "Don't forget to say if they're real or not."

Lorie purses her lips in an oh-you-silly expression.

"Mrs. Johnson," she remonstrates with me. "Of course they're not real." Like lightning she grabs one of the little plush bunnies from her desktop. "See?"

"Yes, *I* know they're not real, and *you* know they're not real, but what if you publish this story? Will other people know? Will you staple the bunnies into the book?" I tease her.

"Well," she says, considering. "I guess so."

Leaving Lorie to figure out what she means by "I guess so," I move along the rows and into Luke's, then Edwin's, and then Allan's corners to find out and note down what everyone is doing today. As usual Allan is sucking his thumb, and Sammy is trying to arrange things so I will sit with him and him alone, by talking loudly and cutting up paper instead of writing. When he sees me looking at him he immediately begins to whine, "I don't know what to write."

I, in my turn, have arranged things so I come to him last. I pull a chair up next to him, make sure his books are on top and his pencil is available, and I get out my own writing notebook.

"You sit here with me and think while I write," I say, putting my chair as close as I can to him. What this one really needs is to be hugged about 85 percent of every minute, but sitting with him, I have discovered, is the next best thing. I raise my voice.

"I'm going to write now, First Grade," I tell them. "It needs to be quiet while I write. I'll stop when the big hand gets to the three." That will be five minutes, and they will be quiet, because it fascinates them that I am writing too. They are equally fascinated when I share my writing during the circle reading, and are always giving me suggestions for what to add or change. Sneakily, I am modeling the conference procedure from a slightly different angle. (I don't take my writing to a regular conference, although I know many teachers who do, particularly in the fourth and fifth grades.) The most important thing about my writing in class, though, is that they can see me going through all the things they do, from not having an idea to being thrilled by the just-right word.

Sometimes during these five minutes Sammy talks to me, but I say "I'm writing now, Sammy," and he stops for a minute. Sometimes, too, a child comes up with an open alphabet book, but I just gently push the child away. If it's Lorie or Charlie, I whisper as I push, "Put the first letter and leave a space. I'll be done at the three." Those two have very short attention spans coupled with real anxieties about nearly everything, and I bend rules for them. Tony-Fonz is the only one who ever complains about the bending.

When I'm finished writing, I get up and look over a few shoulders. Caleb is writing at a breakneck pace, as always, and I take a minute to acclimate myself to his spelling. This was part of a continuing story about a dog.

> I saw My dog He was frye yellow. I got out. My gun. I shot a Bllet. ZOOM!!! I

"Looks good," I comment. "What color yellow was he?"

"Like fire," says Caleb, making his hands spiral up like flames.

"Tell me how to spell *fire*." I put my hand over *frye* and nudge his dictionary closer to him.

"Uhh, uhh, *fff–iii*?" sounding the letters "*er*?" asks Caleb. I open to his *F* page.

"Close, very close," I approve. "What has to be at the end to make that *I* say *I*?"

"Silent *E*," says Caleb with a big smile, as I write *fire* on his *F* page.

"Spell it," I say to him. He does, and picks up the pencil to fix it. I look at Jim's. Not much there, but a start.

After I have rechecked with the most difficult ones, the big hand is on the five, and it's time for the group conference of the day.

"Okay, Yellows," I call. "Please bring your books to the table for conference."

While the Yellows are getting themselves ready, moving over to the big table in the back of the room, I check very fast on what Edwin and Lorie are actually doing, and to see if they need any other words. Allan, this day, has stopped sucking his thumb and, after throwing his book on the floor once (which I ignored — I only have to notice when he tips the desk over too), he is writing some more on his story about a cartoon of the Chipmunks. Some children, the very young ones, grow backward during the early spring.

At the table are Caleb, Charlie, Angela, Kris, and Cory. They have their writing books but not their pencils. I pull up a chair and mark *C* with a circle around it in the spaces by their names on my checklist.

"Okay, Yellows, who's first?" I ask.

"Me!" says Caleb, before anyone else can speak. The others stop chatting. Caleb's stories are always wonderful to hear.

> "Me and Craig. Me and Craig were driving our dirtbikes. I saw something. It was a HAUNTED HOUSE!!!!!!!!!!!!!!!!!!!!!!!! Me and Craig dove our dirtbikes behind a bush. I fliced the flashlite on. We went in. We looked into a room. I saw FRACINSTIN I . . I code not belevit. I saw DRACLE!!!!!!! We went up the stars!!!!!! I saw a gost be hind the gost I saw My dog He was fire yellow. I got out. My gun. I shot a Bllet. ZOOM!!!"

He looks up, pleased with the noise he has made with his *!!!!!*s. He looks at Kris. "What do you like about this story, Kris?"

"I liked when you met Dracula and Frankenstein," says Kris.

"What did you like, Angela?" asks Caleb.

"I like the gun," whispers Angela. Picking the last thing is a common response in conferences.

"Cory?"

"I like it all," says Cory.

I leap in. "That's great, Cory; now tell Caleb what part you liked best."

Cory tilts his head to one side and zaps one arm out very fast. "'ZOOM!!!'"

"Mrs. Johnson, what do you like?"

"I like the part where you said 'I . . . I could not believe it!' That sounded just like what you would say in real life." I always try to make my "like" about the language or the style of the piece rather than the content. Understanding of style will be a longer time coming to many of these children, but that doesn't excuse me from exposing them to everything I can think of.

Caleb smiles and repeats "I . . . I could not believe it!"

"Now ask your friends what you need to add or change to make this story even better," I remind him.

"Wait, you forgot me!" interrupts Charlie.

"Charlie, what did you like about my story?" he asks.

Charlie has been listening. "Where you left your dirt bikes behind the tree."

"Bush," corrects Caleb.

"Bush, tree, whatever," says Charlie. "And what I want to know is what did you shoot?"

"Yeah, that's what I want to know," chimes in Cory.

"Did you shoot the dog?" I ask.

"No," Caleb says emphatically. "I shot the rope."

"What rope?" nearly everyone says together.

"The rope the dog was tied with," says Caleb patiently.

"Is the rope in the story now?" I ask.

He looks. "Oops," he says. "I'll put it in, and then I'll say I shot the rope."

"Great," I say. "Who's next?"

Kris begins to read while I note on my checklist *dog tied* and *shot rope* next to Caleb's name.

> "The giijoe is a snowmobile. I like the gijoe snowmobile. it gows fast. The gijoe can knock skyfire out from the sky. The gijoe is a jet. One day the gijoe was flying and minding his on business!!! and out. . . ."

Kris looks up. "It's not finished," he says.

"Ask what they like so far," I encourage him.

So he asks, finding out that Charlie also has a G.I. Joe, that Angela likes it when he's on his snowmobile ("But I'm not in this story," Kris corrects her), and that I like the phrase "minding his own business."

"What can I do next?" Kris asks. "What do you think, Cory?"

"What did Skyfire do?" Cory wants to know. "Did they fight?"

"Yeah," says Kris. "That's what I'm going to say next."

"That's what I want to know too," says Charlie. "Tell about the fight."

Angela's attention has wandered far away. I can see that no one else is going to ask, so I say, "Kris, I'm mixed up here. What *is* a G.I. Joe?"

"It's a kind of fighter plane," says Kris. "And it fights with Skyfire."

"But at the beginning of your story you said it was a snowmobile."

Kris smiles.

"Is this a story about a jet or a snowmobile?" I rephrase my question.

"G.I. Joe's a jet," says Charlie. "Everyone knows that."

"I didn't," I say again. "And Kris wants the people who read this story to know exactly what he's talking about, so I think he needs to take the snowmobile out if G.I. Joe isn't one." Kris gives a slow nod. He's willing.

"Any other ideas for Kris? Okay, Cory."

> "One day I saw a pirates ship. The flags whr red. A pirate came out withe a knife. He said into the cabrin I said o rite. I was turning into a vampire. It was very very very darck. Good thing it was nighttime. I whent out I kiled the pirate."

Cory gave a big grin. "What do you like about my story . . . Mrs. Johnson?"

"I like it when you say *Good thing it was nighttime.* I like that phrase."

"I like it when you turn into a vampire," offers Angela.

"When you killed the pirate," says Charlie making a knifing motion.

"Yeah, me too," says Kris.

Cory is grinning from ear to ear. "Thanks," he says.

"Ask them what you can add," I remind him.

"I'm not gonna add nuttin," Cory says. "This story's over."

"You're not going to tell how you turned into a vampire?" I ask incredulously.

"I just did," says Cory. "See? Right here" he points to his book and rereads "*I was turning into a vampire.*"

"Yes, but how?" I ask again.

"How'd you get the knife away from him?" Caleb wants to know.

"I didn't," Cory answers impatiently.

"How'd you kill him then?" asks Kris.

"How do vampires kill all the people?" Cory asks, getting mad at our obtuseness. "Aarrrghhh," he demonstrates, thrusting his wide open mouth onto an imaginary neck in the air in the middle of the table.

"But the people reading this story won't know that!" I exclaim.

"I don't give a care," says Cory, folding his arms. "This story is finished."

There is a little pause while I weigh the advantages of pushing his stubbornness against the knowledge that this absolute stall is very rare among first graders, and then I look at Charlie.

"Will you read us your story, Charlie?" I ask.

Charlie pulls a stuffed rabbit out of his sweatshirt. "It's about him," he says, smiling. He reads "*I love my rabbit. I love him.*"

"What else do we want to know about this rabbit, Yellows?" I ask. There is no point in doing the I-like routine on this short a beginning, so we don't.

The suggestions come from all around the table: what he looks like, what he is eating, where did you get him, what's his name. I note all these questions on my list as Charlie nods.

Angela is last. This is too bad, because her voice is so soft they will not readily listen anyway. I decide to read it for her. "*I have a cat. The cat is pretty. He has a flecolor to. I like my cat.*" I look around. "Ask them what you can add to this story, Angela," I finish.

She asks, gently, and gets some typical requests — for color, size, age, and so forth. "Does she sleep with you?" asks Caleb. Angela nods and ducks her head.

"Put that in, too," I tell her. "Anything else anyone needs in this conference?" They are getting up. "We've still got some writing time left — keep working on what people suggested to you."

The Yellows drift back to their places and I resume my circuit of the room. This conference lasted a little less than fifteen minutes.

Notice Caleb's spelling back there. This is one of the most obvious differences between Movement VI and all the earlier Movements. This spelling is invented to a fare-thee-well, and what's more he doesn't seem to change it much from one story to the next. He does, however, sit down with me and edit when we both are sure that a story will not be continued to publication. Every day, too, I insist that enough words and punctuation are correct so that I can read it the next day he works on it.

Allowing for invented spelling, or phonetic spelling as it used to be called, or developmental spelling as the trailblazers of the teaching profession are now calling it, sounds like a contradiction of what I said in Chapter 7, so I will try to explain myself. This story of Caleb's, and the others written with nonstandard spellings this day, were stories in Movement VI. In my opinion, any story that is not yet finished doesn't have to be perfect. The flip of that, however, is that stories that get published do have to be perfect, "so that," as Meg said, "anyone can read them." How to achieve that perfection is the function of editing, which comes after all the revising and conferences are over.

Caleb's spelling here is not the same thing as a kindergartner's writing *IYTFAWKISOADUK* meaning *I went for a walk. I saw a duck*. My difficulty with that kind of invented spelling, as opposed to Doing Words in the kindergarten, is that the child is not using to write the language he will have to use to read. Another problem is that his learnings in phonics change so fast when he first begins to learn about sounds that he himself may not be able to tell what that says the next day. In that case, the teacher may feel called upon to annotate his writing with her version of it. If she's going to go to that trouble, why not just Do Words anyway, and have the added advantage that the child is using, and looking at, and working in standard English?

All the things I have said about this spelling albatross, though, only apply at school, and by and large only apply during writing time. I am always getting messages on the board, or notes, or intercepting kid-to-kid notes and messages, in which the child feels entirely at ease writing and spelling any old way. Doing Words doesn't seem to inhibit spontaneity, nor, as we have seen, productivity.

At home, however, until the child asks for help with spelling and printing, leave him alone. Those letters to grandma and the captions of the pictures of the dog are just fine the way they come out onto the kitchen table. The very first ones, the squiggly lines and odd letters at random, are important excursions by the child into the world of print. Soon more letters will plop themselves onto paper, in entirely random order and shape and position, backwards, inside out, and every other possibility. Great. The five-year-old feels wonderful when she writes love notes to Daddy. Daddy may have a problem, but he can always tell her he loves her back, and ask her to read it to him, "so I will know it twice as well."

What I want the child to bring to school is not expertise in his language, except orally as much as is possible in his circumstances. What I want the child to bring to school is not carefulness, or even fear, because he's been told that he doesn't spell right. What I want the child to bring to school is excitement and curiosity and the expectation that he will be able to do even more reading and writing than he has already done. Undoing caution is the hardest thing a teacher has to do. Comment mightily on what he has to say, not how he says it; on his pride in writing, not his periods. Later, when he has a dictionary at school, maybe he will want one at home. Fine, if he does. A Movement VI child usually writes more stories at home every night, and sometimes brings them in to school to read or revise there. There is a unity inherent in that behavior that has to be beneficial, and none of us, thank goodness, has killed the enthusiasm.

After the Yellows conference I will go around again, looking at everyone's work and pointing out the capitals and periods and the spellings that are unintelligible. I try to get them all on those stories that are not likely to be worked on anymore, so that they can be readily reread anytime. I catch only the worst errors of spelling and punctuation, like Caleb's and Angela's, those that prohibit comprehension, on those pieces that are going to be continuing tomorrow. I misjudge sometimes, needless to say, because even the child doesn't always know what's going to be on his mind tomorrow, and some princess stories get crowded out by Aunt Lyn having a baby or a big storm; but at least I know that by ten o'clock any of us could read it tomorrow if we had to.

Sammy needs some special attention now — he went over to the painting table during the conference, leaving his writing on his desk. At least he did this quietly today, so I let it go. When I get to him and his writing I see that it is one of his favorite stories (Movement V) slightly reworked. *I love you. Today it is April* The most he ever does is about four sentences, so this is fine. I remind him about the period after *April,* and congratulate him for the capitals on *Today* and *April.* He says, "I been good today, ain't I, Mrs. Johnson?"

By now it's nearly ten o'clock. I just may have the three or four minutes I need to go over Jessica's story for editing if we hurry. I call her to the table.

Making editing part of the child's work is an important part of the writing process, as it has been important to the work of Doing Words all along. The difference is that in Movement VI the editing is often done after several days or weeks of working on a piece. Older children can do editing with each other, running down a checklist that the class has decided on. Since I am the first place the children hear of editing and are expected to do it, I have to teach them how.

The easiest way to edit with a first grader is to read the story aloud. I did this with Angela and a little bit with Caleb as I went along with my checklist earlier, instead of waiting for editing time. I had a feeling that the story Angela was writing about the cat might not have gone on another day — as it happened, I was wrong. Caleb's was simply not clear to me as I passed it by, so I did that bit of instant editing for spelling with him, as I did punctuation with Angela. None of this takes more than a minute. Even the editing with Jessica takes only two or three minutes. If there is more than that to do, take two days to do it. The writer has other things to work on.

What we are editing for at this age is not a whole lot: beginning and ending punctuation and spelling, for everyone; quotation marks and commas for some; and, by the end of the year, paragraphs for a few. So I read the writing aloud and stop where there should be punctuation. If it's already there, we're both happy, and if it isn't, the writer can tell easily that it should be there and put it in right on the spot. Then we check for odd spellings, using the alphabet book to find and enter needed words, and have a couple of tiny phonics lessons as the writer corrects the spelling. The child does all the changing and erasing and rewriting: I try very hard never to touch a pencil or a pen to a child's writing book.

In Jessica's case, there are two missing capitals, a now/new confusion and the eternal to/too confusion, and that's about it. After we go over these and she writes in the corrections, she decides on a title and writes it on top. Then she puts the piece in the slot on my desk where the typing aide looks.

The children in this kind of class do tend to do more of the other activities of the creative vent than the children in Chapter 8. There are games on the shelf, some matching games, cards, and Rack-O; and there is always paint; several have brought their own dolls and toys, to write about and to play with. Most of the hour for writing is used by most of the children for writing, or for conference, or for talking about writing with me or with friends. Writing in the steps of the process is serious stuff, and they buy the idea, as far as they are able, that writers need a pretty calm place to work in. Sammy and Charlie, fluctuating between Movements V (very short, not-to-be-revised stories about their own lives) and Movement VI (working on the same piece for a period of several days, with conferences, changes, revisions, and at the end editing and publishing) need other things to do. Sammy cuts paper inappropriately, so I make or direct him to other activities that will give him the organic outlets he still needs. Others need to know that it's all right for them to take a little longer to write longer stories.

All the children, in fact, write in various lengths and to various stages of completion. All of them have published at least one book, Cory and Rachel and Tina and Jessica did three or four, and the rest in between. There's no rule that says you have to finish every piece you start — I certainly don't, and Hemingway probably didn't either. These children are just as much real writers as Hemingway and I are.

•

It may seem that I have put an unlikely number of children into this group who seem difficult to manage or who have fairly low abilities. I have done this on purpose, and it has happened that there are many who are difficult to manage, or at the low end of the spectrum of average abilities, in the same class. I want to make it clear that Doing Words and the writing process are possible and salutary for all children. True, my expectations of what Sammy and Angela will do in writing are very different from my expectations of Gerald and Kathy in Chapter 8; but then, my expectations are different for every child, just as every child's expectations of himself or herself are different from every other child's. Every class I have ever taught is different from all others. I am never bored by them: I try to pay them back by never boring them.

After recess everyone takes their writing books and sits down in a big circle on the rug. I sit on a chair, still with my writing checklist, with Sammy right beside me. "I'm going to choose the quietest one to start," I say. This invariably works, attesting yet again to the power of children's writing if it is from the inside out. "Rachel."

> "Tomorrow my mom and dad and my aunt and my uncle is going to Las Vegas. They will be gone for a week. I will stay at my aunt Lin's house.
>
> I will play with Lucy and Liana. My cousins like me. Lara gives me paino lessons. There easy after a while! My brother's rabbit's girl friend is going to have a baby. I like my rabbit. It is dead. My rabbit was nice and kudley.
>
> Lucy and Liana are nice to me I will have fun. They play games with me. That's fun when they play games with me!!!!!!! I! will! have! fun!!!"

She looks up and giggles, enchanted by her own writing. Then she looks all around, very much aware of this fleeting moment of power because she can pick the next child to read. "I'm gonna pick the quietest one . . . Jonathan."

> "Once upon a time there was a genie. it was a girl. I liked the girl. She led me in a store. my Mom was a princess. I said WOW!!!!

> My Mom said thank you. She had a white dress. she was beautiful! I loved her! she said thank you again. I said you have powers."

We all know that Jonathan loves his mom, and indeed she is beautiful; it is silent for a minute, while everyone thinks about moms. Jonathan abhors silence, so he swishes his book through the air and says, "Hey-hey-hey Kris!"

Kris's story has one new line since the conference: "The gijoe jet chased skyfire." The snowmobile is still in there, so I make a note to remind him about that during my minutes of checking first thing tomorrow. Kris chooses, as always, Tommy.

> "I have Koba Khan. And I have Prince Adam. And I have Orko. And I have clawful. And I have Triklops. Orko is a magician. Buzzoff spies in the sky. Fisto is a hand to hand fighter. I have a Grambalab. It is rele."

For Tommy this is a lot, so I say, "Wow, Tom, you sure know a lot about them."

"Yep," agrees Tommy, looking around. "Caleb."

Caleb has added *was tide up* after *dog* in his story. After the *ZOOM* it now says, *I cut the rope. It was wild when we got up the naxst stars.*

"That's much clearer, Caleb," I say. "Thank you."

"Sure," says Caleb. "Now I say . . . Jimmy!"

Jimmy has added a little to his report about volcanoes. He hasn't added much, because some of this writing time he was reading in a book from the library about volcanoes. It is, as always, hard to hear him read: another problem I don't know how to solve. I've tried telling him that no one will listen if he doesn't speak up, but it's not true. Everyone likes what he writes.

Jimmy chooses Allan, who has written two sentences on his Chipmunk story; Allan chooses Edwin, whose spelling is, today, retrievable. Some days he can't remember what he's written, even a minute before; so I try to get it to at least this stage before he reads.

> "Oun Day wn thay got up Thay wr happy bcus we ar going too fight. We got too sop the volcano."

Heather has added to her continuing story about princesses and unicorns. She reads it very seriously.

> "Once there was a beautiful princess. She never tried out her wand because she had no power in it. The next morning she ran to the window and tried the wand. There was power. She said Who could have done that? Maybe the tooth farie could have done it.Then she called the tooth fairy"

She looks up. "It's not finished," she tells us.

"More tomorrow?" I ask. Heather nods. "Angela."

Angela's is just the same still. She reads it softly, and I wonder if she is learning anything. I know she is, but sometimes it seems very slow. Perhaps we should put all of these stories about her can into an anthology for her. Hmmm.

Tina is reading, three or four pages more about the swimming party. Then the others take their turns, and by 10:50 we are all finished for today. Jessica's will be a published wallpaper-covered book by tomorrow, and I guess I'd better try to edit Cory's a little tomorrow too. Already I'm making notes on my checklist, and tomorrow is a Red day — a whole new set of children in conference!

Chapter 10

Orthography and Other Conventions, Or, Why Do They Do It That Way?

> Most children appear to be born with a feeling that life is fair, that it must be. And only with difficulty accommodate themselves to the fact that it isn't.
>
> — William Maxwell

WITH ALL THE PRINTING that children do in the Words program, it is silly to spend more time in the day, not to mention a lot more money, on penmanship workbooks and lessons.

The same thing is true of English texts, spelling texts, phonics workbooks. I believe that if we are required by statute, or curriculum guide, or the wishes of the principal to teach handwriting, grammatical constructions, phonics, verb inflections, punctuation, and spelling, we can do it using the writing of the children. Children eventually use all the constructions and letters and words and sounds in their writings that we would want to teach anyway, if they are part of a writing program from the beginning of their school lives on up through the grades. I use their writings to teach all those elements of language, all those skills we are supposed to "cover," including in their daily work lessons built on their writings.

When you have engaged a child in his own writing, when you have hooked him to reading and writing his own very important words, sentences, and stories, the focus of his attention to his work is very powerful. The very choosing of his own Word or story is a commitment to that Word or that idea: he will give it his full attention, the full play of his inner resources. It belongs to him.

Use that power. Channel the power of his own writing into the study of and understanding of the structure of his language.

I use the term "grammar" generically, to stand for all the studies of our language, which can so meaningfully be taught as part of the daily writing program. Not only can they be included, they should be.

I give many small "grammar" lessons every day, in all Movements, as the children write. A child I'm talking to doesn't realize that it is a lesson, because it involves his own writing; he will not mind it, because he wants very much to make his own writing as good and as readable as it can be. The very first Word he traces is going to be traced correctly because it's his Word.

One of the first constructions the writing child bumps into is *gonnu,* a Maine variant of *gonna,* the spoken contraction of *going to*. Many sentences of Movements II, III, and IV begin *I'm gonnu* . . . go to my Grammie's, be Spiderman on Halloween, play cars with Jeff. When a child replies to "What's your Word today?" with "I'm gonnu be Spiderman," I repeat back to him "I'm going to be Spiderman," and write it for him that way. "Why?" is the inevitable question — at least I always hope to hear it, since it should be evident that there's no good reason for this change. That is exactly the reason I give: "That's the way English works," I say. "*Gonnu* isn't really a word. You can say it, but when you need to write it you write *going to*."

"Oh. Okay," is the usual response. Children of five, six, and seven have much of their world imposed on them in just such an arbitrary way, after all. "English does it that way" becomes the common explanation. It is impossible for even Noam Chomsky to explain some of the inconsistencies in English. We accept them. Rules come later, and some of the rules never come to first grade.

Sometimes a child will get mixed up for a while, writing *going to* and reading *gonnu* for the *going*. Since most of them read word for word he stops at the *to,* wondering why it's there; then he remembers and reads what he has written. Later, by Movement IV, he may say *gonnu* when he tells me what his story is, but he will write *going to* as a matter of course when he sits down with the pencil and the writing book. A first step toward the recognition of reading vocabulary as distinct from speaking vocabulary has been taken; reading has, again, been invested with a special feeling. The child is learning to think about the way he constructs his language.

Because show-and-tell is so much a part of the day, the second most common sentence construction in the writings of Movements II and III is "I brang . . ." my Barbies, my Cabbage Patch, my jumprope. *Brang* at least shows the logic with which children learn: they know *sing* becomes *sang,* and most will give you *rang* instead of *ringed,* so *brang* should be it. But I don't allow it.

"No, you didn't brang your marbles," I say, admittedly confusing the issue, "you brought them."

"Oh yes," says the child — Jody always slaps his forehead for emphasis — "on the *B* page." If the child looks blank, another child nearby will probably say, "You brought it. *Brang* isn't a word."

This is, of course, a fine distillation of the argument Mr. Webster's dictionary makers have been having for some time on the subject of when slang usage becomes acceptable. I am very old-fashioned about this: my views on *ain't* need not be detailed. Most of the children in our school are not even aware that *ain't* is incorrect in speech, let alone in writing.

Mark, the other morning, brought his baseball glove but said immediately, "I ain't gonnu take it out first recess 'cause the big kids'll take it."

"Hey, Mark," I said. "Run that by me again in English."

Heavy thought, a couple of pirouettes; then, very clearly articulated: "I ain't going to take my glove out." Some you win, some you lose. Another day Matthew, having whined "I ain't got no pencil" at his unsympathetic teacher, lightened my spirit immensely by changing that to "I don't got no pencil." It's this kind of effort that makes me glad I'm a teacher.

Almost as well entrenched in the home language of many rural Maine children are the is/are and was/were confusions. They appear daily, and are nearly ineradicable. I point them out and ask that they be corrected daily, too, and succeed to a greater extent with Words than I would any other way, I'm sure, mostly because of the power of the child-chosen writing. Lisa's story of playground problems yesterday began *Carla and Jenny was playing jumprope and they didn't let me play.* This was corrected, to Carla-and-Jenny-were, and the hurt feelings inherent in the story will help to fix the pattern in Lisa's mind.

Until Dan wants to say, *Me and Michael was building a snow fort,* he doesn't give any thought to which is correct. Even if I were to present a brilliant lesson on is/are on Tuesday and was/were on Wednesday, he will not bother to remember it. When he is writing that snow fort story, however, my hasty explanation will be reinforced by the excitement of the building. Chances are that this story about the snow fort will need some more was/were choices before it's done: *The big kids said they were going to beat us up. Dick and Kevin were making snowballs and me and Michael were making the walls so next recess we're going to get them!*

I might even get in a lick about *we're,* depending on how good this writer is: one point of grammar per story is about all I count on. It is the spontaneity of the lesson fused to his commitment to the writing that is the basis for both learning and remembering grammar — again used generically — as he writes.

The other advantage of learning grammar by writing is that the child has to read his story out loud at some point in the day, to some friend and to the group. So he hears his story, correctly written and correctly read, and it is very real, very alive, very important to him then. Another day he may start another story using *they was* and will need only the reminder. Most children, too, can be told that is/are and has/have and does/do work like was/were; if they've dealt with any of these in a story, the reminder of their similarity may be all they need to use the others correctly.

But the teacher must take the minute to do this reminding and

teaching. The teacher is essential to the growing consistency of the child's English.

Notice that I didn't change the me-and-Michael construction. Who is the most important person in the six-year-old writer's world, after all? The most defensible rule a teacher can live by in this business of teaching standard English is to enforce the rules that she uses herself. I never say *ain't* myself, but I am often guilty of the *me-and-somebody* construction. I think it's like the chicken and the egg: do I use it incorrectly because I hear it incorrectly used so much by the little ones, or do I accept their use of it because it is natural to me? By the time I noticed the pattern in my own speech I had already been teaching first grade for five years and was hopelessly lost in it.

("You get kept back every year," someone tells me each spring.)

The verb inflections *s, ed, ing* can be brought into relief by the teacher through the needs of the children's writing. By Movement V most children, finding a root word in the dictionary, can make the words they need.

Jodi thrusts her battered dictionary, open to the *S* page, onto the table in front of me. "I know the words I need, this is going to be a long story!" she said, eyes flashing, "but I need *sprayed.*"

"Good," I answer, uncapping my pen. "I like long stories with lots of words you know. But I bet you know *sprayed* too. You know *play,* don't you?"

"*P-l-a-y,*" she nods.

"So what's *spray*?" I ask.

"*S-p-a-y* — no — sprr — I know! *S-p-r-a-y*!"

"Yep," I nod too, "and what's on the end?"

"*E-d*!" She grabs her book and runs to her desk.

"See?" I call after her, "you did too know it!" A grin flashes back at me over a pencil already busy.

The *ing* ending, used much more often by young storytellers, is maddeningly complicated by silent *E* and by the doubling of the final consonant when a vowel precedes it. We work on these as they occur, and by the end of the year most of the children

can do them, especially if I remind them to look for the *E* or the vowel. The others are easy.

"I'm a jumping bean," Deborah wants to write one windy day after the full moon. Aptly, too: she's been doing some bizarre calisthenics in the middle of the room. "I need *bean* but that's all. I have *jumprope* on my *J* page and all I have to do is take off *rope* and put on *ing*."

So I write *bean* on her *B* page while she twitches her hands to an inaudible rhythm in her head. "Thank you!" she says, loudly, and flips her way across the room. I watch her for a minute, bemused; then I get up and follow her. As softly as I can I persuade her to sit down to write, and I extract from her a promise to draw me a picture of Deborah the Jumping Bean when she finishes writing. The chances of the picture being done, or of Deborah staying put, are still remote: but the story will be written.

One of the most fun and most hair-tearing concepts is the possessive apostrophe *S*. That's all one word, of course: possa-fee-s. I find it very difficult to explain. In Movements II and III the children simply copy it. *Today is Eric's birthday. I'm playing with Andrew's car. Debra's dress is pretty.* The first few times I simply say, "This is apostrophe *S*. You use it because the car belongs to Andrew." Later the child can do it alone, but if the pattern changes (*I'm going to Grammy's*) or a plural sneaks in, watch out.

Heather, who always wants to know why, was stumped and then disgusted by this one day. Her story began this way: *Yesterday on my birthday I got to wear Mama's necklace but my sister's didn't.* The urge was irresistible to write *sister's* too. I couldn't let it go by; I told her it didn't have apostrophe *S*.

"Why? It sounds the same as *Mama's*, doesn't it?"

"Yes, Heather, but . . ." — thinking fast — ". . . the necklace belongs to Mama, and nothing in the sentence belongs to a sister. You have two sisters, so they get a plain plural *S*."

(Did that make sense?)

"You can't hear the apostrophe, you're quite right, they do sound the same," I added.

A pause, then "So if I had worn two necklaces there would be a plain *S* on necklace too?"

"Yes, exactly!" I pat myself on the back a little. Then her logical mind moves to the next noun, and with a deep-throated giggle she points to *Mama* on the page.

"Just imagine if I had two mothers — I don't, you know — then I'd get to choose how to write it, wouldn't I, because the necklace would belong to the mothers but there'd be two . . ."

I stop her with a finger to her lips, and I sigh. "You won't believe this, Heather, I know you won't" — another sigh — "but if you had two mothers in that sentence it would be *S* apostrophe." I print it, *mothers'*, on the chalkboard behind me.

Dead silence. Then with great dignity she gathers up her storybook, dictionary, and pencil and gives me a look.

"This language is strange," she says with conviction, and turns away from me.

English is strange, but not as much in its grammar as in its phonetic construction. I teach phonics, the sounds of vowels and consonants, all the time, in every Movement, in combination with nearly all other aspects of grammar, as to Jodi with *sprayed.* Teaching sounds this way ties them to the child's own vocabulary and, more importantly, to the child's own images. Some children need more than others to constantly review phonics. For some, I need to go over at least one word in every story.

Kyle had a very hard time learning beginning consonant sounds. Especially *G,* as in goat, and *J,* as in jump. He knew he was getting them mixed up, and he tried his best not to. Finally one day in late fall he wanted to write about his sister Jane, and after we got all the other words he needed I asked him what *Jane* started with.

"*J,*" he said offhandedly. I oohed and aahed and he ducked his head and grinned. "Well, Teacher," he pronounced, smacking his knee for emphasis, "it's easy when you know it!"

G and *J* are hard enough, but sooner or later somebody wants to write about a knife, or a knee, or a knight.

"And what does *knee* start with, Randy?"

"*N,*" he says, reasonably.

"Nope," I exclaim. I turn to the others and ask for their attention. "Randy wants *knee.* Help him. What does it start with?"

"*N,*" comes a chorus, peppered with "of course" and "boy, Randy."

"Aha!" I say. "No. *K.* Silent *K,*" I inform the now-silent room. "Isn't that something? *Knee* starts with a silent *K.*" As I turn back to Randy's dictionary and print *knee* for him, I hear the comments: "I bet *knife* does too" and "I know! *Know*! I've seen that in my reading book."

And another orthographic oddity is accepted.

Two of the years we've done Words there has been a member of the Wren family in the class, and the *wr* words are always greeted by "oh, yeah, like Wren." No whys are asked about this phenomenon, but it is soon a matter of course for a child who has asked for *knife* and seen me shake my head at his *N* page to say, "Oh. *K.*" And for the *R* sounds the same: "Oh. *W.*" I find this rather remarkable.

Lots of whys are asked about the digraphs, especially *PH*. The reaction of most is similar to Julie's the day she brought her photograph album to school. She was at an I-can-do-it-all-myself stage that week, and she'd written *fotograf* into her story. I told her about *PH.*

"Why?" she said. "They could've used just *F,* like I did, and that's only one letter to print!" But she went away to fix it, shaking her head over English.

To be aware of these odd and not-so-odd ways of sounding and spelling is to be alert to the language all the time, which is exactly what good readers and good writers, of any age, must always be.

We lose sight, I often think, of what language really is as we try to "cover" it as teachers. Language is not just the sum of its parts, the cohesion of its fragments. You don't write an essay or a story, or give directions or tell an experience, in bits and fragments of language, no matter how logically sequenced. You don't use all the nouns first, then all the plurals, then the vowels, then the punctuation, then the adjectives. That's ludicrous. Of course you don't use it that way. But when we teach "grammar" out of context, when we fragment the language and try to do it a bit at a time, it is just as ludicrous, just as meaningless, and, in the end, just as useless.

Look at an exercise like this, from an ordinary elementary text (and it might be a reading text, or English, or penmanship, or spelling):

> Change the following verbs to the past tense by adding *ed*.
> want jump learn walk

Any child can do this. But when he wants to put into a story a sentence like *The unicorn jumped over the river,* it is not at all a sure thing that he will write *jumped.* It's equally possible that he will write *jumpt,* or maybe, because he is totally baffled by the dissonance of sound and ending, *jumpted.* The *t* is for the integrity of his understanding of sounds, and the *ed* is for the teacher.

You may have to unteach something to this child before he can internalize how *ed* works in English.

It doesn't make sense, and it is certainly a waste of your time, to dilute or contradict the power he has invested in his own written language. Just as you help each child as he needs a point of grammar, just so you can teach the whole class at once with their own writings.

Even if you try to give examples, to use the textbook lessons, look at what you have for material:

> The girls walked to the store.
> A dark cloud covered the sun.
> The dog rolled in the grass.

These sentences have no relation to anything in the students' lives. When they are done correctly, with the blanks all filled in, they will still have no connection to the students except as "Didja get your English done?"

On the other hand, *One day a ship landed at my house and some green men climbed out,* which is the beginning of a story

Sunday
Monday
Tuesday
Wednesday
Thursday
Friday
Saturday
October Tally
yesterday
today
tomorrow
OCTOBER
Thursday
Friday
Saturday
2
3
4
9
10
11
16
17
18
24
25
calendar
Dates
30

Cory wrote a few weeks ago, used *ed* just as well and would be incomparably more interesting to his classmates as a lesson than any book's sentences. If you use this one, with a few others also written by members of the class, very close attention will be paid by everyone. They all know the stories the sentences come from, too, because the writers have shared every day either in conference or in the whole group.

The eagle swooped down to get the cat, was an event in one of Brett's animal stories at about the same time. Heather wrote, insistently, *I yelled again at the genie, but she didn't answer me.*

I collect these sentences as the children read their writing every day, and for a lesson after recess I put them all up on the board in my best printing.

> One day a ship landed at my house.
> The eagle swooped down to get the cat.
> I yelled at the genie again, but she didn't answer.

Three or four is usually enough for first graders, but you can use more for older children, and you can put them on the overhead projector if that's more your style. I ask Cory, Brett, and Heather to read their own sentences. The rest of the class will be very attentive — this is, after all, a kind of publication even though it's only one little bit of a story. Then I say that we are looking today at how to put *ed* onto words — or verbs, if we've used that designation — and who can tell me the words in each of these sentences that we'll be looking at? (This is a little reading and visual discrimination review.) Either I call on a child to tell and I underline each *ed* word, or I call on a child to come underline it and give the chalk to another child for the next one, and so forth. This give-the-chalk ploy keeps everyone's attention and shares the three sentences among several children.

Then I say, "What's the base word in *landed* in Cory's sentence?" and get it spelled, printing it beside the sentence. I do that for each one, and then erase the *ed* words I wrote originally so the board looks like this:

land	One day a ship ——— at my house.
swoop	The eagle ——— down to get the cat.
yell	I ——— at the genie again but she didn't answer me.

And there is the English lesson for the day, as well as a penmanship lesson. If you'd rather, you can put the whole thing onto a ditto for homework.

The power of ownership is the force behind this lesson that will make it stick as no anonymously authored text can. First graders will always listen to each other's writings, partly because listening to each other is built into Doing Words and into every process writing program, but mostly because they are curious!

Another day we might deal with the kind of *ed* that requires dropping silent *E* first, or the kind that requires doubling the baseword's final consonant first. I collect some sentences from the children's writings just the same way, put them up, have them read, and when the time comes to separate the base words, I check to be sure that they know why they have to make the changes they make. The best way to find out what the rule is is to ask, so on the day we do sentences with *tagged* and *stopped* (Erica's *You couldn't be tagged if you were on the raft* and Todd's *We stopped and looked into the volcano*) I might ask them to add a sentence of their own which tells what they did to make the *ed* words that day. They ought to be able to do this in writing by late spring, although you would probably be teaching about *ed* this way much earlier.

After you have done lessons on each of the *ed*s, you can do a set that mixes them up. I am very wary of doing this, since it does demand that they have completely internalized the skills involved, but it is one way to find out if they have. The best way to find out is to simply watch their writing. Never, ever, ever do a mixed set first, even in third grade. It's not fair. Even if you do it in the name of diagnosis, the child will probably come out of it garbled and you will have more to teach anyway. It's not fair, and it's not necessary. You've got time, and you've got material. Don't think for one minute that the wonderful sentences about the eagle swooping and the girls playing tag in the water are the only wonderful sentences you will see all year. There is new material every day, and to use it reinforces its already great importance to the writer: so use it. It will be fun for all of you.

Was/were, is/are, plurals of all configurations, possessives, *ing, er,* comparative adjectives, quotation marks, all kinds of punctuation — whatever they're supposed to "do" with you — can be done this same way. I write up sentences the children have written that illustrate the point I want to deal with, have the writers read their sentences, discuss the reason, have the base words, if any, spelled and written. As an ending to the lesson I ask what the rule is.

If you are much more organized than I am, you can follow up this board lesson with a duplicated exercise using the same words on the next day. These papers can be kept together, by the student, in a folder in his desk, as his own grammar book. He can refer to it when he has a question about the uses of his language, and you can refer him to it, too.

Into this same folder can go spelling. Spelling also belongs under the generic title "grammar" because English now has very set spellings and so it is essential to proper usage to spell correctly. (I do occasionally think it would be so much easier to live in an earlier time, a few centuries ago, when you could spell however you wanted to: but I know I wouldn't have been able to stand the smells.) Parents and teachers have traditionally worried and fussed so much about spelling that it has an inordinate importance, so that it seems to exist for its own sake, instead of as a tool for writing. Spelling has traditionally been done with spellers and lists that have nothing at all to do with the child's other work, either writing or reading. The power of the child's ownership of his writing has not been focused on spelling at all, and that's wasteful.

I take the spelling words for the class from the writings of the week before and post them on a big chart on Monday. These are words that some children are having trouble with, and they are often among the most troublesome words English has: *does, what, know,* and words like those, words the children will have to use all the time. (There's another one: *have to.*) This week one of the words was *genie* because there is currently a spate of stories about genies coming from all over the room, and the variants of its spelling are seemingly infinite. I start first graders on five or six words a week, and work up to ten by the end of the year. In higher grades, I suspect spelling could be done individually, with individual tests of ten words a week, but I haven't tried that lower than third grade myself. A class list will work as well in second and third as in first.

I put the words up on Monday, and into the folder goes a ditto sheet of them too. Home goes another paper, on which the children have copied the words three times each. No matter how you do spelling, parents always say "I want to help him learn his words," so send them home.

Then every day there is Something To Do with the spelling words during the work time after morning recess: alphabetizing, putting into sentences, finding opposites, finding synonyms, finding rhymes. Dividing the list into nouns and verbs and others might be an activity for a class whose curriculum included parts of speech; giving definitions, with or without illustrations is another possibility. You only need three, after all: the test is on Friday.

It is helpful to the children if the activities are predictable, that is, if they know that on Monday we copy, Tuesday we alphabetize, Wednesday we do definitions, etc. You can even make a song about it, like the old pioneer women did with their chores. "Today is Monday, today is Monday. Monday, Washday, is everybody happy, well I should say." Or, "This is the way we wash the clothes, wash the clothes, wash the clothes. This is the way we wash the clothes, so early Monday morning." Pioneer women had so much to do that the routine of the song gave them several fewer decisions to make in their too-busy lives. Children usually do well in predictable situations, and goodness knows we do keep them too busy.

I always do these grammar lessons with the whole class. It

never hurts either the bottom or the top to go over what the middle needs, and it never hurts anyone to be stretched out a little for the specific benefit of either end of the average. Any time, every time, whether the lesson is new or review, it will have the kids' own stuff in it, and they will be enchanted.

Language is a whole, an integral and integrated whole. Children use it, whole, to write and to read. If they use it this way to write and to read, they can also, in the second place, use their writing to dissect their language and play with its parts. This is absolutely the opposite thing to learning about the pieces and trying to put them together. If the language, the writing they are dissecting, belongs to them, they will care. They will want to know more about it; perhaps they will even be delighted by it.

If not, not.

In *Zen and the Art of Motorcycle Maintenance* Robert Pirsig talks about the way in which, even as we learn, we humans discriminate among the details of our world, absorbing some, rejecting others. This discrimination sorts for us an otherwise overwhelming set of data, so that some of it we notice, and the rest we let go by.

> We could not possibly be conscious of . . . and remember all of them because our mind would be so full of useless details we would be unable to think. From all this awareness we must select, and what we select and call consciousness is never the same as the awareness because the process of selection mutates it. We take a handful of sand from the endless landscape of awareness around us and call that handful of sand the world.
>
> Once we have the handful of sand, the world of which we are conscious, a process of discrimination goes to work on it. . . . We divide the sand into parts. This and that. Here and there. Black and white. Now and then. The discrimination is the division of the conscious universe into parts.
>
> The handful of sand looks uniform at first, but the longer we look at it the more diverse we find it to be. Each grain of sand is different. No two are alike. Some are similar in one way, some

> are similar in another way, and we can form the sand into separate piles on the basis of this similarity and dissimilarity. Shades of color in different piles — sizes in different piles — grain shapes in different piles — subtypes of grain shapes in different piles — grades of opacity in different piles — and so on, and on, and on. You'd think the process of subdivision and classification would come to an end somewhere, but it doesn't. It just goes on and on.

This sorting activity, he goes on to say, is only one of two ways to look at the world. One might add that it is only one of two Western ways of looking at the world. "Classical understanding is concerned with the piles and the basis for sorting and interrelating them. Romantic understanding is directed toward the handful of sand before the sorting begins." That is, one can understand the sand as sand and as a whole, or one can define it by separation into (some of) its parts. The point may well be taken that both points of view, both ways of seeing the world, are necessary, and that it is the "or" in that last sentence that causes all the trouble.

When children are learning about the world, it seems to me, they approach it with both of Pirsig's understandings. They don't, at first, notice similarities and differences. That is, they don't weigh the fragments and images of the world as the world presents itself to them. After a long period of simply connecting themselves to the world, learning to believe that they in fact exist, they merely collect data. They collect, for example, animals. A child of three or four knows what a dog looks like, a cat, a rabbit, a mouse; some know horses, cows, rats, pigs; children have seen birds, pigeons and robins at least; some also know gulls, eagles, pelicans, chickens. Each of these creatures is as important as each of the others to the child as he encounters them, unless one or another has a special significance about it because of the circumstances in which it was encountered. A bleeding skunk on the road is a stronger image than an eagle floating a mile over his head.

These will be classified as the child gets older. They will be classified when the child is in school, a child who comes to school to me, and it will be a rediscovery period for him to do this. Light bulbs go on all over the place when I talk about what makes a mammal, for instance. Everyone has an animal to put on the mammal list, and they can readily see that chickens and frogs don't belong there. They can do this the other way around, too: given all the mammals, they will eventually tell me what the common characteristics are. And this is almost as thrilling as seeing the white-tailed deer standing by the road in the first place.

I think this kind of ordering the world is very exciting for the child. I think, too, that it is necessary. To have a system of classification in your head for mammals, behind which you can tuck what you know about them, leaves the front of your mind freer for noticing and absorbing new grains of the world's sand as you come across them. Children keep right on doing this, all the time. And once they have a class named, the discovery of bits to add to it is great fun.

We talked a few weeks ago, as a class, about the amazing and wonderful apostrophe *S*. Several children had used it in their writing, so we asked various writers to read theirs; a few other children recreated those uses in writing on the board for a grammar lesson. Not a day has passed since then that Lindsay has not tiptoed up to me at some point in the day with wider-than-ever sparkling blues to silently, and gleefully, point out an apostrophe *S* in some bit of print — a book, a song, a worksheet, her writing. She is still collecting, but her collection has been focused for the moment on that particular thing. She has a cubbyhole to store these data in. It's lots of fun to fill it.

It is often said, by the gurus of writing instruction, that until a writer (any age) has some text written down to look at, whether on paper or monitor, the writer can't begin to exercise the writing process. Revision isn't possible until there is something to work with. In much the same way, classification isn't possible until there is stuff to classify. It doesn't make sense for me to explain what apostrophe *S* is to Lindsay and her classmates, and then tell them to write something with apostrophe *S* in it. I am sure that they could do such writing: but it would have no organic connection to them. Their use of apostrophe *S* would not have grown out of their own need for it, and they would not have learned it.

Children discover the world and their place in it; they collect and process and store infinite amounts of data while they are living and breathing their way through the first, prepuberty, years of their lives. What I do, in school, is to lay grids and structures and outlines over their data, so that they can classify their information and their discoveries. Then they can more fully synthesize what they know. Light bulbs do occasionally go on as I "teach" first graders, or sometimes grown-ups who have chosen to come to school to me; but these light bulbs are always the blinding realizations of synthesis. The eurekas come when two ideas or facts bump next to each other and make a new one in that mind for the first time. That's exciting: but it's not something I do, I merely allow it to happen.

And at home that's what is going on all the time. When Beth is playing — there's that word again — I mean working with her Play-Doh, she knows because it has happened to her that the hard part of the heel of her hand is the best for pushing it around, and the soft parts of her fingers are much more likely to get sticky. If she has had a chance to mess around with Mom's Play-Doh, too, that she makes into bread or pie crust, Beth has more data to put with her own reconnaissance of clay. Perhaps she's got a feel for mudpies, too — depends on the Mom. So she intuitively knows, in those three realms of experience, that the thicker the stuff, the less sticky it is; and the fleshier parts of her will stick to it the best. She also knows that the most fun is to squeeze any of these things through her fingers — in addition to popping up between them in a nifty and often uneven way, the dough always sticks there.

When I, then, begin to talk to her about matter, about the physical properties of solids and liquids, she reclassifies those experiences into "learning" and has a new base from which to experiment. And when we talk about heat and cold, and warm-blooded and cold-blooded creatures, and what heat and cold do to various substances, she will "learn" that the folded places and the fleshy places in her body retain heat, and that heat is ever so slightly melting the dough between her fingers. I didn't teach her a thing. She knew all she needed to know. I helped her to classify her data, and to sort of clean off her desk so she could go on to discover more.

Where education in America has made its mistake, I think, is to give too much power to the grid or the structure. Somehow it has gotten turned around. Here is this classification system, they think, for the information of the world, and now we have to be sure that each new member of each new generation has something in each of the spaces on the grid. So we'll put it there, fit it onto his brain the way the metal dividers fit into an ice-cube tray, and fill it. Whether the child has any data for that space or not, whether that has ever been important to him or available to him or not, whether he is ready to grasp that information — that is, attach it to his own structure of the world — or not, we'll just pour information into this grid-mold. Then, since it's easier to do a lot of these pourings at the same time, the classroom becomes the factory, where subjects have to be covered, and children have to be filled with knowledge.

They are, however, already filled with knowledge. What they do learn in school, too often, is that their knowledge, their own work of the last few years, is inadequate, wrong, untrustworthy. It's very easy to get from that state of mind to "I'm inadequate, wrong, somehow untrustworthy." And from there to "tell me what to think," "tell me what to write," "tell me what to read," "tell me what to be," is a dangerously small step.

When we in school allow the children to own their language, it is likely that they will come to a sense of ownership and meaning of all their learning, as they had when they were still toddling through their preschool world.

English is just about the richest and most complicated and layered language that humans have yet come up with during their tenure on this planet. Share that with the children you teach. Let them be frustrated and fascinated by their own language. Let them be proud of its incredible depth of synonyms: nearly every noun and verb in English has a Germanic, a Latin, and a French-from-Latin root, not to mention the Indian and Greek ones. Let them be enchanted to find out that the funny *know* has the other one right in it. Let them be thrilled to find *love* inside of *glove*. English is exciting. Let it be exciting. Exciting is better than tedious any day.

Chapter 11

Revision, Or, "I've Got Lots More To Say"

> "What is *real*?" asked the Rabbit one day. "Does it mean having things that buzz inside you and a stick-out handle?"
>
> "Real isn't how you are made," said the Skin Horse. "It's a thing that happens to you. When a child loves you for a long, long time, not just to play with, but *really* loves you, then you become real."
>
> "It doesn't happen all at once. You become. It takes a long time. That's why it doesn't often happen to people who break easily, or who have sharp edges, or have to be carefully kept. Generally, by the time you are Real, most of your hair has been loved off, and your eyes drop out and you get loose in the joints and very shabby.
>
> "But these things don't matter at all, because once you are Real you can't be ugly, except to people who don't understand. . . . Once you are Real you can't become unreal again. It lasts for always."
>
> — Marjorie Williams

THE KEY ELEMENT of the whole writing process is revision. The word means "to see again," and that is what I ask young writers — and old ones — to do. "Look at this again, and see if there is anything you want to add or change."

Very little written revision occurs during Movements I through IV, although there is a lot of revision of thought during the conversations that precede the work of those Movements.

The first kind of revision, adding more to a story, is easy for sixes, although not all of them ever have or take the opportunity to do it. Revision can be simply a change of name, or a period here instead of there. The kind of revision that requires cutting and pasting, whether literally or not, is harder. Revision as such, that is changing words or sentences, or changing the order of events in a piece, or changing the voice in which a piece is written, seems to take a long time to "get."

Revision of any kind, whether adding or changing, comes as the result of a conference. A group conference elicits the most ideas for a writer to choose and use, or not, but in a roomful of writers all four kinds of conferences aid revision. Some stories require several different conferences.

Holly was a fairly typical example of a writer who was just beginning to deal with internal changes. Her cat story was a long rambling thing that had several strands, not all of which held together. In the middle of it she had spent a couple of days putting down the first half of the poem, *'Twas the Night Before Christmas*. The story was about a girl named Holly and her little brother, but the main action involved a lamb. As far as I could tell, neither the girl nor her brother figured in the story after the lamb was introduced. In the first draft the last sentence was, *The lamb pulled them up and down the hill.*

When she read this in conference with the other Yellows, Holly learned that they didn't think the *Night Before Christmas* belonged in this story. They told her in no uncertain terms to take it out, and to be sure that Holly came to the party for her brother Gerald. They didn't seem concerned that the lamb was so central. She did take out most of the poem, but in the end couldn't bring herself to take it all out.

When she had a conference with me alone, the next day, I said to her that she had three stories going.

"What do you mean?" she drawled. Holly is a child who keeps the information and skills she gets, but takes some little time to come to her understandings. This question, which in another child might well have been a delaying tactic, in Holly was a genuine request for clarification.

"I mean I can't quite tell what this story is about yet," I tried again. "Is it about Holly or Gerald or the lamb?"

She looked puzzled. "It's about Holly, and Gerald, and the lamb comes to Gerald's party." She flicked her eyes to my face to see how I was taking that.

"Did Holly come to the party?" I asked. "Are you going to have her play with the lamb too?"

Holly considered this, but shook her head. "No, she didn't," she explained patiently. "The others are Gerald's friends. Not Holly's friends. Holly was in the house."

"Oh," I said. "Is she coming back into the story later? What's she doing in the house?"

Every now and then, with the best of intentions to only reflect and elicit what the child already knows, I suggest something. Holly lit up, inspired.

"She's playing with her cat!" she exclaimed. She picked up the book and began to walk away. "Now I know!" She moved back to her own seat, stopping by her cousin Rob's desk to say something. He replied with a smile, his own pencil stopped for a second to answer her. Later I realized that he'd okayed the use of his name for the cat Holly was about to introduce, incidentally reintroducing the character of Holly. This was as close as she got to giving unity to this piece.

> Once upon a time there was a girl. Her name was Holly. She had a mother. Her name was Amber. Holly had a father. His name was Brett. Holly had to go to school. She had to stay inside. But she snuck outside. Her mother saw her.
>
> It was the night before Christmas when all through the house not a creature was stirring not even a mouse.
>
> Amber had a baby. His name was Gerald. Gerald couldn't crawl yet. But his birthday was today and Amber called all of his friends up and one of his friends didn't come to his birthday. Because he was sick.
>
> Three friends came. One of the friends brought a lamb. And he left the lamb outside. He forgot to tie him and the lamb stayed there. The friends took him for a walk. The lamb pulled them up the hill and down the hill. They went back home.
>
> Holly was in the shower. Holly got dressed. Holly went for a walk. Holly saw a cat. The cat's name was Robbie. Holly picked

> Robbie up. Holly forgot to close the door. Her cat followed her out. Her cat's name was Jamie. Robbie jumped out of Holly's arms. The two cats loved each other. They both lived with Holly. The end.

This story was finally recopied and hung on the wall, entitled "Holly and the Cats." She was proud of it, and I was glad it was finished. Or, perhaps I should say, over with. This was Holly's first attempt at seriously revising a piece, and it can certainly be said that there was a lot more that she could have revised. My expectations for Holly at this point in her development as a writer, however, were two. I wanted her to realize that details and sequence could be changed, and to begin to see that a story needs to have a focus.

One of the besetting sins of writers of every age is the tendency to assume that the reader knows more than he really does. Jacob, who had started the year with a pronounced secrecy problem, never wanting to let the reader know anything, had developed a severe case of this. He was one of several primary writers who had or longed for a three-wheeler (I think it's a fat-tired kind of dirt bike). They wrote flat-out fantasies about all the things they might do with these machines if only their moms didn't think they were too little.

> Once upon a time there was a boy. His name was Jason. Jason had a three wheeler. And he took off. And he found a boy his name was Eddie. Eddie had a Honda and he took off. And caught up with Jason and Eddie passed Jason. And Jason caught up with Eddie. But Ed speeded up.
>
> And Ed said, "I'll have a race." And Jason won the race. And Jason said I won the race." Then Ed chased Jason in the woods. And around the house and up stairs too. and over the house. And they had a race.

At this point he thought it was finished, but he was quickly disillusioned by the Greens in conference.

"How can they go over the house, anyways," said Jason.

"A bike can't go up stairs in a house like that, Jacob," chimed in Stephanie.

Jamie, who'd been listening hard, summed up the reaction of the whole group with a sad shake of the head. "That doesn't make any sense," she said with regret.

"Well, they did, too," said Jacob belligerently. "I know they did." But as much as we questioned him, he wouldn't tell how. We went on to another child's story, then, and after the group left I kept him with me to talk about it a little more.

This conversation was about the difference between something that is make-believe but could have been real and something that is make-believe but couldn't really happen. (I find this a useful first distinction between fiction and fantasy.) Jacob insisted that "it was a real story, except Eddie's bike isn't a Honda," and they did too go over the house.

"Tell me again how they did that," I said, in as neutral a voice as I could manage.

Jacob sighed a patient sigh and began gesturing. "First they chased around the house, then they went through the house, and then they went over it." He looked down at the floor for a minute, thinking. "And then they went in the woods," he finished up unhelpfully.

I was intrigued by the spatial sequence he was trying to convey in this story, but no nearer to understanding how it was done, when he seemed to give up on me, picked up his book to leave and said, as casually as anything, "they build another ramp in the woods."

Light dawned. I'd asked the wrong question, that was all. I'd been saying "how" and I'd needed to ask "what did they go on?" All was now clear. And after a brief disagreement, which I lost, about the propriety of running these vehicles through a house and up its stairs ("What did their mothers say?" "They didn't like it and told them to go outside."), the final draft emerged with details added.

Ed and Jason

Once upon a time there was a boy. His name was Jason. Jason had a three wheeler. And he took off. And he found a boy. His name was Eddie.

Eddie had a Honda. And Eddie took off.

And caught up with Jason. And Eddie passed Jason. And Jason caught up with Eddie. But Ed speeded up.

And Ed said, "I'll have a race." And Jason won the race. And said "I won the race." Then Ed chased Jason in the woods. And around the house. And upstairs too. And over the house. And they built a ramp on the stairs. And over the house.

And they made a ramp in the woods. And the Honda couldn't make it over the ramp. And the Honda flipped over.

And Jason laughed. the end.

There were still several things that could have been taught through this story of Jacob's, most obviously the repeated "And ... And ..." routine. But he'd shown that he had a working knowledge of paragraph form and of quotation marks, so I left the *And*s alone.

Sometimes a story seems to come out whole on the first draft, with no need for revision or rethinking at all. There are very few of these in any given year. Handel wrote his *Messiah* in three weeks without stopping or erasing anything, they say, but there are very few of these that any writer can claim — the kind of piece that seems to write itself.

A few loose ends, perhaps, but remarkable unity of thought and action characterized Gerald's story "The Snow Beast." It was spelled *snow beste* throughout, because in January when he started it we had just been talking about how silent *E* makes the other vowel long: he applied the rule. When the final copy was done for submission to a state contest, he did look it up and spell it with the *A*.

Once upon a time there was a snow beste. Nothing could go through it except fire. A snow beste is a monster made out of snow. The snow beste lived in a mountain. At the top of the mountain the snow beste had a cave. He didn't have anything to eat except ice. At the top of the mountain the snow beste went sliding. He made lots of snow things. He even made himself. He made dragons and ghosts. He made so many other things he hardly had any space to slide in. He saw another snow beste. They started to fight. They knocked down the snow things. The first snow beste won the fight, because the first snow beste had stronger arms than the second snow beste. Then the snow beste made the snow things again. The snow beste didn't know there was a snow snake behind him. The snow snake strangled the snow beste's leg. The snow beste fell on the ground. But the snow beste rolled over and smushed the snow snake. The snow beste noticed that he was hungry. So he went to get some ice. But little did he know that there was a hunter coming over the hill. The snow beste didn't know that the hunter was waiting for him. When the snow beste came the hunter looked up at the snow beste. The hunter dropped his gun with his mouth wide open. The hunter had to look up twenty-seven feet high, because the snow beste was so tall. The hunter ran as fast as he could. But he wasn't fast enough for the snow beste. The hunter hid behind one of the snow things. The snow beste ran past the snow thing that the hunter was behind. The hunter looked out from behind the snow thing. The hunter ran away. The hunter ran home. He told his wife what had happened. His wife said "who cares?" She was having supper. The hunter left without having supper. His wife said "wait." Because he didn't have some supper. The hunter's wife ran out the front door saying "wait" "wait" but the hunter didn't listen to his wife. Meanwhile back at the snow beste's cave the snow beste sat worried because he didn't have any friends. The snow beste wanted to do something about it because he didn't have anyone to talk to. And anyone to play with. So the snow beste got up and went outside. There he found some hunters plus the hunter that the snow beste had scared away. The snow beste ran. But he wasn't fast enough for the big guns. So the biggest snow beste in the world is dead. The End.

This story was read aloud several times as it was being written. The whole class liked it: we were all sad when the snow beste, inoffensive creature that he was, got done in by the hunters. Gerald comes from a long line of hunters, so it was entirely fitting from his point of view, and the other children agreed that hunters get to shoot animals. I kept still about that myself, and only wished in my heart that Gerald hadn't put in the part about how lonely he was just before he was shot. It was Gerald's story, not mine.

Another story that didn't get revised at all because it came full-blown on the first draft was Becky's picnic story. The only thing the other Yellows wanted, in conference, was what they ate. Becky decided it didn't matter.

> Once upon a time there was a boy. His name was Michael. He had a friend. The friend's name was Becky. They went for a walk. It was a nice day.
>
> Becky said, "boy it's a nice day!"
>
> They brought a picnic basket, to stop and eat.
>
> And then Becky said, "Now that all of the food is gone don't you think we should go home and tell mom what a great time we had?"
>
> Michael said, "Yes, I do think we should go back."
>
> So they went back home. They got home all right.
>
> The End

Many stories don't get revised for other reasons. Chief among these is that the first draft was never completed, and the child simply lost interest in the whole thing. Some don't get revised because there simply isn't time to do them all. Some are coherent and exciting enough to suit everyone in the first draft, as Gerald's and Becky's were. And some are not worth more work.

This last was the case with Amber's story about Gandhi. She worked quite hard on it (for Amber — she was one of the most endearingly dilatory children I've ever had), but at no time did it make any sense, even to her, and her interior comments reflect this. The easiest way to put it is that it didn't get revised because she didn't know any more about it when the first draft was finished than she had when she began it.

> I saw the movie Gandy. The man who was named Gandy was the man who led his country. He was on a train. And Gandy got in the wrong car. And Gandy got thrown out of the train.
>
> Then Gandy brushed himself off. Then Gandy waited until the train went by. Did you know Gandy went to jail 12 times. Because he kept going to the other peoples country. He did not do it on perpus. He only did it by accident.
>
> Since Gandy went to jail 12 times he had to go to something like a triyl. Why Gandy was gone the country started to break

up. And Gandy told them not to break up but the country disobeyed him. Then when Gandy came back. The country did not like Gandy. They were screaming. At Gandy. Gandy looked at his people. Then he layed down. I think on top of a castle. I didn't know why. Then a man cam up in the steps. And in the part that Gandy was in. And he pulled out a piece of meat. And put it on Gandy's bed. And said, Here eat here eat," he said. But Gandy didn't take it. Cause he wanted to convince his people. And he did it. I don't know how he did it.

Probably her mother and father really wanted to see this film, and just took the children along. Probably they had a fine time; but Amber didn't have any idea what it was about. She did tell me, though, a week or so before she began to write this, that it was a very long movie. "They stopped it in the middle and I got up and Mama got me some more popcorn."

Michael wrote his only really finished story of the year about coyotes. Coyotes were big in his class, written about almost as often as Luke Skywalker. In the first draft of this story the action was very cut and dried, and not well connected.

Once there were two coyotes. Their names were Weylon and Michael. Michael saw a rabbit. His name was Kyle. Michael killed Kyle. Then a bear came. Then a girl came. Her name was Josh. The bear ate the girl the end.

The main questions raised in conference were, What happened to the coyotes? and What did the bear do? So in the final draft he pulled it together a little more, and incidentally decided not to kill the girl.

The Coyotes

Once there were two coyotes. Their names were Weylon and Michael. Michael saw a rabbit. He started to chase the rabbit. His name was Kyle. Michael killed Kyle. The other coyote just stood there watching him.

Then a bear came. He was a good bear. He didn't have a home so he made friends.

Then a girl came. Her name was Josh. Then Weylon, one of

the coyotes, chased the girl through the forest. She fell on a stick.
The coyotes went home. They went to sleep.
The end

Weylon wrote a story about coyotes, too, and its revision was painful. When he was writing the first draft, he kept adding explanatory details after the coyotes killed the bear, and the whole sequence was very confused.

> Once there were two coyotes. Their names were Weylon and Michael. They saw a squirrel. His name was Kyle. They killed Kyle. They ate him. They were full. They howled. They went to there den. It was nighttime so they went to sleep.
>
> A bear was waiting. They woke up. They killed the bear. They were hungry so they ate it. Then they went to sleep. When they had killed the bear they used there claws They jumped on the bear and ripped the bear apart. The end.

The first revision only seemed to make it more complicated. The details were wonderful: it was the sequence that was not. He reworked the last paragraph several times.

> A bear was waiting outside the den. They woke up. They killed the bear. When they had killed the bear they had used their claws. They had jumped on the bear. And the bear didn't know they were coming.
>
> A bear was waiting outside there den. The bear was backwards. The coyotes jumped on the bear. When they had killed the bear they had ripped the bear apart.

It was hard work to get it all straight. In conference with me, he put numbers in front of all the sentences to try to get the sequence more logical, and in the end he succeeded. Finally, in all its gory detail, "The Two Coyotes" was published.

> Once there were two coyotes. Their names were Michael and Weylon. They saw a squirrel. His name was Kyle. They killed Kyle. They ate him. They were full. They howled. They went back to their den. It was night time so they went to sleep.
>
> A bear was waiting outside the den. The bear was backwards.

The coyotes woke up. And the bear didn't know they were coming. The coyotes jumped on the bear.

When they killed the bear they used their claws. They ripped the bear apart. They were hungry so they ate the bear. Then they went back to sleep. They were happy. The end.

Kyle himself hardly ever killed anyone off in his stories. He is a talented child graphically, and his story about the cats is very visual. It was written after the coyote stories, and he can hardly be blamed for dispatching Weylon and Michael. Kyle's problem was capital letters: he routinely forgot them, because he wrote very fast. But unless he had those capitals in the right places in this story, it was incomprehensible. This is the published version.

Once there were five cats. The cats' names were Blacky and Squirrel and Chipmunk and Bird and Blacky. Bird liked birds. Squirrel liked squirrels. Chipmunk liked chipmunks. Blacky liked black. Blacky liked black too.

Squirrel called Blacky. Both Blackys came.

"You nit wit. I called Blacky," said Squirrel.

"We are Blacky," said both Blackys.

"Gee whiz!" said Squirrel.

Blacky said, "there's a squirrel, Squirrel." Squirrel chased the squirrel. The squirrel's name was Weylon. Squirrel caught the squirrel. Squirrel was happy. Weylon got ate. Blacky asked Squirrel a question. The question was why Squirrel called them. Squirrel wouldn't answer this question.

Blacky said, "there's some black." Both Blackys played in it. Squirrel went on hunting for squirrels. Squirrel caught another squirrel. The squirrel's name was Michael. Squirrel ate Michael.

Chipmunk had no luck. Bird had no luck, too. Squirrel had some luck. They went to bed. They woke up in the night. They went hunting. Everyone had no luck. They went to bed. The end.

This story was a disaster without capital letters, so that was the major work Kyle did on it. The other thing he changed, from the first draft, was adding the last paragraph, to tell what the other cats, Bird and Chipmunk, were up to. We could also have worked on *Everyone had no luck,* in which the negative should be in the pronoun, or the *got ate* construction (Kyle consistently read that as *aten*). I feel strongly that two changes are about all a child can handle in a revision. Certainly two new ideas or suggestions are all that I expect a child to remember from a conference, and all that I write down when I'm making notes during conference. To expect children, even superstar writers, to turn a piece into flawless perfection, is to overwhelm them as much as it will overwhelm grown-up writers. The danger of too many suggestions is that the writer will begin to think that none of it is any good, and that's not true. Kyle's story about the cats and Holly's story about Gerald's party were worthwhile, pridemaking stories for each of those children. I'm not teaching writing as a vehicle for discouragement.

Jason C.'s baseball story required mostly editing, not changes in content, but it amounted to a revision because the editing was done on the verbs. He'd written a sentence or two a day about the progress of his Farm League team, kind of journal-entry sentences, and hadn't intended to put it together into a story. Then one day in early May he came to me with the book and asked for a conference.

"I want to publish something," he said.

"What story do you want to work on?" I asked. He spread his hands out in the I-don't-know pose. "Do you want to add more to your baseball stuff, maybe give a description of a real game?"

"We haven't played any real games yet," said Jason C., ever matter-of-fact. "I mean, we're just practicing still."

"Will it be good to make this a story about practice, then?"

"Okay." So Jason C. sat down and we went over it. When we'd finished changing the tenses and he'd copied it he was proud of it. When his mother came to get him for an appointment a few days later, he zoomed her to the wall to read it before I even knew she was there. She was proud too.

Baseball

I am going to have practice. I might play second base or pitcher in the baseball game. I am the only seven.

> We have practice Monday, Wednesday, Thursday, Friday. I hope I am going to be in Patty's team. Because Shawn is on that team.
>
> Tonight we have practice but it is cancelled because it is raining. We are going to have it Monday. It is at 6:00 to 7:30.
>
> I pitch but in a game we are going to hit off the t-ball. The t-ball is a black base that has a black rubber bar. The baseball sits on the t-ball and you hit it. We pitch and hit off the t-ball and we play pass with a partner.

It is inevitable that children want to write about "unacceptable" things, and when they do I get rather direct in their revision work. "Bad" words crop up all the time, of course, on the playground, but also in the phonics lesson. One day, long ago, I asked a class to help me make a list of words that rhyme with *truck*. (I was younger then.) We made a little list — *duck, luck, buck, tuck* — and they settled down to illustrate them. In the middle of this working time one of the mousiest of all the little girls in the room appeared at my elbow.

"I know another one," she whispered. "But it's not very nice to say."

"I think I know the one you mean," I whispered back. "Do you think we should put it up there on the chalkboard?" I added curiously.

"Mm-mm," she said, still whispering. "Better not."

"Okay," I whispered back. "Thanks for telling me about it though."

She nodded and went back to her seat. Two minutes later, there she was again.

"You know," she said, as grown-up as could be, still whispering, "it might be all right. I remember now, my Daddy told me, it only means a girl dog." She looked at me, kindly leaving it up to me to tell the class.

"Right," I said. I had to swallow a couple of times — laughter? indignation? pity for the child who heard Daddy calling (Mom?) this compound word she had in her head — before I could go on. "I think we have enough words, though. We'll leave that one in your head."

She was happy. I was too. Sometimes, although I never ask for *truck* rhymes anymore, that very word comes out loud, for the effect of it.

Effect is the main reason I ever see any of the "bad" words in writing. Boys, especially, seem to have to put the *pee* and the *poop* in their writing. Not often, but often enough to keep me on my toes, a story will move along perfectly fine for a few paragraphs or pages on Mars, or in the prince's castle, and then all of a sudden the writer "gets weird." (On their report cards I usually refer to these excursions into scatology as "inappropriate language.") When someone uses this sort of language everyone gets to giggle during the first reading — *peepee* gets double the giggles of *pee*. Then I Step In. Almost always, the writer was just trying out the words, and my same old *ain't* line, "You can say this but you can't write it," suffices.

I must confess I guide some revisions. Occasionally we get an acute manifestation of the bathroom-and-body fascination, and even the writer's friends who hear it unfolding day after day feel uncomfortable. I watch the listeners as closely as I watch the writers. I have to: I am too old to get giggly about bathrooms. Sex is more likely to claim my personal attention, but fortunately it doesn't come up very often. Very few six-year-olds, thank goodness, know very much about it.

Once I had a child who wrote about a boy who romantically kissed his mother, and when he read it aloud, nobody laughed. After a minute another boy said, "That's weird." The next day I told him I wanted him to revise it with me, right then. "What's all this kissing for?" I asked.

His eyes slitted shut over silent giggles, and he put one hand over his mouth in a classic tee-hee gesture.

"She was kissing him on the mouth, like on TV, Teacher," he said, "and they were holding onto each other." "Do you think that's what mothers do?" I asked as mildly as I could. As the words left my lips I thought Oboy, if he goes home and tells his mom I asked that she'll think I meant her. Oboy. I mentally crossed my fingers.

"No," he answered, surprised. "This is a story, Teacher, this isn't real."

"Well, you know, it's hard to tell that it isn't real, and I think it bothered some of the other kids," I said, trying for a man-to-man kind of tone. "I'd like you to leave out that part." My mental fingers were aching.

"But I like it," he said.

"There are a lot of good things in this story," I agreed. I struck a pose, as if I'd just had an idea. "Hey! Maybe he could just have a girlfriend that isn't his mother! How about that?" And after a little more talk, in which we discussed what her name might be, he did change that part. The story never did get published, but the girlfriend's name was changed — to Mrs. Johnson. . . .

My behavior with this story was very skewed from my normal nondirective pattern. I think there were two reasons why I wanted to suppress the sexy part of this story. First, it simply made everyone uncomfortable. For most of the children, having a mother be a girlfriend is "yukky," a generic epithet that translates here into abnormal. For them, it wasn't enticingly weird: it was off-puttingly weird.

It made me uncomfortable, also, because of What Other Grown-ups Would Say to me for allowing it. This feeling does me no credit, I know: but it is real.

By comparison, the *truck* rhymes and plain old *damn* and *shit,* which appear from time to time, pale into ordinariness. I don't allow them, either, but I don't feel as badly as I do when stories like the mother-kissing one come up. Underneath writing like that there are problems that the child cannot cope with: and I don't help.

Blood and gore, somehow, are not a problem for the other children. Only when there is indiscriminate killing, perhaps reflecting an abnormal preoccupation in the writer's mind, do I step in. Mostly, peers take care of this.

A killing story surfaced last year, with lots of detail. Several people were killed — not, as far as I could tell, immediate family of the writer — and in various interesting ways. The listeners were fascinated by the detail, as was I. The first person was killed by a truck, the second by being dumped in a well, the third by being blown up — with good, plausible descriptions. Then, the second time she came to conference, the writer had added another death by being dumped in a well.

"That's the same," accused the conferees. "The other hunter fell in a well."

"What can you do about that?" I asked.

"Well, no, see, this one was already dead," she said.

"How did he die, then?" asked another child.

"Uhh . . . poison! First he drank the poison and then he fell in the well."

"Put that in," I said. "Please." Nobody seemed to mind the Stephen King grossness. It wasn't "weird," so it was acceptable. I didn't love it, mind you, but it didn't seem that the class needed protection from this revision.

Drafts are not always revised. No one revises and publishes every story. Depending entirely on the class, I insist that everyone publish at least one or two stories in the year. Many do just that; many do much more. Almost always, though, a draft is given some kind of closure. The day after Christmas vacation Pat had a lot to say about vacation, but there was an unfinished story in his book. He thought about it for a while, and then he wrote *He got away. The end.* This neatly finished off his robber, and he could begin his new piece.

Gerald's story about Santa Claus, written as if no one knew the legend at all, ended, *And for all I know Santa will always go out on Christmas Eve.* I congratulated him on this ending, and asked him where he'd gotten the idea. Usually if a child has borrowed an idea, he will tell me so proudly.

"Oh," said Gerald, shifting his weight nonchalantly. "I just thought that up last night."

•

It has become obvious by this time that all writers of once-upon-a-time stories take the names of their characters from among their classmates and, much more rarely, from their families, and only occasionally from anywhere else. In this story about astronauts by Lance, this leads to an ambivalence about whether they are men or boys. Lance paragraphed this:

> Once upon a time there was a boy. His name was Josh. He was in the storage room of a space ship. The space ship was in space. There were three other men. Their names were Vince and Luis and Jason. They were in a different Solar System.
>
> Then they landed on a fireball. The space ship was made to land on fireballs.
>
> The men had fire proof suits on. Josh saw a lot of fire proof suits. Josh got a fire proof suit on. The suits were black. Also they had jets on them. The suits looked like space suits.
>
> Josh saw a door. He went towards it. It was locked. Josh was trapped in the space ship.
>
> Josh saw a window. He broke the window. It was the window to the back door. Then Josh got out.
>
> The other men had guns. The guns fired rays. The rays were green and red. Josh found a gun in the suit.
>
> Luis was taking samples of fire from the biggest fire ball in the world. Luis had 100 sample takers. They were glass.
>
> Then the ship blew up. But luckily the men had four miny speeders. They heard a noise while they were going to get on the speeders. They shot it. They got on the miny speeders. And they went back to Earth. The End.

Lance has clearly bought the idea that each paragraph has a new or slightly different subject. Once we'd figured out, in a Blues conference, what these astronauts were up to, and paragraphs two and seven had been added, the story hung together nicely. He said he didn't know and didn't care what the noise was that they shot at: none of the Blues suggested that it was probably Josh, so I didn't either. Josh was Lance's best friend at the time. The story made sense, so it was published.

As time goes on, more writing is fiction or fantasy than not during writing time in the morning. Children come to be at ease with revision, conferences, editing, and publication of these stories. It seems to be true that several months of writing in the process, in Movement VI, is necessary and enjoyable for most children. If this occurs in first grade, as it has where I have taught, then second graders need new worlds to conquer.

To recapitulate Movement VI in first grade: a child works on pieces of his own choice, deciding which ones to take through to publishing, having conferences of various kinds on virtually all his beginnings, understanding the difference between real stories and make-believe stories as he writes them, and understanding the difference, within make-believe, between fiction and fantasy. He has the sense that the language he uses is whole, that he is in the end responsible for how it works in his own writing. He is proud of his work.

At the same time that we are Doing Words in the morning, though, we are often writing social studies reports and scientific observations in the afternoon. Even in the morning it's not all wild tales. In connection with other areas of the curriculum, then, or because he wanted to do so in writing time, he has explored other kinds of writing a little. He may have done some poems, or some letters, or some reports. These have been, for several months, optional. By the middle of second grade, this exploration needs to be codified into curriculum.

Genre needs to be introduced and modeled, just like everything else about the writing process. The idea that certain audiences demand a certain style of writing is impossible to understand if you do not have quite a lot of experience as a writer and as a listener to and reader of others' writings. Now, when children are at ease, we can expect them to use several different kinds of writing, Letters, their form and their style, including the difference between a letter to Grammy and a letter to the principal; reports, with the rudiments of note-taking and bibliography; poems; and even how-to pieces are all appropriate to introduce and require of old sevens and eights. They are writers, now, if they've been Doing Words, and they will be delighted to know about new forms and styles and audiences. Practice can be required occasionally: by second grade the children have observed the structure of school long enough to know that there are a lot of things they Have To Learn; and they have been self-confident writers long enough to accept the teacher's requirements from time to time without losing their own belief in themselves.

Once the children get into the writing process, they expect to move through it. They think, and write, and think, and write some more, and talk to someone, and write some more, and talk some more, and have conferences to revise, and revise, and think, and have an editing conference, and publish. They see the sequence of the process, and they are comfortable with it. Some of the models for changing the way a piece looks physically on the page as a result of revision are now internalized and used by the children routinely.

As children write and think of more things to say it is easy to simply add them to the end of whatever they are writing. If they think of, or if a conference suggests, clarifying details or expanding something that is already surrounded by print on the paper, what can they do? I think it is a bit much to ask any child to recopy each time he wants to add something new: I think copying the final draft is plenty, unless the piece becomes illegible because it's been changed so many times. Even then, if there are twenty pages and the mess is on two of them, I would only ask that the two be recopied so that the writer will be able himself to read what's going on in the piece.

One of the basic things to do when children are doing revision as a usual procedure is to have them write on alternate lines of the paper. Tell them to leave a whole line in between each one they fill, so that if and when additional material is needed there will be plenty of room. An age-old device, the caret, is often the handiest and most direct way to use this space. Grown-ups know about the caret and tend to dismiss it as too easy: both first and second graders to whom I have introduced the lowly caret think it is a very nifty gadget. When a six or seven is revising, it can be daunting enough to have several pages of print to keep track of. To have to search through them to find the added parts that wouldn't fit where they belonged can cause real despair. If the writer can put a ‸ exactly where he wants to add something, and then write the addition there, he will feel much more at ease with the whole thing.

Carets win over stars hands down, but stars can be helpful when there is a lot to add. *This horse was very lucky because it lived in a special place,* someone wrote in second grade. *Then the next day a little girl came and they. . . .* In conference everyone wanted to know what made its place special. The writer knew very well, and had kind of assumed that the rest of us could read her mind. A special grass grew there, the rain only came in the evening, there was a tree with yellow apples — much more than any caret could usefully redirect. So she put a big, noticeable star next to *place* and wrote its description on the other side of the paper. When she was rereading the piece, in conference with herself or her friend or the group, she knew she had to read the other side when she came to the star.

Both carets and stars sound foolishly simpleminded, and it might seem unnecessary to describe them in this much detail. I know about them, you know about them — doesn't everyone?

No. Not beginning writers. We are talking here, remember, about six- and seven-year-old children. They need to have both of these simpleminded aids to revision modeled, demonstrated, and explained, and more than once, too. I usually do this as a minilesson, a whole-class demonstration, writing a little story on the chalkboard or the overhead or a chart and showing how I would use the ‸ or the ★ in these ways. I don't use both in a demonstration, either. These are new to the children, remember. New skills need to be taught.

While the caret and the star have been around nearly forever, there are new ways to rearrange material in a draft. Chief among these are spiderlegs. Children love spiderlegs even more than carets.

A spiderleg is a narrow strip of writing paper on which the writer writes the sentences he wants to insert into his draft. The sentences about the "special place" in the story we just went by could have been done on a spiderleg. When the additional writing is all there, the left end of the spiderleg is stapled or taped to the paper exactly where it goes. It's kind of like making the paper itself grow a little where you need it to. Sometimes a page has several spiderlegs, sticking out on both sides. When it is read, then, or copied, the writer simply reads to the joint, reads the spiderleg, folds it over and keeps reading what's on the paper. I use them myself, now.

Spiderlegs, too, must be modeled. I tape a big piece of chart paper up on the chalkboard and write a short beginning of a story on it with a marker, asking the class to read as I go. When I've used up about half the paper I ask for someone to read the whole thing. Then I ask, "What can I do to make this a better story?" As the suggestions come I repeat them, saying, "Where should that go?" Sooner or later — usually very soon — someone says a new bit must go in the middle of what's already there. Someone else in the class usually comments, under their breath, "Now she's gonna have to copy it over." So I take a slice of paper, write the new bit on, and tape it to the chart where it goes. The children invariably giggle, because the "leg" droops instead of lying flat, as it would do if the paper were on a desk. I do a couple of these, and then ask the class to tell me what I did and why and what it's called, as a review and winding up. This takes about ten minutes. Usually they will begin using them right away in their own work.

It is very helpful to keep a stack of half- and quarter-sheets at the writing table, or the paper shelf, for use in this way. Generally speaking, the teacher is a less wasteful paper cutter than the children are.

The end of school presents special opportunities for young writers, as well as occasional frustrations. Ruth wanted to publish one more thing, and it was the next to the last day. She didn't bother to discuss it with me, or arrange a conference, or move through the normal sequence of events. She simply wrote a diaryish entry, proceeded to copy it over immediately, and put it right up on the wall that very day.

A Activity

Tomorrow is the last day of school. I brought a Activity Book. I am sharing it with Courtney. It's fun. I like writing in it.

Jock, at about the same time of year, thinly disguised his feelings in this short fictional piece.

The School

Once upon a time there was a boy. His name is Craig. A boy came. His name is Jason.

They went to school. They had a teacher. Her name is Mrs. Johnson.

They were happy because there were five more days. The end

Kate was writing a very long story, about forty sides of lined paper, which the stapler was beginning not to go through. One day, the seventh of June that year, I made an announcement to the whole class at the beginning of writing time.

"If you want to publish the story you're working on, First Grade," I told them, "you'll have to finish it and have your editing conference on it by Wednesday." Then I began to move toward the table.

Kate appeared at my hip. Her arms were folded across her chest, her foot was tapping, and the light of battle was in her eye.

"What do you mean I have to be edited by Wednesday? Why Wednesday?"

"Well, Kate," I said, laughing, "I can't get anything published if it's done later than Wednesday. Friday is the last day of school."

She dropped her arms and took a step back, incredulous.

"School can't be over yet," she said with decision. "I haven't finished my story!"

Chapter 12

Time on Task, Or, Keeping Up with the Real World

> "Look!" Charles Wallace said suddenly. "They're skipping and bouncing in rhythm! Everyone's doing it at exactly the same moment."
>
> This was so. As the skipping rope hit the pavement, so did the ball. As the rope curved over the head of the jumping child, the child with the ball caught the ball. Down came the ropes. Down came the balls. Over and over again. Up. Down. All in rhythm. All identical. Like the houses. Like the paths. Like the flowers.
>
> — Madeleine L'Engle

YOUNG CHILDREN DON'T LEARN the way grown-ups or even older children do. Young children learn by observation of their environment and by interaction with it, be that environment physical or social or linguistic. (It's this interaction that makes the Twos so Terrible.) They learn, as Piaget and others have shown, progressively and also recursively. They watch, experience, experiment, repeat, imitate, devise new experiments from their experiences, watch, imitate, observe — all these things over and over. Some get stuck or sidetracked on one step or idea or item or word in their environment; some on another. They set their own agendas and live through their own sequence charts.

"I can't understand where Meg gets her interest in worms — I hate them, and her brother never paid any attention to them when he was four," a thirtyish mother said to me. "Why worms?"

"Why not?" I said.

"Well, I can't imagine that I would have a daughter who's a scientist!" the mother said, with a little laugh.

"There's no way of knowing that you do," I told her. "The most we can know about Meg right now is that she is fascinated by worms and is exploring them. Maybe next month it'll be hair ribbons. She doesn't have any idea that her behavior is that of a scientist. She's only interested in worms."

"Well, I wish she'd get to hair ribbons soon," said Meg's mother, forgetting to smile. "Maybe I should take the worms away and give her something else."

"Don't you dare!" I said, not smiling now either. "That's what childhood is for: to make your own choices, to decide what to do and when to do it and how long to be interested in it. That's how children find out who and where and why they are. Soon enough they'll be told what to do. Leave Meg with her worms now. Leave Meg with herself now."

In a way, this Meg is prewriting her life. The data collecting she is doing about worms is her task right now, set by her, and its integration into the rest of her life may not be apparent for some time, if it ever is. This makes grown-ups who want to see "results" a little uncomfortable.

Grown-ups try so hard not to be recursive and unpredictable, because somewhere American grown-ups have picked up the notion that they have to be logical and linear, like an assembly line. Not so Meg; nor my first graders, yet. Perhaps the reason is that they haven't been in school long enough.

The other day Allan, a first-grader who is six, was deep in the four-and-a-half personality he still uses, and he spent forty-five of the fifty minutes of Word time sucking his thumb with his feet up on his desk. Finally he sat up and wrote, *I like my Mom.*

Allan is mostly in Movement V, although he certainly didn't need his dictionary this day. The sentence was Key for him: his mom had just come home after leaving him with two teen-aged babysitters for two weeks. She'd gone to San Francisco for a little R&R with his father. Allan had been sullen and exhausted while she was gone, and I have no doubt that he had also been feeling abandoned.

So this little Movement III snippet, from my point of view, was a legitimate story, and the thumbsucking had been a legitimate use of that child's time that day.

The principal picked that morning, though, to come in and look around while the children were writing. And since Allan sat — or in this case lolled — in the front of the classroom, naturally the principal stopped by Allan's desk. At recess he said, with some restraint, "Allan didn't do much this morning, did he?" I explained about the Mom and the trip to San Francisco, and he said, "Oh, yes," in an accepting kind of voice. I could clearly see and I clearly felt, however, that from his point of view I hadn't kept that child On Task in a meaningful and verifiable way. Allan didn't produce much that day, it was quite true, to show for all the work he was doing.

I knew, though, that the day before, Allan had written three sentences about the babysitters; and the week before that, he had written a couple of sentences each day about the trip to San Francisco and his Mom and how he was going to stay with the babysitters, and all the rest of it. Since that day, Allan has done much more than a Movement III "I like" every day. He's been doing more and feeling very good about doing it by himself. Yesterday, even, two weeks after the *I like Mom* day, he informed me that he didn't have any more to say about the story he'd started on but he would, because writing time wasn't over, begin another one. Fortunately I was sitting down, so I didn't fall over.

Knowing what is going on with the writers in my classroom is important to me, to them, and to anyone else who wants to know. That doesn't mean that I tell them what to do, except to give a framework for their day; it does mean that I know what might be a useful or fascinating next idea or possibility to make present in the classroom. These behaviors of mine don't do anything to ensure either precision or uniformity in the writing or in the class. Precision and uniformity are in many ways antithetical to the writing process.

The now popular idea of Time on Task is seeming to me to be more and more inimical to what writing is. The Time on Task people assume that every task is clearly definable, that completed tasks can be readily evaluated, and observed. Recursive experimentation with a task after it has been evaluated is undesirable and unnecessary.

In the writing process, however, these criteria can't be met. Neither beginning writers nor accomplished professional writers work in straight lines and discrete parts. Except perhaps for publishing, the stages of the writing process — prewriting, drafting, revising, editing, publishing — can't even be described except in terms of the next stage of the process. Revision, by definition, is recursive: a writer has to go over and over and redo and rethink, because that's what revision is. Prewriting insinuates itself into and between all the other stages, and it can rarely be identified, leave aside observed. Writing is riddled with work that can't be defined as On Task.

There was Allan, with his feet up on the desk, his thumb in his mouth, his brain squirreling around, and maybe a few minutes of near-nap: and I say, bravely, that he was prewriting during the bulk of that time. The only way I know that for sure, though, is that he did reach and perform at the next stage, the draft stage, when he put his words on his paper. He reached a place in his interior ruminations where thought was crystallized into a sentence, words were chosen, letters identified as necessary to those words, pencil grasped in a fashion that would produce controlled marks, body posture altered to provide the balance and muscle direction necessary to mark the paper with the pencil in the squiggles that could be interpreted by a reader as the letters he intended to use to transcribe the words his thoughts had become.

The convolution of that sentence is intentional. What actually goes on in the head of a six-year-old — or a thirty-six-year-old, for that matter — as he is "writing" is as nearly ineffable as anything can be that has a tangible result. It is also true that all of the activities I listed in that sentence are going on absolutely all at once, and I bet those are only a small fraction of all the activities taking place in Allan's mind and body as he transcribes *I like my Mom.* I can't reduce my perceptions enough to program them all out.

Even in the drafting stage, then, where there is a result to observe, the task defies delineation and analysis. Strictly speaking, the task of drafting isn't observable either until it is over. The difference between these two is that prewriting can only be seen in the next stage; drafting can be seen in itself.

What happens next is the recurrence of prewriting and drafting together, a stage called revision. The same interior activities go on during this stage, with many stops and starts and much mental thumb-sucking. Between thinkings, sentence by sentence and word by word, are transcribings, all those unconscious physical alterations over and over again. The Task here could be, inadequately, described as choosing, or imaging, or relating, but until it is over, until something is down on the paper again, the writing teacher has no proof that anything whatever has occurred. Indeed, it could probably be argued with as much proof that nothing has occurred at all, that the letters and words he transcribed simply appeared that way. But I don't believe it. I don't believe that Allan was merely copying a string of characters on a display, as it were, on the inside of his forehead. I believe that he is a writer.

Lisa came to school one fall morning, bright and shiny and golden as always, with an additional purposefulness in her step. She marched in, stood a few feet inside the doorway observing the environment. She looked first to the left and then to the right, checking out the room to see what was new, reassuring herself that this was her place. Her chin was high, her shoulders were back. From across the room at my desk, I could feel electricity.

"Good morning, Lisa," I said. I tilted my head a little sideways at her, the tilt acting as a stop for the twelve other things I was trying to do in that moment. I froze myself for an instant for her, responding to the importance of her presence. "How goes it?"

She moved, then, toward the coat rack, unzipping as she went; after two steps she turned almost coyly to her left a little to look back at me. This conversation and movement took a total of about six seconds; it feels false to stretch it this way, but a lot was going on.

"I've got a story," she began casually; but it was too big for this nonchalance she was trying on. She stopped, turned all the way to face me, spread her still-jacketed arms wide. As if she'd invented the phrase — which she had, the words were hanging in the air clearly newly minted — she said, "Have I got a story for you! Wait 'til it's writing time!"

I beamed. She beamed.

Joni swirled away from the coatrack where she'd been rummaging in her school bag and swung herself toward me as if she'd get through the twenty feet in one lunge. She knocked Lisa off her balance, and the moment was broken. It became Joni's moment instead. Her "Sorry, Lisa" was spoken to the air behind her.

"I can't wait, Lisa," I called to her jacket. Then I braced myself to grab Joni in a slowing-down hug as she finished her lunge.

Lisa's prewriting for that day was already completed. I had had neither control of nor proximity to it. It had happened on the bus, or in bed, or talking to her sister, because of the adventure she had had the evening before at her house. As it turned out the story was about riding horses, and the ride she and Angela had had the afternoon before with the horses in the field next to her house. The story was the caption, *I went riding yesterday,* and the transcription of it was the first draft of her writing for that day. When it was written down, her revision instantly began.

When she showed me that sentence in her writing book, she went on talking about the ride, and what Angela had done, and as she talked I asked a few questions. After a minute, then, or maybe only fifty seconds, she was through another prewriting stage and into the revision of her story. Unless I taped the conversation, though, there would be nothing observable about this prewriting either, even though it did occur in class. Her revision, when it was transcribed, was the simplest and most common kind: adding detail. It didn't even look like a revision, in that nothing on the page had been changed. But the whole piece was changed, lengthened, altered, refocused by the addition of the new material. It was an entirely legitimate revision.

And it is only the transcribing of the revision that can be seen.

Notice that the prewriting that brought that revision was done with me. Does that make it any more On Task than Lisa's first round, or than Allan's at his desk? No. It is only more observable: I could have recorded the conversation Lisa and I had, which I could not have done with Allan. That doesn't make it better. Those children had to do their writing in whatever ways it worked best for them. For each of them.

It sounds more efficient to put children in groups and tell them to all do the same thing at the same time, and then you know they've all got it and you can go on to the next thing and they'll get that, too, especially if you're really careful and separate the concept into teeny tiny steps and be sure they do everything in sequence.

When this is done in a factory, the products come out on time, built with nothing left out, and exactly alike. In addition, no one expects them to change, except perhaps to become a little less of whatever they are when they're new.

That's not what we want for humans, is it? That they be identical, immutable, unchanging, and deteriorate right from the start?

The Maine Department of Education, on a nationwide bandwagon, published a brochure in 1984 called *Increasing Educational Effectiveness*. One of its major recommendations for action was that local schools "institute precise instructional strategies" in order to improve schools. This idea of precision in teaching is scary to me. It implies a uniformity, an interchangeability of children's minds. The notion of precision suggests to me a bow-and-arrow and a target: the child's mind is the target; the teacher loads the arrow with a lesson, an objective, and lets the child have it, twang. In this image it is the aim and the bow-and-arrow that are important: the brochure's first recommendation is "to institute clearly defined learning goals," that is, to decide what gets loaded onto the arrow. The positioning of the target, that is to say the readiness of the child to receive that loaded arrow, that objective, seems to be of secondary importance in this metaphor.

The implication that teaching and learning can be precisely laid out, sequenced, and bullseyed into children I find hard to believe. Not that I have anything against sequence: I think Madeline Hunter is right when she says that any child can learn "the next thing to what they know," and that many problems have arisen because teachers — and departments of education — have arranged lists for learning with gaps and steps left out. I have found, however, that when children are learning to be writers and readers, sequence is hard to determine, and useless to copy from someone else's lists. *Precision,* and *clearly defined,* and even *goals* are not words that describe writing, not words that describe the combining and recombining of thought and language and transcription to create writing. Keeping these young writers On Task is even more impossible than the ordinary old-fashioned "nose to the grindstone," because of the nature of writing. Most of these same remarks can be made about reading: it has become more and more evident to writing teachers and to researchers that reading and writing are analogous to the point of being inversions of each other.

When children are hooked into Words, grindstones aren't necessary.

While I agree that laying out steps and listing sequences can occasionally be useful, the lists must not be cast in stone, and must wait upon the readiness of the child. Now lost in the mists, the idea behind all this curriculum development was perhaps the sensible one, that wherever the child can connect to the subject

matter, that's where the child should enter the lists. Somehow the lists have become the purpose, and we have become convinced that they are more important than the children themselves. During the Vietnam War, there was a particularly outraged public outcry about a village of noncombatants that had been totally destroyed by our bombs. The poor lieutenant who was on press duty that day had to defend the indefensible: he said, "We had to destroy the village in order to save it." Somehow we've lost the idea of waiting for the child to find or need the ladder of sequential learning. We set it in front of every child at a certain age and say "begin."

When connections and hooks work for a person of any age, the product is ownership, by that person of those events and data and understandings and emotions. In writing, this is easy to see, because a story written about her new shoes is going to be a lot more interesting for a young author to write than any topic I could possibly think up, and the ownership shines from every word.

To the question I often ask myself, "What's organic about social studies?" ownership is again the answer. Hands-on experiences are most suitable for young children in developmental terms, and my experience has convinced me that Piaget's concrete stage is a true description of the way children work. Ownership of a concept through concrete activity makes the connection necessary for the child to "learn" it. Of course, the logical corollary is that there should be much less theoretical stuff for the children in ages of three to eight. While they are Doing Words, children rediscover the language all the time. It can be the same for science, social studies, math, reading, public speaking, cabinetmaking, and anything else we try to subdivide ourselves into. Writing is, then, the paradigm for all the disciplines.

The grown-ups of Meg's and Allan's world have made the divisions, the boundaries of knowledge with names like "science," "math," "history," "grammar," "medicine," and so forth. These are utterly artificial, after all, when you think about it. Meg doesn't know that as she collects and compares and feels and describes her worms to and for herself she is doing science and math all at once, interwoven and edgeless. She doesn't know that she is an American sociological phenomenon, being a female child enjoying snakelike creatures. She's nowhere near those descriptors. She's still collecting data for herself. She is self-directed, as the jargon goes; self-motivated; childlike in her eagerness and singlemindedness.

No one told Meg to learn about worms. Equally importantly, no one (I hope) told her *how* to learn about worms. As soon as she begins to be told what and how to learn, she will stop being self-motivated, self-directed. She will stop being eager, too. She will no longer be childlike in her learning.

Wait until she is no longer a child, until the bulk of her initial assimilation period is over. Wait to direct her learning until she is well along in data collecting and in self-esteem. Probably she will continue to direct her own learning just fine. In the meantime, just as you have from her first day home from the hospital, put her environment in her path. Squeeze that funny terrycloth frog in her week-old face; hang the glinting chrome sailboat-mobile above the crib; invite your friends to hold her and feed her; sit on your hands while her daddy flies her around (before, not after a feeding); play your Beethoven or your Michael Jackson when you need to; let her decide whether she wants to sleep on her back or her tummy or her side; let her feel the cat. Be reasonable about it, don't overload her if you can help it (i.e., restrain the grandparents and restrict the television), and use common sense. She can decide how she sleeps, but not if she will; let her touch the cat as an infant, but don't let the cat touch her.

When she goes to school, if she's lucky, she will meet more elements of her world, more people, more possibilities for exploration and assimilation and imitation. If she's lucky, she will have teachers whose own priorities do not intrude upon her too obviously, and a school where it is recognized that during those first years most of what is mandated to be "covered" will come up naturally if the environment is open. Kids and curriculum will come out even in the long run.

By the time Meg is pushing nine, the intensity of her growth will have subsided, providing a welcome lull before the very different but equally intense time of puberty. So in third and fourth grades she will be ready to be excited all over again by the arrangement of the information she has been collecting all this time. "Look!" the teacher can say. "Look at all these words you have been using to tell how a thing looks and feels. These are called adjectives. In fact all of your language fits into a pattern called grammar — here is the pattern, see if you can fit it together." If the school hasn't killed Meg's natural curiosity and confidence, such an invitation will be fun, not a chore; new, not a repeat of stuff she was expected to grasp in the abstract since kindergarten.

Young children don't deal in abstractions very much, if at all. Piaget says they won't be able to think exclusively in abstractions until about age fifteen — I have no data on this point myself. The difference is just that, though: data. Preabstracting children collect and observe and make connections like mad, all day long and probably all night long in their dreams. But until they are six or seven or eight, they can seldom see the patterns of what they are collecting. They cannot at all see a pattern before they have data. Seeing the patterns into which their world may fall is the next mode of learning after observation and exploration. Observation and exploration may accompany abstraction; the other way around doesn't work. It would be like cooking the apples in the pie pan and then trying to put the crust under it. The example isn't exactly analogous, but the impossibility is.

What difference does it make? you may ask. If the children will eventually be told that all those words are adjectives, that all those animals are mammals, why not start out that way? Why not provide the grid-spaces and fill them right up? Why wait until they can see patterns? Think of the time and energy you would save the children!

This was what was wrong with the New Math, which had everyone on their ears some years ago. It seemed like an efficient idea to give children the reasons why numbers relate the way they do at the same time as they were learning to use numbers. More or less at the same time, transformational grammar hit the English books, trying to do the same thing. I found that very exciting, but the children I was teaching, and my own children who were trying to learn, did not. They weren't, in a word, ready.

We were trying to give the theories first to children who had no data. New Math was fascinating to me, as to many adults. (An equal number, of course, many, many parents, were terrified of it and resentful that they were made to look like they didn't know anything.) Fascinating, but just as frightening to me as math had always been. I felt for many years like a complete fraud teaching math, and I did it with workbooks because I knew I didn't understand it — I wasn't "a math person."

Then, about five years into my teaching career, I went to a math workshop and was given a bunch of chips and told to do a certain problem, 9 + 3 — I knew how to do that — and separate the answer into tens and ones by putting a blue chip in a column marked *tens* and two yellow chips in the column to the right of it marked *ones*. Then I was told to change to Base 6. I got to fiddle with those chips and the idea, and found that I had to use two blue chips and no yellow chips instead. I had never, ever understood the concept of bases in math before, and I remember clearly being baffled and frightened by it when it was first presented to me in high school. After playing with those chips for part of an hour, I connected to that concept and I understood it — two ways of saying the same thing. What that understanding has done for my self-esteem and my confidence in myself as a "math person" is remarkable: I now consider math my second-favorite thing to do with the children in my classes.

It is intriguing to me that I responded to the concrete manipulation of this concept, although I am older by far than the span of years Piaget labels as typical of the second stage of intellectual development. It could be that in math I never worked through the concrete, manipulative stage as a child, so that day of the workshop I really was six again. As a human who has lived longer than six years, I could deal with — that is, remember and parrot — the abstractions and theory of math, even New Math; but because I had never connected to them concretely I "didn't like math" all those years.

For the humans still in the data-collecting and discovery stage, it was not and is not at all an appropriate style of learning.

Efficient, yes. Like a factory, which is the model our schools are indeed now based on, instead of like a home where everything is mixed and jumbled; instead of like life. Of course it is easier to keep track of what and how the children are learning — or at least of what you think you are teaching — if there is no variation in the materials they are using or in the sequence of the skills they acquire. If each work paper is easily reduced to some numerical equivalent, and if anecdotes are not relevant, records can be flawlessly kept. Clipboards were invented for use in factories, I'm sure. A problem with this kind of teaching is that it requires nearly robotic children and teachers, and a nearly sterile classroom environment.

Another problem is that it doesn't seem to be working.

During the past few years there has been a cry for educational reform, following upon the realization that many of the children who are graduated from high school still can't do very basic kinds of academic stuff, like read and write and figure percents and find anything on a map. Fewer than half fall into this category, fewer than a fourth, probably, but enough to worry about even so. The numbers vary from state to state and from economic subculture to economic subculture, although I have heard that there is less variation than one would have expected.

Much more important features of the graduates of today, though, in my view, are that they are bored bored bored and that they have great difficulty doing any analytical thinking. Most of the young people I have known in the past twenty years since I was one have an attitude of entertain me, make me be interested in life, work, whatever. Some manifest this politely, some antisocially. It seems to me that these attitudes result from being told at the beginning of school that someone else had the agenda for their lives and learning; so why bother to think for yourself? Because these features don't lend themselves to numerical measurement, however, they are not at the hub of most of the reformers' tracts.

The reforms that have been proposed and shouted about range from extending the learning-in-school time from nine months to twelve, beginning children in school at three instead of six, and making big changes in the way teachers are trained and examined. All of these reforms, including the Maine one about "precise educational strategies," are really talking about redesigning the factory, not changing — re-forming, or re-formulating — its purpose.

Children are doing all this work before they come to school, connecting to the world they find themselves in, trying out its patterns and its goods, fitting into it. They do these things when they need to or when the environment is right, or sometimes both, and they are rewarded for this behavior. Even if three-year-old Tommy only hears from the others of his species a "That's nice, dear" when Mom looks at the pail of stones, he has his sense that this day of stone-finding fit his life that day, and his feeling of accomplishment as rewards. He also has the new knowledge or the connections or the insights he has come to in the course of this work he has been doing, a reward many adults long for in their own work.

And then he comes to school.

How many families have you known where a child is required to raise his or her hand before speaking?

How many households require children over the age of three to announce when they are going to the bathroom?

How many homes have twenty-five children all within eleven months of age of each other?

How often, at home, do loud bells change the activities of their children?

This going to school business causes major culture shock first of all! The required behaviors implied in these rhetorical questions are only a few of the overt ways school is different. Much worse is the insidious notion that play — the kind of work the children have been doing for five years — is only appropriate at certain limited times of the day in certain areas of the room or the grounds. "We come to school to work and play, good morning, good morning," runs a particularly vapid first grade song from a book of idiotic inventions called *Songs Children Will Like*. And since play is only for recess, the rest of the time is work. This kind of work — schoolwork, workbooks — is like nothing else the child has ever done. The play is not like anything else the child has done either — in crowds, and for exactly ten minutes at exactly the same time every day.

The child has been doing real work, self-directed, self-assessed, and self-assigned. Nowhere near enough of this kind of work exists in school. Too often, even if it does, it only comes after the child has proved someway to be able to handle it. Before you can read on your own, look at books and begin to make sense of them, you have to do that mysterious thing — learn to read. And you can almost never simply count stones, or compare leaves, unless it's math work, or science work, and everyone else is doing it too at the same time.

Books and pamphlets have sprouted from every state legislature and many foundations and assorted unlabeled citizens. Some of them are even written in English, as opposed to Education.

One of the most erudite of the lot is *The Paideia Proposal*, by Mortimer Adler. Its very erudition may be a major flaw, but its suggestions are intrinsically allied to the idea that the individual is the most important element in an individual's education. That may seem obvious, but it isn't true of education in America in general. As a society we have adopted for education the model of the factory. The assumption is that somebody else knows best what a child needs and wants to learn, and the easiest way to teach is by groups, in sequence, and with uniformity. We in school kind of hope that along with the mastery of the material the children will automatically learn to (1) behave and (2) think.

Thinking. Thinking is what separates humans from other animal species. We have these big brains so that we can remember, compare, and analyze what happens in life and alter it. A long time ago there was an educational system built on a very different model from the factory model, wherein the teacher had failed if the student did not become different from all the others. The student was led and followed through all the byways of his own mind until he reached the outer edges of his own understanding. I use the *he* here deliberately, because in the culture I speak of there was no consideration given to educating females in this way, if at all, and that was one of many reasons this culture didn't last. But the Socratic dialectical inquiry method of questioning is a sound one if the underlying principle of the culture is that the individual is central and unique. Much of what the Greeks put together about the world and our place in it remains fundamental to our understandings 2,500 years later.

The industrial revolution changed our culture radically, and not least in that it paradoxically changed our concept of the individual. Before the weaving machines were invented, things were done by hand and had individuality, but they took so long that an individual's life was almost indistinguishable. As a result of having all those weaving machines, the products are indistinguishable (and often undistinguished as well) but the individual has more time to find out who he or she is. As a result of the industrial revolution, then, we have an immense amount of leisure time; but instead of using it for individual expansion we have allowed ourselves to be factory-served by our schools and, lately, by the television.

The Paideia Proposal has, underlying it, the idea of the worth of the individual and each has a potential that is different from everybody else's potential. These potentials might be exactly the same. Just so does almost every child write a snow story in first grade, and all envelopes of kindergarten Words have Mama and the dog's name in them. I can predict that most children will get certain Words during Movements I and II, and may look just the same when they are all done, but each one did it separately. Each one grew in his own way; each one developed through her own stuff. It can be generalized about afterward, but not prearranged.

The same is true of reading. Empirically I have known that even though I may hear the same page of the same book read to me by five different beginning readers perhaps on the same day, to have them discover that vocabulary and that story as a group would deny each one the individual discovery of it, and the connecting to his or her own soul. Another of the best of these change-education documents is called *Becoming a Nation of Readers,* and it suggests strongly that children be allowed to do reading that is interesting to them. Children should be allowed to connect themselves to what they are reading, too.

Patricia MacLachlan, who writes literature for children, says that is how she starts writing for them. "What I always need is a connection, between the present and the past. There are bits of children in every child, and I begin by making connections." Readers will, too.

It's how each person connects, comfortably, and at the same time with a certain amount of tension, to the rest of us and to the universe and to the world and the country and the school and the family and to the house, not to mention the bars of the crib and the skin of the mother, that is the important thing. It needs to be said again and again and again. Each person is unique. "This above all," said the most amazing mind of our language, "to thine own self be true."

The epigraph at the beginning of this chapter, about the children Charles Wallace sees in the town ruled by Evil, is not about the lack of freedom. Those children are a paraphrase of factories, an exemplar for interchangeability and the elimination of the individual. I am reminded, too, of Arthur's visit to the ants in T. H. White's *The Once and Future King,* which White wrote as a paraphrase of Orwell. It is the implied interchangeability of minds that is wrong with the factory model of school. We really must be on guard against our own Orwellian instincts all the time. None of those ants was able to think.

Children don't know how to think nowadays, we say to each other. "My Sara loved to experiment with words when she was in preschool," a woman I met on a plane told me, "but now she's afraid to write. She thinks she'll get it wrong because her teacher has marked her school writing so much for errors in grammar and spelling, so she never writes at all unless she has an assignment." Second grader, this Sara was. The seventh grade English teacher asked the class to read some Greek myths, for discussion and as a writing model, and brought a map of Greece to the classroom to provide some historical and geographical background.

"What's that map doing here, Mrs. S.?" they asked her. "This isn't social studies class."

If we don't have an informed electorate, say the statesmen, how can democracy as we know it — or think we know it — continue? In a 1983 speech at Vassar College Meryl Streep said that when journalists from the United States and journalists from Europe interview her, their questions are always the same except that the European journalists always ask her opinion on world events and political issues of the moment. After they ask, she says, "How do you manage to combine family and career? and How does your husband handle your success? and What is your real hair color? there would inevitably be a category of questions on the state of the world. It was just assumed that as a member of the human race I had one or two thoughts on the subject. This from . . . everybody but the home team." The American journalists assume that because she is a woman and because she is not in the business of government or politics, she knows nothing and cares less about the world.

In schools on the factory model, how we feel about what we know and what we can do is not of the first importance. If we come to expect someone else to decide what's important for us to know, come early to expect that the work of school will be largely irrelevant to where our own interests lie, we will not become thinking, synthesizing, eureka-ing, caring adult citizens. Leave aside democracy, I say sweepingly. I wonder if humanity can possibly survive the process we call education in America.

Chapter 13

Writing Past First Grade, Or, How To Catch Up

> To every man, in his acquaintance with a new art, there comes a moment when that which before was meaningless first lifts, as it were, one corner of the curtain that hides its mystery, and reveals, in a burst of delight which later and fuller understanding can hardly ever equal, one glimpse of the indefinite possibilities within.
>
> — C. S. Lewis

IT IS MY FIRM BELIEF that children who have been raised on organic writing, so to speak, that is Doing Words from kindergarten, rarely need any help with prewriting in the upper grades. They will still need modeling of new genres and new revision and editing methods, but they seem to have enough that they want to write about to never lack for a topic. If writing is begun in second or third grade, however, some prewriting strategies are helpful. Here is one way you might begin second or third graders on the writing process if they've never done it.

The easiest way to start is to give each child a writing book, a dictionary of their own, and ask them to think about five things or adventures or ideas that interest them. Have them write these on the inside cover of their writing books. You do it, too, for yourself, in your writing book. These entries can be single words, or phrases, or whole sentences: *eagles*; *when me and Ben went fishing*; *The Terrible Green Monster.* Then set a timer and ask them to write for six or seven minutes, and you do it too. Take some time to share a little, a few writers, every day. You share too.

Do this for a few days, just to get wet feet. Be relaxed. Then you can begin a more formal and systematic introduction of the writing process, perhaps with a prewriting activity.

The prewriting strategy that children use with great success and glee is webbing, also known as clustering. It's fun. All you need is one word. This must be modeled several times, but every time will be a lot of fun, and it will teach the children not to be afraid of thinking.

I put my word in a circle in the middle of the chalkboard and make several lines out from the circle, like rays. I put circles at the ends of the rays. The day I did this with the second grade my word was *salamander.*

"I want to write about salamanders but I don't know what to say," I told them. "I need some other words and ideas in these other circles. I can put one in, and then maybe you can help me. I like spotted salamanders best." I wrote *spotted* in one of the circles.

The suggestions came thick and fast. "They live under rotting logs." "Salamanders hatch from eggs." "Toads eat them." "Newts are red." "Salamanders are brown and live in the water."

I wrote *rotting logs, eggs, toads eat, newts, live in water* in the other circles. From the *newts* circle I drew another ray outward and put *red* in a circle at the end of it. I made another ray from the center next to the *newts* ray and put *brown* at the end of it. Then I drew a line between those two and the one that said *spotted.*

"We know there are lots of colors, don't we?" I said, when there was finally a lull. "Sometimes it's fun to connect the parts of the web that seem to go together, like I just did with these three," I told them, tracing the lines I'd just put between the colors. "What else can we put here about salamanders?"

After ten minutes we had thirty-two words in this webbing. We were all impressed. "Now take a clean piece of paper from your own writing folder," I directed them, "and choose a word to put in the middle of your web for today." I watched, moving around the room now, while they did this. "What's your word, Tim?" One by one I asked them to read their words to the group. "Now go ahead, make some lines and circles and fill them up!" To the question, "How many lines?" I usually answer, "How old are you?" (It might be a good idea to remind them that there were more minds working on the *salamander* web, so perhaps they won't get thirty-two, in case someone is anxious; or you might not say that until anxiety has reared its ugly head.) After ten minutes the webs were counted, to see who had the most.

This technique is for them to use. After they feel comfortable with the procedure, they can say to themselves, in the middle of a piece, too, "I think I need to web this for some more ideas," and go right ahead and do it. During the first modeling, they can see right away that there are no right or wrong answers, and the teacher can see that they know how to do this webbing. She needs to be sure that they can repeat the activity another time, on their own.

If I had time, or if the teacher wanted to do it, the next step would be to put all those circled words into sentences in a first draft. It will be choppy writing, probably, but it will be down on the paper and the writer can go on with it from there. Webbing is useful as prewriting in two ways: to get ideas out of the child's head about the topic he has put into the center; or, to bring to the front of his mind something utterly unrelated to write about. When a child says, "Now I know what I want. I'm not going to write about this webbing," you know you've unlocked even more than you were hoping for. It's a good moment.

Another way to start writing with older children is to go right through the process.

On the first day of school, model a prewriting strategy on the board, like the webbing I did with the second grade. Take about ten or fifteen minutes to do this. Talk about why you are doing it: to help find lots of things to say about the topic you have chosen.

Then have each child choose a topic of his own and put it in the center of his paper and web it. Don't start until everyone has the center word. Let them take about ten minutes to do this, and you be walking around to check. Ask, then, if anyone would like to read all the ones he's thought of. Usually you can find one who will share, even in fifth grade, and then another two or three will want to. This reinforces the idea that anything is acceptable as a topic, that there is no one right way to do this.

This reinforcement is important. The older the child gets without doing much writing of his own in school, the more afraid of it and reluctant to do it he becomes. That is a fact. If organic writing has never been done and the child has been in school for three years, he thinks, rightly, that he knows about school: it's a place where he'll be told what to do. Writing doesn't do that. Writing he has to do from himself. That can be scary.

The webbing exercise has taken about thirty minutes. That's probably enough for the first day. Have the children save the webs in their writing books or folders, and you copy the one you did on the board. You'll use it tomorrow.

After prewriting, it is time to do a little drafting. On the second day, model writing a draft from your web. It will be clearer if you have copied your web onto a large sheet of paper, to tape up near the chalkboard space you will write on. They will feel comfortable with its familiarity, too. Write your title first. Titles often make tentative writers feel better.

Salamanders

"I think I'll write about the colors first, since I have several," I said to the class. "Can someone read the colors I have for salamanders in my web?"

Timmy C. read out, looking, "Spotted. Red. Brown."

"Yes," I said. "Now I could write *some salamanders are red, some salamanders are brown, some salamanders are spotted.* Would that be a good sentence?" I looked for a hand. "Crystal?"

"Combine them together," said Crystal. "*Salamanders are red and brown and spotted.*"

"Good idea," I said. I wrote that down under my title. "You know what? I want to tell what color the spotted ones are, too, even though that's not in my web. Can I put that in here too?" I asked them.

"Sure," said Jeremy. "You can put in anything you want as long as it's about salamanders, can't you? I caught a spotted salamander last year."

I wrote, *Spotted salamanders are black with yellow spots. I like them best. I wish I could catch one.*

"Now what?"

"Write about where they live, you know, in water," said Josh.

"But they don't live in water, they live on land, under rotting logs, remember?" argued Wendell. "That's where I catch them. I've never seen a salamander in the water."

"What do you call an animal that lives part of its life in the water and part of its life on land?" I asked. Silence. Then Josh smacked both hands down on his desktop.

"Amphibian!" he shouted, as one might say "Eureka!"

"Right," I said. "How about this?" I wrote, *Salamanders are amphibians. They live in the water and they live under rotting logs on land.*

The story was plainly growing before our eyes. After we worked through one more circle, I recapitulated.

"What are we doing?"

"Making up sentences about the salamanders," said Erinn.

"We used each of those words in the web in a sentence," said Jeremy. "And you put some other stuff in there too."

"And what have we got now?" I asked.

"A story about salamanders," said Timmy C. impatiently.

"We have a beginning of a first draft of a story about salamanders. Right. Now I want you to do the same thing with the web you made yesterday. Get out a new sheet of paper, put your web in front of you, and write sentences for your circles. I'm going to finish mine while you do that." I sat down and copied the sentences we'd made, and wrote some for the remaining circles. Then I began to circulate around the room, watching.

It is least threatening for the children to simply make up a sentence for each of the spokes in the web they have made. After ten or fifteen minutes of writing, ask for some stories to be shared. Again, the children will see the variety of topics and sentences and know that there is no right or wrong. They will be fascinated to hear each others' works.

The next day, write yours up and talk about how to revise it. Simply talk them through your thinking as you look at your story. "I want to say some more about how they look," you might say. "I'm going to add that they are cold to touch unless they're in the sun, and then they're hot." You would write in the new stuff. "And I want to add that they have neat names. There are newts and there are efts." Write more sentences onto the draft. "And I think I'll put in about what I'd do if I caught one." Write *if I caught one* onto the story.

"There," you could say. "Now I've started to revise my draft. I'll write a little more now about putting him in a terrarium and stuff, and you begin to revise yours by adding more to it just like I did. I'll be coming around to watch and help in a few minutes." Then sit down and write.

Don't do too much revising on your own in front of the class — maybe five or so minutes, two or three sentences. You don't want them to get discouraged. Let them write for fifteen minutes, circulating after you've written a little, and then have a sharing time again.

Sharing is very important. They get the most ideas from each other.

Writing yourself is important in several ways. It is a trick a teacher can use to make writing much less threatening. It shows that writing is very important, if the teacher is going to do it too. And, since their teacher is the mystery of their lives, they are enchanted to have glimpses into her through what she writes. (They are always astounded to see me in another place, like the supermarket. They don't believe their eyes: I don't *belong* there, you see.) I find, too, that I can hear a pin drop while I'm writing myself.

The next day after the revising, the fourth day, choose three children who won't mind and model a group conference in front of the class. Use the procedure described in Chapter 8:

The child reads the piece.
Each listener says what he liked about it, specifically.
Each listener gives a suggestion to the writer of something to add or change or clarify.
The writer asks the group for any specific help he needs.

Go through this routine at least twice, four days of thirty minutes each. Then your writing lab will have some form, and you can begin operating without the models. Once every couple of weeks or so you can introduce something new the same way: it might be spiderlegs, or interviewing, or poetry, or outlining for reports, or the form for a book report, or peer conferences, or any number of editing strategies, or how to keep an idea book.

Notice that as I model the steps of the process I name them, casually refer to them by name as we go along. Children like to know the names of things. Knowing the words *prewriting, draft, revision* and using them makes them feel that they are in charge of the process. That's exactly what you want them to feel.

After the children know how the process works, they may not remember that teachers have always told them what to write. You can always hope that they work themselves naturally off what Donald Graves calls writers' welfare. Most of them will. One of the things you're trying to teach through writing is responsibility.

Your writing time, then, will be similar to the routine described in Chapter 8. For the first few minutes you go around to each child with a checklist to find out what he or she is writing, where she is in the process, and if she needs a conference with you soon, either alone or in a group. Note all this down.

Then sit down and write yourself for at least five minutes.

Next, go to your conference table or corner and call the children who are having a group conference that day. You will have determined this through the check you just made, coupled with information from the day before. Have your conference, which under no circumstances should last more than twenty minutes: fifteen is much better.

Then you have time for an editing conference or for an individual revision conference, neither of which should last more than five minutes.

A child who came right in and sat right down and began writing has now had thirty minutes of uninterrupted writing time. That's a lot. For the next fifteen minutes, if you have them, have some stories shared — don't forget to share yours too — or do a modeling lesson, or, if you have time, both.

Then go to recess. You've all earned it.

Another way to begin a year with children who have never written before is with a rap-session kind of conference. On the first day, gather four or five children together and just talk. They will talk, almost show-and-tell talk, and you can say, "Gee, that sounds exciting. You could write about that." After ten minutes, after all have talked, send them back to their seats to "write it just like you told it to me." Then do the rest of the children in similar groups until they've all gotten an idea.

On the second day, call each child for an individual conference. "What are you writing about? What ideas do you still have to add? Where are you going with your piece?" They are eager to share with you what they've written, and you can make sure everyone is moving. They, on the other hand, learn that whatever they've written is okay, and they can go do some more. About two minutes each is the maximum necessary for this.

On the third day, call four for a group conference, and show them how to be helpful to each other, giving specific suggestions. The others can be writing, or if they finish they can read.

On the fourth day, take ten minutes for a skills lesson on an editing point — capitals, punctuation, paragraphing — before having a group conference and others writing.

After about three weeks of this pattern, the time will feel smooth to you, and to the children. They may begin to object to having their time for writing cut into by a skills lesson!

Next you will have to begin modeling revision strategies. The ways to insert material described in Chapter 11 are not, strictly speaking, revision strategies. They show how additional information and reorganized material may be incorporated into a draft, not how to help or lead children to formulate or discover those changes and additions.

The primary path to revision is talk. As Sylvia Ashton-Warner says, "It is the conversation that has to be got." In these Movements of the writing process, the conference is the arena for most of the talking and the source of most of the revision. You model group conference procedure so that the children can use it when they talk to themselves and each other as well. Just so, you model other ways for them to make changes or additions to their pieces so that they can do these things by themselves, too, taking full responsibility as writers.

One of the most fun and productive ways children can "talk to themselves" is a revision tactic using the five senses. I do it first with and for the whole class, modeling it as many times as they seem to need, so any one of them can use it on their own. It's most useful with a piece whose outline or plot is okay but whose bones are bare. When I model this, I use chalk and an empty chalkboard. An overhead or a big chart probably works as well.

A big spider named Harriet lives in my porch, I began on the second grade's chalkboard one day. Various voices were reading this quietly as I write. *This morning when I went out she came down from the rafters. She walked over my foot. I didn't know she was there. I yelled.*

Josh, a typically bloodthirsty eight-year-old, said, "Oboy. And then you stomped on it. Squissshh!"

"Yukk, Josh," squealed Jessica P. and Erinn together.

"Hold it," I said. "You're right, I want you to help me revise this, but first we need it read." I looked around the room, murmuring, "Who looks like a good reader?" All hands went up, waving madly. "Can you read this beginning to us, please Clark?"

Clark read the whole thing.

"Do you like this story?" I asked. "What do you think, Jeremy?" I knew Jeremy wouldn't be caught dead writing such a boring story.

"It's okay," said Jeremy, wanting to be polite. "There's not much in it, though."

I looked at the board, nodding. "Yeah, it's pretty boring this way. I want to add some details to this that will use my five senses." I held up one hand's fingers. "What did I see," I ticked off one finger, "smell," I ticked off another. "What else?" Several hands went up, I called on three more, ticking off my fingers, and we had the list of five. From this point on I called on hands.

"Now," I said. "*A big spider named Harriet lives in my porch*. What can I add to that sentence that I could see? Jeannie?"

"What color is the spider, you could see that," said Jeannie.

"Okay," I said. "What color is this spider?" Several suggestions were made, and the consensus was gray, so I wrote *gray* with a caret above the first line. "What else? Mick?"

"Does she live in the porch, like in the wood? Where is her web?"

"Good question. Her web is way up above the rafters, on the wall. She usually sits up there. How can I put that in?"

Mick answered first. "Put *way up on the wall* next to *lives*." I did that. "That's something you can see too," he said.

"What can I add to the next sentence? What can I say about *this morning*? Could I smell something? Feel something?"

After some discussion I added *it smelled like spring* after *out* and *the porch floor felt slippery with the dew* as another sentence and *silently* after *down*.

"How did you know she walked on your foot?" asked Jeremy, reading ahead. "Did it tickle?"

"I bet that felt gross," said Crystal, shivering.

"Ooh, do that again, Crystal," I said. I shivered with her. "Can I put that in?"

"*She walked over my foot and her legs tickled. It made me shiver all over,*" dictated Crystal. I wrote that on the board.

"Now what?" I asked.

"I don't think you can say that next part," said Josh. "It doesn't make any sense. *I didn't know she was there.* You did too know, she just walked on your foot."

"That's right, I did. Shall I take that sentence out or move it somewhere?" I asked the group.

"Take it out," said the majority. "It doesn't tell any senses, anyway," added Jessica P.

"Okay. *I yelled,*" I read. "What shall I do with that? Is one of the five senses in that sentence?"

We got bogged down here for a minute or two while they tried to decide what I should have yelled. Finally I cut off the discussion by taking one of the suggestions and writing it into the story. Then I asked again for a reader, and Wendell read out the new version.

> "A big gray spider named Harriet lives way up on the wall of my porch. This morning when I went out it smelled like spring. The porch floor felt slippery from the dew. She came down silently from the rafters. She walked over my foot and her legs tickled. It made me shiver all over. I yelled, 'Get out of here, gross gross gross!'"

"What do you think, Second Grade? Is this better now?" I asked, grinning. They agreed, with matching grins, except for Josh, who said again he thought I should squish it. I ignored this suggestion.

"Okay, now I'm going to read it and you stop me when we get to something I could see." I read, they yelled *stop,* and I circled *big, gray, way up, porch, porch floor.* Then I read it again and underlined the words and phrases they stopped me for hearing: *silently, yelled.* Then we went through it again for touch and smell.

"There isn't any tasting in this story," pointed out Jeannie accusingly.

"Who'd want to taste a spider?" said Crystal.

"There isn't anything to taste," said Josh.

"Jeannie's right," I said, "but I have to go now and I think we made it a lot better with just four senses. Thank you."

Another revising activity that is also a prewriting strategy I call the 5*W*s because it asks who what where when why. Once again, I model the activity so that the children can use it independently when they get stuck. All you need for this one is a single word. I have heard many second graders say "I want to write about my" rabbit or Grammy or whatever "but I don't know what to write."

"I want to write about a dragon," I said when I visited these second graders on another day, standing by their chalkboard with my chalk at the ready. "But I don't know what I want to say." I wrote the five *W* words on the board, and the word *dragon* at the top like a title.

"Who is the dragon?" I asked. "Does anyone have an idea?"

"Yeahhh," said Jeremy in a Fonz voice. "He's a mean and fierce dragon who eats teachers!"

Everyone cracked up, including me and the teacher at her desk. I turned shakily back to the board and wrote, *This is a mean and fierce dragon who eats teachers,* and crossed out *who.*

"Thanks, Jeremy," I said. "Now, we know what he eats: What else does he do? What happens?"

A little thinking silence. "One of the teachers fights him?" suggested Erinn tentatively. "Maybe Mrs. P. can teach him to be nice," chimed in Cherry.

I wrote those ideas down, and crossed out *what.*

"Where are they?"

"The dragon lives in a mountain," said Josh, leaning across his desk to be sure I heard him. "It's dark and scary and black in there."

"Okay," I said, writing *He lives in a dark and black and scary cave.* "Any other *wheres*?"

"Sometimes he comes to school," said Cherry, still on her own track.

"Good," I said, writing *school.* "*Sometimes* sounds like *when* to me. When does this happen?"

Several suggestions are raised for *when,* and also for *why.*

"Why does he eat teachers?" Mrs. P. wanted to know. "Are teachers the best-tasting things he knows about?" she teased.

That stopped Jeremy. I leaped into the pause.

"Thanks for helping me with my dragon story," I told them. "When you can't think of what to write, try answering those Ws."

After this is modeled a couple of times the children can use it when they get started on a piece that doesn't have much in it, that's "boring" like this story was at first. You can just say, "Try putting some senses in it," and they can go on by themselves.

It is a lot of fun to model an activity like this, but don't enjoy it so much you forget the point: what you are after is for children to be able to make meaningful revisions without you, to use strategies like these by themselves. I don't mean to suggest that you must refuse to model it again if you think some of the children didn't "get" it; I only want to reemphasize that making children dependent on you is not the aim of a writing program. To be a teacher in a classroom of children who depend on you to direct all their revision and, in reality, all their thinking may sound like a powerful position, but such a teacher is really power-less. It can't be done, there isn't time, and you will all have to give up independence and growth in such a classroom. By doing writing with young children we are allowing, encouraging, enabling them to find and use their own power, for their own best growth. The less the teacher controls children, the more they will grow in self-esteem and in writing ability. You are working to make them ever more independent.

I have purposefully given several different ways to begin a writing program if you don't begin by Doing Words in kindergarten, just to show that there isn't one way. There are as many ways to implement writing in classrooms as there are teachers, and there are as many ways for children to become writers in school as there are classrooms.

There are, though, two irreducible foundation-stone rules for a writing program, I believe. Consider that this paragraph is written in neon ink:

Children's writing comes from the children themselves, or it has no power; and *The teacher must feel comfortable with the way writing goes in her classroom, or it won't work.*

All that I have written in this book can be reduced to these two rules.

Chapter 14

"Tomorrow Is Thanksgiving," Or, Twenty-seven Minds with But a Single Thought

> To do the thing properly, with any hope of ending up with a genuine duplicate of a single person, you really have no choice. You must clone the world, no less.
>
> I have an alternative suggestion, if you're looking for a way out. Set cloning aside, and don't try it. Instead, go in the other direction. Look for ways to get mutations more quickly, new variety, different songs. Fiddle around, if you must fiddle, but never with ways to keep things the same, no matter who, not even yourself. Heaven, somewhere ahead, has got to be a change.
>
> — Lewis Thomas

YESTERDAY was December first, and all of a sudden it's Christmas.

Christmas is just around the corner, wrote Hal quaintly. I wonder if it's his mother or his grandmother who says that. It is still a magic time for the sixes of our world: there is nothing trite at all about Christmas from their point of view. As far as Hal is concerned no one else — except his mother (or grandmother) — ever said Christmas was just around the corner. He was giggling while he wrote it, and he chuckled as he read it to me.

"That means it's coming up," he explained to me concisely. "That's just a 'spression, you know, there really isn't a corner to come around." I told him I was glad he'd noticed it was an odd thing to say. Why did English do that?

Hal twirled his writing book in the air thoughtfully. "Maybe because *Christmas* and *corner* both begin the same way? I don't know. Why do they say that?"

"I don't know either. I think it's fun to think about, though. Do you want to make up a reason and write about it?"

He shook his head. "That's okay, Teacher, I know what I want next." Hal went back to his own desk to write some more about Christmas, about his aunt and uncle and cousins who were going to spend it with him and his brothers.

For some, the level of surprise about the language or excitement about the holiday is much more subdued. Audrey wrote:

> my Grammy is getting me a Smurfette for Christmas. And a snomobile suit. and new boots.

Audrey is a placid child whose emotions, if she has any, rarely show. She is well taken care of, it would seem; every wish anticipated, at least by Grammy.

"What are you going to get Grammy?" I asked, after we had discussed beginning new parts of the story with capital letters. Audrey gave me an expressionless look in reply. Perhaps the notion of a gift *for* Grammy was a wholly new idea. I was about to rush into another question when Audrey opened her mouth.

"Mama will buy her something from me," she answered softly.

Oh. Too bad.

December ninth, Thursday. Last night the wonderful television networks in their infinite wisdom played, back to back starting at eight, "Rudolph the Red-Nosed Reindeer" and "A Charlie Brown Christmas." No child in the entire state went to bed before nine o'clock.

So, today is a lethargic day in first grade. As it happened I didn't watch television last night, so I got my first clue from Shawn, who came up to me with his dictionary open to *W* and asked for *watched.*

"What did you watch?" I asked him, as I underlined *watched* on his *W* page.

"Rudolph."

"Did you like it?"

A gleaming nod with shining eyes answered this silly question.

"What time did you get to bed?" A short stare — Shawn does a brief inward stare before most of his communications. I think it's because he's the youngest of a lively bunch and he's learned to wait for their attention. Then he shrugged. I should've expected that: first graders very seldom look at clocks, although I am doing my best to teach them to tell time.

"Do you know what you're going to write?" I asked next, giving up on foolish questions. "Can you do *Rudolph* by yourself?"

The stare again, and a decisive nod answers me. "I'm going to copy it from the book," he told me, waving toward the shelf where the Christmas books were set out.

"Good idea, Shawn!" I exclaimed. Good for him. It's so nice when a child actually uses the print environment of the classroom.

Shawn's story, when completed, was much less interesting to me than his decision to copy the title. It was perfectly fine to him.

> I watched Rudolph the Red-Nosed Reindeer last night. My brothers watched it too. My brothers liked it. My mother liked it too.

Tiredness takes each child differently. Shawn's story was boring; Sam's printing fell apart today.

"Rudolph the Red-Nosed Reindeer" happens every year. Once a few years ago one of the kindergarten children wanted *Rudolph* for his Word. It was Mickey, who was adult to the point of seeming gifted, who very politely did exactly as he pleased in school. It was impossible to confuse Mickey with the facts, his mind was thoroughly made up. He didn't change much, gradually settling into the "capable" rather than the "gifted" category as he went up through second grade. Then he moved, and we heard he was at a parochial school instead, where I have no doubt he is blithely directing the nuns.

Mickey wanted *Rudolph* after the television show that year. His teacher printed it for him on a card.

"Excuse me," he said when she finished printing. "I think you've made a mistake here on my Word."

"Oh?" she inquired, interested. "What seems to be wrong with it?"

"You see," he said gently, "here at the end. You put a *P* and *H*. I wanted *Rud Off,*" he sounded for her carefully. "I know *off* is *o-f-f,*" he said. "You've made a mistake. This should be *R-u-d-o-f-f.*"

And no amount of explanation that *PH* says *F,* no reminders about *phone,* which he knew, would shake Mickey that day. Finally he smiled a sweet pitying smile, took *Rudolph,* and went away. Later his teacher found his Word copied neatly on the chalkboard several times, spelled the right way: *Rudoff.*

Good for Mickey, too. He was using the data he had. There is very little that is logical about English spelling, and names are probably the worst. Now that I think of it, why does Mickey get both a *C* and a *K* in his name? Surely the sound of one should be sufficient.

I have said several times that I model the responses I want children to learn to make to their own and others' writing. In conference I validate their reactions to their own and other people's images, as with Rob and Jason. I do not, ever, give them my own or any other person's images and say, Use this. Therefore, their personalities are much more whole and their minds are much cleaner in writing time than from that other source of images in their lives — television.

I'm going to make an unabashed plea here about television. If anyone who arranges for, or advertises on, television should happen to heed this plea, so much the better. This plea is directed, however, to parents and to other, as the expression now goes, child care givers.

There are so many things to say about television, and most of them have been said before. The main thing I want to say is that it may not make as much difference what is watched — that is perhaps a surprise, and I may take it back in a page or two — as how it is watched.

It's really too bad that there aren't slot machines for quarters in all television sets, just as there used to be in England for hot water heaters. If there were still slots for shillings on the hot water heaters of the Western world, perhaps the energy crisis would not have got so far out of hand either. It's hard to recognize when progress isn't really.

If there were some system whereby each television program that was watched was paid for on the spot, there would be a great deal more selectivity among the watchers. It seems unlikely that television sets would be left on in empty houses, or on in the living room when everyone is in the kitchen or in the bathtub. People who come home from work might be less likely to plunk down in front of it and go to sleep instantly. Those people might not then have to go to chiropractors so often because their backs have been squinched around in the chair for several hours; and they might not have to take so many sleeping pills, either, because they can't get to sleep when they finally do go to bed.

An even greater benefit — or at least change — that would occur if television watching were more selective among us is that the people who sit together in the living room of an evening to watch it, or who lie together in their bedroom later at night to watch it, would have to spend some of that time making conversation instead. It is a lost art, conversation; and lest anyone feel that to call it an art is to automatically exclude great numbers of people from being able to practice it, let me add that it is also a great sport. But the most important thing about conversation is that it allows you to show and tell another person who and what you are, and allows you to hear who and what another person is. If the other person is one you are presently sharing your house and life with, this can only be a beneficial thing.

Conversation is a lost art because no one practices it anymore. Whole days can go by when all you have to say is Yes, No,

Really, I mean, like, you know, and occasionally, Neato (or the current equivalent). Somehow we've allowed ourselves to invest those empty words with the power of communicating. It's harder to communicate this way over the phone, I grant you, because a lot of body language is used with these words, but it's being done.

Except that what is being done is not communication, by any wild stretch of the imagination. What's going on is interpretation. The listener reads into these words whatever he or she wants to "hear," and that will happen with all parties to the "conversation." This practice is sad because it's isolating the talkers; it's scary because it is atrophying the language.

It isn't surprising, though. Everyone under the age of forty-five has had the television set, especially its situation comedy shows, as a model for conversation and communication between humans since they were able to notice. I think the ubiquity of television has grown in those forty-five years, so that for today's children it is The model. If parents were talking to each other, communicating, and brothers and sisters had learned how to do that a little, we had that model, too, but it rarely had the power the television had, or the number of minutes per day that the television grew to have.

When television first came into people's lives, it was a wonder. The power of the wonder of it is hard to estimate, but it is related to the power of seeing Santa at Christmas in the mall when you're four. Pretty powerful. Then, too, at the beginning there was quite a lot of "good" dramatic production being aired; most of the trashy shows, and in the 1950s trashy meant merely silly, were for the kids, and the kids were only watching between five and seven P.M. The kids didn't watch the news. They were already in bed, or on the way, or being read aloud to. This is no longer true.

Of course all these early images and people were removed from reality to some extent by being in black and white. I would say that probably the power of the early television, the wonder of it, was almost balanced out by that attribute. Now, of course, it is all in too-glorious color, too-real reality.

Television has power over the written word. I have always refused to watch the television version of *Charlotte's Web* or the Tolkien books, because I want to keep my own images of those very meaningful stories. Once a child has seen someone else's images, a book has lost a lot of its power to spark an imaginative response. A picture book is a picture book: Curious George can't come any other way, Babar is Babar in everyone's mind, Max and the Wild Things look the same to everyone. But Judy Blume's Margaret, Harriet the Spy, Johnny Tremain, and even Frank and Joe Hardy look different inside my head from the way they look in yours. In combination with our absorption of the text, we create images of these characters. When someone else creates these images for us, our integration with the story, with the written word, is diminished.

Television also has power over the spoken word. Particularly subtle is the power of the situation comedy, whether for adults or for children. (It's important to remember that all television shows are for children, in the long run. Sooner or later they'll see nearly everything, even in unusually strict households. They can always go to someone else's house, for one thing; and now that the VCR is a household item, there's no such thing as "I missed that show.") The people talking in the film on the box are just as real as members of the household with whom a child lives. Conversation, on television, is a special kind. Even on the best of the television series, in which list I put "M.A.S.H." and "The Cosby Show," there is rarely an extended interchange between two people. Most of the time, one person sets up another person, the second person responds, and the first one zings in a one liner, either terse or hilarious, which brings out the canned laughter or the mood music or even the credits, and that's it until the next snippet of "conversation," which will probably be between two other people, certainly on a different topic. "Hill Street Blues," which I also love, is madly guilty of this hopscotching. The dramas on public television usually are guilty of the same things, except that the canned laughter is so blessedly absent: but many many fewer people watch public television. Besides, it rarely presents the same kind of "situation" on a continuing series that the Jeffersons or the Punky Brewster gang or the Archie Bunkers have presented: folks just like us.

The naggling thing is, if these are supposed to be people just like us, why can't I talk that well? I don't make an unseen million people laugh when I snap back to my husband, or wife, or teen-ager, or mother. And besides, the person at my house that I talk that way to doesn't seem to like it.

All of this contributes to the perception by the watcher of television that: (1) he isn't somehow as good as he should be; (2) nobody at home appreciates him; and (3) the purpose of talk is to make a hit, a point, a snappy remark at someone else's expense. No suggestion, or rarely, that talking to someone is to find out about him; not even a whisper that talking to someone is to find out about yourself.

Would you ever make to any of your friends and relations some of the remarks that go by on television routinely and are considered funny by the laugh-making machines? I used to catch my breath four or five times in each episode of "Archie Bunker," and "The Golden Girls" aren't much better. It is irrelevant to say that these are adult shows. In the first place, many children watch adult shows; in the second place, the adult shows have an insidious reincarnation in the four to six P.M. slot, opposite Big Bird (who has problems of her own), and thereby become kid shows. The point is not only, however, that kids hear this talk. The grown-ups hear it and therefore begin to allow it and even, occasionally, to imitate it in their own conversations — such as they are — within their own circles, modeling for their children.

Conversation on television as a model for the behavior of the watcher of any age, then, is very subtle. As an intellectual model, it is terrible. Shut off the picture anytime, and you will very likely have no clue about the content or the story line of the show. When you read Shakespeare, who after all wrote drama, aloud, you know exactly what is happening and what is going on because the text gives clues and definitions and introductions as it goes along. This is not true of television drama today (if ever).

Conversation on television has to be fast, too. Is this because the pace of life is quicker these days, or why is it?

Impatience with words, with using whole sentences, with finding the right word when *neat* or *groovy* or *nice* will fill that bit of air just as well has become the hallmark of talk and by extension, perhaps, of any interaction between people. Whether it is between man and woman, man and man, woman and woman, doctor and patient, mother and son, son and father, daughter and son, friend and friend, it doesn't matter. It just has to be fast. I'm in a hurry, Mom. "Talk to you later" has become another way to say good-by, not a promise. Conversation is not thinking time, and I'm not sure that it is even communicating time.

What television has done to the language is discouraging, to say the least. I have watched the vocabulary of my six-year-olds diminish over the years, and mine has too. But what television has done to the sophistication level of children is frightening. Where is childhood, now? Is it necessary for Jeremy to describe the gas chambers of the German concentration camps when we are having a discussion about death? Why does he need to have that image in his six-year-old mind? It was an image, too: as he talked he gestured in the air, trying to make for us the picture he had seen on television of "a lot of people, walking up a hill real slow, into a great big oven." I see no reason for this to have been part of his experience. Nor do I see why Tony should be able to tell me (and the other kids, who flatly refused to believe him) that the way parents and big kids have fun is to have sex, which he described calmly and accurately — in its most common form, I suppose I should be grateful for that — ending with "and usually the man takes off the woman's clothes first." And Henry, a few years ago, who would stand up behind his desk, stick out his chest, tell me he was the Incredible Hulk, then heave the whole desk over with a great crash. He believed that he was, then, the Hulk. He believed that he had thrown the desk across the room, as the Hulk could have done.

How does this happen? Children watch television by themselves. No one is with them at all, or maybe an older sibling or a teen-aged babysitter, which may be even worse than being alone: the teen-ager will have an agenda of her own as she watches.

Parents need to be there, with the young children. With all their children would be even better, but there are other things going on, like separation, between teen-agers and their parents, so that's a little unrealistic. If parents watched television with their children when they are young, talking about what was happening, responding to fears and confusions and reinforcing good language and appropriate behavior of the actors, I'd like to think that by age twelve the child would have learned some discrimination.

Parents should watch with the kids. They don't send them to the movies, after all, at age six or four, by themselves, to see whatever they want to or someone has told them about. I didn't go to the movies by myself until I was at least eleven, and then my mother had doubts about letting me see *So Dear To My Heart,* in company with four other eleven-year-old girls. We went on the bus and paid eighteen cents to get in, I remember.

When *Friday the Thirteenth* came to the movie houses, members of my first grade were not taken to see it, to watch the people being sliced up and murdered in hideous detail. The next year, though, when it came onto television as a nine to eleven o'clock movie, several watched it. They were pretty distraught the next day, and we did a lot of talking, which we shouldn't have had to do, and which was much less useful than the same conversation would have been the night before, during the show. I don't mean to suggest that I don't like to talk about children's fears and anxieties in school, far from it: but this conversation should have been going on during the film.

That's assuming, perhaps unfairly, that a parent would knowingly let his child watch an overtly gory or violent or sexual film or program. No one would, you say. Well, a lot of parents of my current students were not helped to learn to be discriminating themselves with television, and it may not have occurred to them that it's bad for their young children. So I say there are two ways that parents can deal with the problem: if it's okay with the parent that children see adult programs and films, they must sit with them to watch, to interpret, and to teach. Better yet, bite the bullet and don't let the child watch. You will survive the "But Mom, everybody else got too" whine.

In general, if you have a standard about movies, apply it to television. Leaving aside the time problem, letting them stay up (it was on Friday, and that's different), what made it okay for the child to see *Friday the Thirteenth* at home when it wasn't okay at the theater?

I wish I thought I could stop here. It isn't *Friday the Thirteenth* and *Animal House* that are the problem, of course. As you have been reading the last few paragraphs you have been saying to yourself: What?? Is she nuts? Of course I'd never let my kids watch that stuff. I just let them watch good shows, like "M.A.S.H." reruns and "Happy Days" reruns and "Punky Brewster" and "Family Ties" and if they've been real good, "Knight Rider." But these teach, respectively, war, and that compassionate people who don't believe in it are powerless in our society to do more than pick up the pieces; disrespectful behavior to parents, managing a foolish mother, and being a bigger success if you drop out of school than if you stay in; children manipulating their grown-ups; parents made of cardboard, seeming to be very young and innocent, dense and never questioning or giving limits; the edges of unreality masquerading as reality with the help of trick photography and stunts, not to mention routine lawbreaking in the name of law and government. I love "Knight Rider" myself, and I wish VCRs had been invented when I could have taped all the "M.A.S.H." shows to be mine forever.

But I'm a grown-up. Even my teen-agers needed some handholding when the first "M.A.S.H." stories were aired fifteen years ago: I made it a point to always watch with them.

That is my message, now. Watch with them, even — maybe especially — the Saturday morning cartoons. Look at the kinds of expectations and images of life and love and death and hate that are replacing your children's natural images. The children need you to model for them some appropriate reactions to all of this; they will not become discriminating grown-ups themselves, otherwise. And they need to have some room in their heads for their own images, their own interpretations of what they hear and read and imagine, and to feel that theirs are not inferior to the television's images.

Part of what writers do is to use words accurately and aptly enough to create in the reader's mind the image that was in the writer's mind, connecting the reader with the writing. That's why I say, as often as I can, "Oh, that makes a picture for me," and hope that the children will look for those pictures as they help each other, as writers, in conference. But each writer's mind filters images differently, even images for which the same words can be used. *Horse* says very scary things to me, because one ran away with me once; to Stephanie (Chapter 8) the word brings very different feelings and memories. These differences and these filters are what make our images our own; our images are what make us ourselves. Television can imprint every mind with the same images, and then we are in danger of all being the same.

Writing, Doing Words, can't do this.

Particularly but not exclusively at holiday times there may be as many as twenty children who write essentially the same thing, because it is each one's thing for that day. There is always at least one, too, who begins December with "Twenty-five days until Christmas." Every day of the month one or two will use the countdown sentence as the first sentence of their Movement V writing.

Fifteen more days until Christmas, wrote Jessie. *I can't wait until Christmas. I love Christmas. I love Mama and Daddy.*

This effort had as many sentences as Jessie could easily do, and all the capitals in the right places. It was rote work from my point of view, but fresh and intense from Jessie's. It gave her practice in writing, spacing, capitals, periods, and a little drill on *until.* (That word gives everyone fits because they say it *intul.*) All was well until she read it aloud to the group.

"No sir!" called Susan. "Sixteen days! That's what I wrote, look," she insisted, waving her book at Jessie. Into the same air boomed Jay, with "There are fourteen days until Christmas, right Teacher?"

Then they were all going at it, and I just grinned. After a minute or two they calmed down and noticed that Ben had his hand in the air. Ben will grow up to be Chief Justice. I hope.

"Ben?" I said, in a let's-listen voice.

"Jessie's right, and Jay's right and Susan's right too, Teacher," said Ben easily. "It can be all those numbers."

Incredulity and argument babbled around the room. I raised my own hand this time, and got quiet.

"Can you explain that some more, Ben?" I asked.

Unconsciously he got to his feet. "I counted like Susan did, starting today: tenth, eleventh, twelfth, thirteenth, fourteenth, fifteenth, sixteenth, seventeenth, eighteenth, nineteenth, twentieth, twenty-first, twenty-second, twenty-third, twenty-fourth, twenty-fifth," he re-counted, using his fingers. "That's sixteen. But we're already in the tenth, that's today, so Jessie didn't count it, so that's fifteen." Shifting his weight to one foot, he bent the other knee and balanced the toe on a chair behind him, clasping his ankle. "And to get *to* Christmas, not counting it and not counting today, that's fourteen, like Jay said."

Ben smiled beatifically at twenty-seven open mouths and sat down again.

Into the extending silence Julie, hands on hips, actually said "Hummph!" Exhibiting an unexpected spirit of scientific inquiry, she marched over to the calendar and began counting the spaces. Susan subsided, muttering, "I'm right anyways." I picked up my pen to write down Ben's impeccable logic.

It's tempting to be bored by some of these stories, the same old thing about Christmas, or getting a new bike, or the unicorn in the woods. These stories are only boring for you, the adult, though. The children think they are fine, and the writers think they are brand-new. They are absolutely right: Shawn never wrote about Rudolph before in his whole life, and Jessie never wrote about Christmas. Nothing is trite if it's brand-new and your very own. The idea that a piece of writing is trite is a teacher idea only. The teacher has to be careful not to let that show.

In Movement V someone retells the Christmas story, or the story of Rudolph, nearly every year. One enterprising child last year tried to give a synopsis of the Grinch story, but it is so visual it was difficult for her to stick to the facts: the television images got in her way. "And the Grinch got nice, and his heart got big and red," was her ending.

In Movement VI retellings occur, too. In Ben's class we got most of the old favorites retold: Sam did *The Three Bears,* LauraJean did *The Three Pigs,* Jay did *The Billy Goats Gruff,* and Heidi did nearly everything else. Last year was the year of the Jedi.

Jason N. was first with this notion. He came to me the morning of November third with the beginning of "The Darth Vader Story." "I can use the book (*Return of the Jedi*) when I need words," he said, identifying his resource. We talked a little about whether he would use all the same words the book did, or tell the story with his own words. As it turned out, it was a wonderfully clear one-page synopsis of that very complicated story. I learned more about the plot from Jason N. than I did watching the film.

Later, Jason N. wrote another Jedi story in a style fairly common in Movement VI. These stories are a lot of fun: clearly derivative, but with the names of classmates pasted in as characters. In this story, "Vince on the Deathstar," I wondered what Vince had done lately to annoy Jason.

> Once upon a time there was a boy. His name was Vince. Vince wanted to be a scientist. And in two days he would be 21. Then it was his birthday, so he got the job.
>
> The next day he had to take a flight. The ship was about to blastoff. 10. 9. 8. 7. 6. 5. 4. 3. 2. 1. 0. Blast. it went. He was going to the moon. On the way he met another ship just as he was running out of fuel.
>
> So he jumped out. But he had a jetpack so he wouldn't float.

He landed on the other ship. He jumped in the ship. The pilot on the other ship was named Luke Skywalker.

Vince said "hi I'm Vince."

Luke said "do you want to look around my ship?"

"OK. Luke, there's a ship."

"Don't worry, that is Han. He's going to the Deathstar" said Luke. "That is where one of our enemys lives. Do you want to go to the deathstar?"

"OK let's go launch the ship," said Vince.

"OK but it is very far," said Luke. "And you have to be careful."

"OK" said Vince.

Luke said "I don't want you to get hurt."

Then Vince said "OK."

But Darth was waiting there.

Luke gave Vince a light-saber for safety. When they got to the Death Star they opened the door. They were surrounded by Storm troopers. One of the Storm troopers shot at Luke. But Luke jumped and the Storm trooper hit another Storm trooper. Luke giggled.

Darth said "you fool." Darth took his light-saber out. Luke was not looking.

But just then Han ran in. Luke didn't see Han. Han said "Luke watch out!" Luke took out his light-saber. He turned around. And shot Vince instead of Darth. Darth laughed.

Luke said "shut up." Luke took his light-saber out. Darth took his light-saber out. They started fighting.

Luke won.

the end

It is interesting that I have never heard a child say, when similar stories or retold stories are read aloud, that "Jason copied," or "Susan copied Jessie." "That's the same as . . ." somebody's, they sometimes note, and they are usually delighted by the similarities. The idea of "copying" as equated with "cheating" rarely arises in first grade: I think I've only heard it in connection with math. When the negative connotation of copying is heard of at all, it comes from an older sibling. It's a learned response, I'm sorry to say.

On the December day after Ben arbitrated the calendar dispute, seven children wanted *snowing*. When they came to me with their *S* pages opened I asked them to give me the second sound. Of the seven, six got the *N*; one said it began *SO*. For four of the seven I wrote *snow* and asked them to tell me what the rest was, which they did; of the other three, one couldn't tell me when I asked (an incorrect assessment of readiness on my part); and I just gave the whole word to the other two.

Each one is in a different place in the unending work of connecting reading/decoding skills with writing/word-building skills. None of the children will get either set down pat by the end of first grade: my responsibility is to see that each one makes as many and as complicated connections as she is ready for.

On that day, three of the "snowing" stories were variations on "I like snow" and the others were more individual treatments of the theme. Even those three, however, came to it through their own brains, on their own tracks, each owning anew that same old story. If all twenty-seven of them want to write about the same snowstorm, that's fine. Having the idea and writing that idea, even if it is the same idea that others have, is still important and unique to each one. What they do with the idea is their own work, their own image.

Here is a snow story with very little personality:

> It is snowing. I like snow. The snow is pretty.

This story would be an easy out for many, and I would ask for more to be done with it. "What makes it pretty?" I might ask. "Is there anyone who doesn't like snow? What's the best thing you like about it?" For a typical child in Movement V, and certainly for a child in Movement VI, this would be only a beginning.

But when Kevin wrote that story, Kevin who the next year was placed in the special class, I cheered him, and I shouted for joy inside myself. It was whole, it was beautiful, and it was his. No one else in the world ever wrote that story, nor ever will.

Envoi

All through this book I have made pictures and told stories of young children, mostly five and six and seven, writing and reading, reading and talking, talking and listening, listening and sharing, sharing and writing. As they have done all of these things, they have been thinking in as many ways as they were, each one, capable of. They have been growing as much and in as many ways as they, each one, could grow.

They have been doing all these things in school, in structured settings, with many other children their same age doing the same kinds of things at the same times. They have all had Word cards; they have all filled pages of lined paper with sentences; they have all discovered the joys of "I likes"; they have all written and revised and published stories; they have all learned about their language, English, by using it to read and to write; they have all written what they read about and read what they have written.

And there are no two alike, still, after two whole years of school. No two children, in all my years of watching, have grown through this magic in the same way. Within the framework of the Movements of Doing Words, choice has been theirs exclusively. I say only that they must write; they find their own ideas and write what they want and need to write about. I can generalize only about their pride in themselves and in their work.

They are luckier than humans who are older than they, because they can reach right into themselves still and bring out "the stuff in their heads" for their subjects. "Whether the stuff is coloured or dun," Sylvia Ashton-Warner said, makes no difference. It is theirs. They reach into their minds, their hearts, their souls, their lives. Those five or six or seven years have been filled to the limit, after all, with work, discovery, love, sorrow, pain, joy, and puzzlement: everything imaginable in life. Any five or six or seven years in any life are filled just so, too, but the older we humans get, the harder it is to reach inside ourselves, and the harder it is to accept that what we find there is good.

When children Do Words, they learn that what they are and do and think, each one, is perfectly valid and acceptable, each one. As they assimilate the skills and understandings of writing and reading, they believe that they are, each one, worth writing and reading about. They know that they can do this new work; and they know that it is theirs. Each one can say, "I am me. I am good. I am worth it."

That's why I think there is great hope in children's writing. Children who Do Words know that every individual is unique and uniquely able; they take responsibility for their own work and growth, and accept as a matter of course that all other people are as important as they. In the grown-up world, this is known as tolerance, and it is very hard to come by.

Sooner or later, too, in the first three years of school, the children use all the English that they will want to be sure they know, and we, as teachers and parents, can help them with the confusing or rough bits as they need them. As they need to learn the way the physical world holds together, and why numbers work, they can be connected to those learnings too.

If we learn when we need to learn, we keep what we learn. This is called ownership, when we connect what we need inside with learning from outside, or what we know inside with what we need from outside. It only works when we are ready for it, and then it works wonderfully well. To present learning to children before they are ready and hungry for it is, at best, a waste of everyone's energy; at worst, it imposes perilously on the child's view of self, and can destroy it.

Teachers who Do Words and adults who accept what a child is curious about are allowing the child to be more important than the grid of learning and knowledge into which, for better or for worse, Americans currently subdivide their universe and their experience. Let the children find their own places; let them choose which squares to fill and when; let them use their own energy to do this, and it will be done better. Nor will adults have to feel drained of their own energy, nor be guilty, frustrated, disappointed, angry. If all of us allowed the children to fill the grid in their own time, individually challenging themselves and proud of their work and their worth, maybe, just maybe, that pride and those individualities would bend and burst the sides of the boxes and rid us of them forever. We grown-ups can't do this: we're locked into the grid we have made. We are afraid to trust what is inside us. We were all told, implicitly and explicitly, in school, that what was inside us was not good, not right, and we began to learn that what we were was not good either. How we feel about ourselves is what makes reform so hard. "We have met the enemy," said Pogo, "and he is us."

This is why I Do Words, trying to change the school, too, from the inside out. To me the most important thing of all is that young children at the beginning of their schooling come to feel good about themselves: I believe that all else follows upon self-esteem. Doing Words builds this, even as it hooks the young mind to the world's work of reading and writing. It is exciting to watch, to help, to be present at this magic.

Jeremy came to Doing Words in kindergarten, and loved it. By most standards in today's America, Jeremy was deprived, culturally as well as economically. He didn't know that, though. He buzzed through Movements I and II with great delight, moving from the inside out with ease and glee. There came a day when he began Movement III, eagerly.

Sitting near the teacher, he traced the letters of the sentence he had chosen that day and then took up the pencil to print it. Great concentration and inner drive took him, finally, to the period. He looked up at the teacher, beaming.

"Hey," he said, grinning through the aura of pride and Jeremyness that wrapped him round, "hey, Teacher, can I be a writer for the rest of my life?"

Bibliography

Adler, Mortimer. *The Paideia Proposal: An Educational Manifesto.* New York: Macmillan, 1982.

Ashton-Warner, Sylvia. *Teacher.* New York: Simon & Schuster, 1963.

———. *Spearpoint.* New York: Alfred A. Knopf, 1972.

———. *Spinster.* New York: Simon & Schuster, 1958.

Britton, James. *Prospect and Retrospect.* Montclair, N.J.: Boynton/Cook Publishers, 1982.

———. *Language and Learning.* London: The Penguin Press, 1970.

Calkins, Lucy. *The Art of Teaching Writing.* Exeter, N.H.: Heinemann Educational Books, 1985.

Derrida, Jacques. *Of Grammatology.* Translated by G. C. Spivak. Baltimore: Johns Hopkins University Press, 1976.

Elkind, David, and John H. Flavell, eds. *Studies in Cognitive Development — Essays in Honor of Jean Piaget.* New York: Oxford University Press, 1969.

Graves, Donald. *Writing: Teachers & Children at Work.* Exeter, N.H.: Heinemann Educational Books, 1983.

Moffett, James. "Integrity in the Teaching of Writing," *Phi Delta Kappan,* December 1979.

National Institute of Education. *Becoming a Nation of Readers: The Report of the Commission on Reading.* U.S. Department of Education, 1985.

Piaget, Jean. *Play, Dreams, and Imitation in Childhood.* New York: W. W. Norton, The Norton Library, 1962.

Sizer, Theodore. *Horace's Compromise — The Dilemma of the American High School.* Boston: Houghton Mifflin Company, 1984.